Poetry and Speculation of the Ṛg Veda

HERMENEUTICS
Studies in the History of Religions

GENERAL EDITOR
Kees W. Bolle
UCLA

Stephan Beyer, CULT OF TARA
Edward A. Armstrong, SAINT FRANCIS: NATURE MYSTIC
David R. Kinsley, THE SWORD AND THE FLUTE
Marija Gimbutas, THE GODS AND GODDESSES OF OLD EUROPE, 7000–3500 B.C.
Henry Duméry, PHENOMENOLOGY AND RELIGION
Wendy Doniger O'Flaherty, THE ORIGINS OF EVIL IN HINDU MYTHOLOGY
Åke Hultkrantz, THE RELIGIONS OF THE AMERICAN INDIANS
Kees W. Bolle, THE BHAGAVADGITA: A NEW TRANSLATION
Robert D. Pelton, THE TRICKSTER IN WEST AFRICA
Bruce Lincoln, PRIESTS, WARRIORS, AND CATTLE
Willard Johnson, POETRY AND SPECULATION OF THE ṚG VEDA

POETRY AND SPECULATION OF THE ṚG VEDA

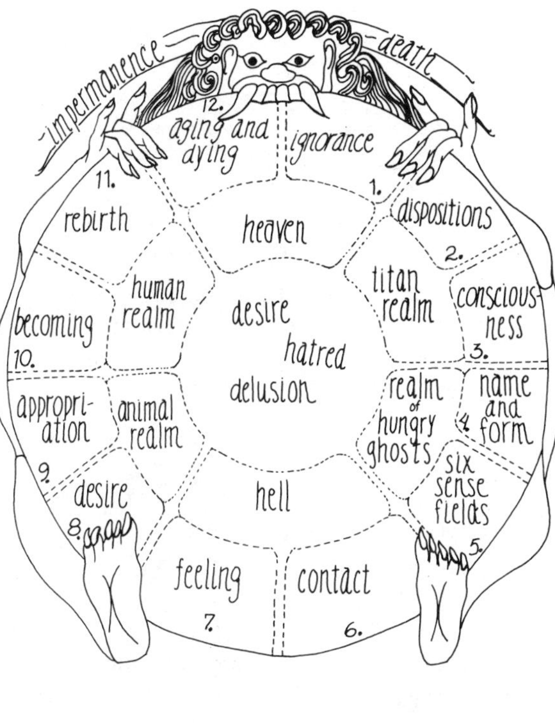

Willard Johnson

UNIVERSITY OF CALIFORNIA PRESS
Berkeley Los Angeles London

University of California Press
Berkeley and Los Angeles, California

University of California Press, Ltd.
London, England

Library of Congress Cataloging in Publication Data

Johnson, Willard L.
Poetry and speculation of the Ṛg Veda.

Bibliography: p. 181
Includes index.
1. Vedas. Ṛgveda—Criticism, interpretation, etc.
I. Title.
BL1115.A38J63 294.5'9212 80-14040
ISBN 0-520-02560-1

Printed in the United States of America

To my parents
and in memory of Richard H. Robinson
sácasvā naḥ svastáye

Taking such liberties with sacred Writ, as are by no means allowable upon any known rules of just and sober hermeneutiks.
—*Oxford English Dictionary*, A.D. 1737

Every poem is created by a journey through darkness and a return to light, the journey from light back to light which cannot be made except through darkness, and the finished poem is the image of that journey. In the poem, you [poets] are reborn; it is a re-creation, a resurrection of the body in which your experience is given blood and flesh and bone; and no man, touched by that poem will be quite the same man thereafter, so infectious, so satisfactory are the joys that spring from the poem's operative truth.
—C. Day Lewis, *The Poetic Image*

Contents

Preface ix

Introduction: "Into a Thousand Similes" xi

PART I: THE ṚG VEDIC SYMPOSIUM AND ENIGMATIZING IMAGES IN EARLY SANSKRIT SPECULATION 1

1. The Sacrificial Symposium as Context of Ṛg Vedic Speculative Uses of Enigmatizing Images 3
2. The Bráhman as Object for Speculative Vision 26
3. The Enigma of the Two Birds in the Fig Tree 42

PART II: SANSKRIT WORLD VIEW BRÁHMANS: MYSTERIES OF SUN AND WHEEL 67

Prologue. Archetypal Images in Tradition, Landscape, and World View 69

4. Enigmas of the Sun, the Eternal Wanderer 81
5. Enigmas of the Wheel, the Eternal Turner 103

PART III: THE ENIGMATIC SENSE OF REALITY 127

6. An Auspicious Enigma: In Memory of Albert Camus 129

Notes 143

Bibliography 181

Index 185

Preface

While I was a representative of the Oberlin Shansi Memorial Association in India (1961–1963), I once visited Banaras Hindu University and happened to meet there a French scholar who could read the Vedas. He told me that the Ṛg Veda was unlike other later Sanskrit texts, such as the Upaniṣads, with which I was somewhat enamored. Astounded by his effusive praise of the Vedas over later Sanskrit works, for years I wondered how the Ṛg Veda was related to the Upaniṣads and to the world view assumed by all classical Sanskrit texts and religions. In this essay, I have tried to make progress in answering this question by approaching some of the most difficult portions of Ṛg Vedic speculation, its bráhmans or enigmas, through a "just and sober hermeneutik." The essay, being a first survey of an untilled and difficult field, has all the defects attendant upon such an attempt.

Many have helped me. I especially wish to remember Richard H. Robinson, who initiated me into Indology, and to thank my Ph.D. advisor and Vedic teacher, Francis Wilson. Along with David Knipe and Murray Fowler, all of the University of Wisconsin (Madison), they provided me with the seeds of this study. I also thank Professors M.

Emeneau, H. Scharfe, G. Chemparathy, and T. Goudrian for their comments on a previous version of chapter 3, and especially Professor Carl Naether for his help with its ornithology. Stephan Beyer commented on the manuscript before I revised it, to my great benefit, and Professor James Santucci reviewed its early chapters, allowing me to correct many infelicities. I also thank Kees Bolle, editor of the series, John A. Miles, Jr., sponsoring editor of the University of California Press, and Gretchen Van Meter, my copy editor. To all these, I extend my heartfelt thanks, as well as to those in the future who will advance the investigation of these subjects.

W. J.

Vista, California
January 1980

Introduction: "Into a Thousand Similes"

> The meaning of all language, written or spoken, is developed by the application of general laws, usually termed Hermeneutics.
> —*Oxford English Dictionary*, 1843

Anyone who sets out to interpret the poetry and speculation of the Ṛg Veda, Indo-European's first "book" and one of the fountainheads of Sanskrit civilization, surely should comment on the methods of the inquiry. In seeking for a hermeneutics that would apply to this recondite material, I have become more and more attracted to the principles set forth in recent literary criticism. I have also benefited from those works in philosophy that seek to clarify language. I have found especially valuable the work of Philip Wheelwright, particularly *The Burning Fountain* (1968*a*), *Metaphor & Reality* (1968*b*), and *Heraclitus* (1964), his model edition with translation and commentary. These, along with the writings of Gaston Bachelard, Eliade, Gonda, Camus, Coomaraswamy, Renou, Charles Anderson, Stanley Cavell, and Herbert Fingarette, have brought me to my present approach to enigmatic language in the Ṛg Veda. The following comments explore some of the perspectives I bring to this essay, the title of which was suggested by Kees Bolle, the editor of this series, as was my reading of N. Kershaw Chadwick's *Poetry & Prophecy* (1952).

"Turn to the image."

> Let us take the poetic image in its being.
> —BACHELARD, *The Poetics of Space* (1969, p. xxv)

In college, some elements of our education were imparted to us whole and beyond criticism. Our professors considered them part of our initiation into the realm of learning. At the end of a year's general biology, the lecturer pronounced that the whole is greater than the sum of its parts. In first-year literature, imagery charted our understanding of the great (and little) works of literature that loomed before us like some half-obscure shore. To illustrate, Professor Pullet presented us with Ezra Pound's "In a Station of the Metro":

> The apparition of these faces in the crowd;
> Petals on a wet, black bough.
>
> [*Personae* (New York: New Directions, 1971), p. 109]

Aside from helping to launch imagism in diverse arts, such poetry led from criticism in the humanities to a renewed appreciation of metaphor and imagery of all kinds. In this case, Pound showed us his subject, the crowded subway station, through an image that juxtaposed two usually disparate things to form a hybrid image that created a unique meaning. This technique is also used in Chinese poetry and the Japanese *haiku* form. Some of our professors of literature dutifully pointed out that such metaphorical language has two levels of reference, the image (*vehicle*) and its application to another meaning (its *tenor*).

Even some extended poems are all image. To the unskilled at poetry, they try patience and test insight to its limits. How often have I sat before an image struggling to penetrate it with insight sufficient to see what it means! Sylvia Plath's "You're" makes poetry a marvelous expression of mystery:

> Clownlike, happiest on your hands,
> Feet to the stars, and moon-skulled,
> Gilled like a fish. A common-sense
> Thumbs down on the dodo's mode.
> Wrapped up in yourself like a spool,
> Trawling your dark as owls do.
> Mute as a turnip from the Fourth
> Of July to All Fool's Day,
> O high-riser, my little loaf.
>
> Vague as fog and looked for like mail.
> Farther off than Australia.
> Bent-backed Atlas, our travelled prawn.
> Snug as a bud and at home
> Like a sprat in a pickle jug.
> A creel of eels, all ripples.
> Jumpy as a Mexican bean.
> Right, like a well-done sum.
> A clean slate, with your own face on.
>
> [ARIEL (New York: Harper & Row, 1961), p. 52]

The poem piles image upon image, all the extended vehicle for a single tenor, the poet's unborn baby. Each image appropriates meaning through its mode of concreteness. The reality expressed by the entire assemblage of images is, as our biology initiation claimed, a whole greater than the sum of its parts. To penetrate these images tumbling out of the poet's motherly imagination allows one to participate in her experience, her wonder, her joy.

Speaking more technically, Plath enigmatizes, or represents in the form of an enigma (extended image) her baby's individuality within the womb, as her unborn infant. To use figures of speech—enigmas and such—to represent what other words can only detail descriptively is common to all imaginative literature, but is uncommon (and dysfunctional) in reportage and in any communication which needs unequivocal clarity. In another equally brilliant poem, "Metaphors," Plath uses the figure of a riddle in "nine syllables" to enigmatize the nine months of her pregnancy:

> I'm a riddle in nine syllables,
> An elephant, a ponderous horse,
> A melon strolling on two tendrils.
> O red fruit, ivory, fine timbers!
> This loaf's big with its yeasty rising.
> Money's new-minted, in this fat purse.
> I'm a means, a stage, a cow in calf.
> I've eaten a bag of green apples,
> Boarded the train there's no getting off.

[*Crossing the Water* (New York: Harper & Row, 1971), p. 43]

The underlying figure, in this case, structures the complex of juxtaposed images toward establishing the configuration of their common tenor, the gestation of a child.

In literature, images have tremendous power because they speak of one in the terms of an apparently different and unrelated other. The basic mechanism of symbolism rests on this ability which brings two together, vehicle and tenor, image and meaning. When the renegade Ch'an Buddhist poet, Han-shan, experiences the psychic oneness and protection that meditation has brought to him, he enigmatizes it in the mysterious figure of the "single robe":

> Now I have a single robe,
> Not made of gauze or of figured silk.
> Do you ask what color it is?
> Not crimson, nor purple either.

> Summer days I wear it as a cloak,
> In winter it serves for a quilt.
> Summer and winter in turn I use it;
> Year after year, only this.

[Burton Watson, *Cold Mountain* (New York: Columbia University Press, 1970), p. 113]

In a few lines of another poem, Han-shan describes himself in a process as creative as Plath's pregnancy, whereby he gives birth to his spiritual self by "digging a hole," that is, by turning within through meditation to discover spiritual riches:

> In the old days when I was so poor,
> Night after night I counted other men's wealth.
> Recently I thought it over
> And decided to open a business of my own.
> I dug a hole and found a hidden treasure—
> A store of crystal jewels.

[Ibid., p. 77]

The crystal jewels symbolize the innate, undefiled mind in which all Buddhists place ultimate trust.

Clearly, such literature cannot be read without interpretation directed at discovering the tenor of its images. Every image vehicle provides a structure upon which to found a meaning, its tenor. Much literature consciously adopts metaphor, the two-sidedness of images, to express its subtlest meanings. Professor Pullet assigned C. Day Lewis's *The Poetic Image,* presumably to educate us so we would not fail to understand literature. That author instructed us to see the pattern of images:

> It has been my argument throughout, that discussion of the poetic image cannot be confined to what is popularly understood as 'imagery'. Once it is conceded that imagination is the instrument with which the poet explores the patterns of reality, and that the images in his poetry are high

> lights by which he reveals to us these patterns, then the questions of subject-matter and of theme become relevant to the discussion of the image [Day Lewis: 1947, pp. 104–105].

Another book, Charles Anderson's *The Magic Circle of Walden*, taught me how to read literature through its images. Ordinarily read as a classic work about the Yankee naturalist, Anderson's turn to Thoreau's images opened a whole new dimension of Thoreau interpretation. He suggested reading *Walden* as a poem!

> To call *Walden* a poem is not to say that its best passages should be extracted and rearranged as free verse, or to suggest that flowery vagueness associated with the hybrid term 'prose-poem'. What is needed is not a vocabulary for praising Thoreau's style but a technique for reading his masterpiece. [Anderson: 1968, p. 16]
>
> To read it [*Walden*] as a poem is to assume that its meaning resides not in its logic but in its language, its structure of images, its symbolism—and is inseparable from them. [Ibid., p. 17]

A purely literal reading of *Walden* does not suffice to illuminate its conscious symbolism. It is, like Bashō's travel sketches (1966), an enigma of the poet's spiritual adventure.

Images tell us as much about the image-makers themselves as about the world they figure forth. Spurgeon believed this when writing of Shakespeare's images:

> Those who have followed my argument so far will, I hope, agree that I have grounds for believing that a study of Shakespeare's imagery throws light on his physical equipment and characteristics—in short, on his personality. I suggest, however, that we can go even farther than this, and that we can obtain quite clear glimpses into some of the deeper thoughts of Shakespeare's mind through this oblique method, the study of his imagery. [Caroline

Spurgeon, *Shakespeare's Imagery* (Cambridge: Cambridge University Press, 1966), p. 146]

In the following chapters, I will examine some of the images proposed by Sanskrit speculation, exploring mysterious reality in hopes of discovering the deeper thoughts of the image-makers who created the Sanskrit world view.

"Into a Thousand Similes"

> Man himself is mute, and it is the image that speaks. For it is obvious that the image *alone* can keep pace with nature.
> —Boris Pasternak, quoted by Bachelard: 1969, p. 104

The ability of images to "keep pace with nature" enhances their effectiveness as communicators of meaning on many levels. Through images, speculative imagination gives form to the unknown, shaping awareness of the deeper meanings of any reality. An enigma is just such an image (hence "enigmatizing image") applied to various tenors pertaining to the unknown it attempts to reveal. The image presents this unknown, abstract tenor in terms of a known, concrete vehicle that is easily identified and visualized. The Oxford English Dictionary identifies the enigma's metaphorical nature as well as its requirement that the reader exercise "ingenuity" in discovering the image's tenor:

> *Enigma*, 1. *a*. A short composition in prose or verse, in which something is described by intentionally obscure metaphors, in order to afford an exercise for the ingenuity of the reader or hearer in guessing what is meant; a riddle. *b*. In wider sense: An obscure or allusive speech; a parable.

The following passage from Shakespeare's *As You Like It* demonstrates the ability of images to enigmatize or symbolize either a moral or a speculative tenor; in this example, Jaques uses the image of the wounded stag:

Duke Senior Come, shall we go and kill us venison?
And yet it irks me the poor dappled fools,
Being native burghers of this desert city,
Should, in their own confines, with forked heads
Have their round haunches gored.

I. Lord Indeed, my lord,
The melancholy Jaques grieves at that,
And in that kind swears you do more usurp
Than doth your brother that hath banished you.

Today my Lord of Amiens and myself
Did steal behind him as he lay along
Under an oak, whose antique root peeps out
Upon the brook that brawls along this wood,

To the which place a poor sequest'red stag
That from the hunter's aim had ta'en a hurt
Did come to languish; and indeed, my lord,
The wretched animal heaved forth such groans
That their discharge did stretch his leathern coat
Almost to bursting, and the big round tears
Coursed one another down his innocent nose
In piteous chase; and thus the hairy fool,

Much marked of the melancholy Jaques,
Stood on th' extremest verge of the swift brook,
Augmenting it with tears.

Duke Senior But what said Jaques?
Did he not moralize this spectacle?

I. Lord O, yes, into a thousand similes.

First, for his weeping into the needless stream:
"Poor deer," quoth he, "thou mak'st a testament
As worldlings do, giving thy sum of more
To that which had too much."

Then, being there alone,
Left and abandoned of his velvet friend:

"Tis right," quoth he, "thus misery doth part
The flux of company."

Anon a careless herd,
Full of the pasture, jumps along by him
And never stays to greet him; "Ay," quoth Jaques,
"Sweep on, you fat and greasy citizens,
'Tis just the fashion; wherefore do you look
Upon that poor and broken bankrupt there?"

Thus most invectively he pierceth through
The body of the country, city, court,

Yea, and of this our life, swearing that we
Are mere usurpers, tyrants, and what's worse,
To fright the animals and to kill them up
In their assigned and native dwelling place.

Duke Senior And did you leave him in this contemplation?

2. Lord We did, my lord, weeping and commenting
Upon the sobbing deer.

Duke Senior Show me the place.
I love to cope him in these sullen fits,
For then he's full of matter.

As You Like It, II.i.21–68

Wherever literature, oral or written, has been composed, wherever persons have become "full of matter," inspired by the inner voice to understand the spectacle of creation, the thousand similes have extended man's expressive reach. Jaques moralizes on the spectacle of the wounded stag's agony, using it to symbolize human indifference and cruelty. In much the same manner, speculative thought uses images to venture descriptions of the subtle and mysterious, the unknowns that motivate humans to seek to know everything.

Two examples, one from Eastern and one from Western scriptural traditions, illustrate the scriptural, parabolic style based on the use of enigma or extended metaphor.

Guenther's translation of the commentaries on Saraha's royal *dohās* or mystic songs shows that the doctrinal verses were constructed on images intended to facilitate meditation on the abstract doctrines through visualization of the concrete images. The commentator sKye-med Bde-chen explains, "Saraha used twenty-three similes to explain his message" (Guenther: 1969, p. 89). Commentators spent great effort elucidating these images as the vehicles chosen by Saraha to convey his underlying tenors or meanings.

A passage from his biography reveals how Saraha himself came to understand the value of such enigma-teaching. The lesson from a young woman arrow-maker, like Siddhārtha's four visions outside the palace walls, completely changed the direction of his life. He had been told in a vision to seek out a woman arrowsmith in the market, and

> went to the big market place and there he saw a young woman cutting an arrow-shaft, looking neither to the right nor to the left, wholly concentrated on making an arrow. Coming closer he saw her carefully straightening a reed with three joints, cutting it both at the bottom and at the top, inserting a pointed arrowhead where she had cut the bottom into four sections and tying it with a tendon, putting four feathers where she had split the top into two pieces and then, closing one eye and opening the other, assuming a posture of aiming at a target. When he asked her whether she was a professional arrowsmith she said: "My dear young man, the Buddha's meaning can be known through symbols and actions, not through words and books." [Guenther: 1969, p. 5]

With this admonition that a lesson's vehicle meant more than its surface connotation (making an arrow), the young Saraha experienced a moment of recognition (*saṃvega*, see next section). Insight lit the darkness of his literal understanding:

> Then and there the spiritual significance of what she was doing dawned upon him. The reed is the symbol for the un-

> created; the three joints, that of the necessity to realize the three existential norms; the straightening of the shaft, that of straightening the path of spiritual growth; cutting the shaft at the bottom, that of the necessity to uproot Saṃsāra, and at the top, that of eradicating the belief in a self or an essence; the splitting of the bottom into four sections, that of . . . [and so forth]. [ibid., pp. 5–6]

The elucidation of each sub-aspect of the image vehicle continues in this careful mode throughout the commentaries.

The image as contemplative object is not confined to the Eastern scriptural style. Jean Daniélou's "The Dove and the Darkness in Ancient Byzantine Mysticism" (1964) shows that Gregory of Nyssa paid close attention to images in his exegesis of Christian scripture. With considerable skill, he defined his ideas in terms of such images from scripture, selecting and commenting on them to provide the bases for his own theological arguments and conclusions.

For example, a discussion of the meaning of death and the immortality of the spirit is based on the Biblical image of the wearing of skins demanded by God after the expulsion:

> After the first men had fallen into what was forbidden and had been stripped of beatitude, the Lord gave coats of skins to the Protoplasts. I do not think that these should be interpreted as ordinary skins. [Daniélou: 1964, p. 272]

With this last sentence, Gregory implies that the skins express God's meaning and will, symbolic of the consequence of the Fall. They are not ordinary skins, but are the vehicle for a meaning (tenor) yet to be elucidated. Gregory raises the question, "Of what species indeed were the animals who were killed and skinned to provide the garment thus contributed?" Since no species of animal is mentioned, Gregory reasons that these must be symbolic rather than specific skins. Consequently, in his meditation on the image, Gregory seeks a generalized, symbolic significance for skin. He moralizes that human mortality, which is the punishment for the Fall, is only adventitious, not essential. He draws this conclusion rather neatly from the image of skins (something put on, something superficial, not pertaining to the essential nature):

> But since all skin removed from the living creature is dead, I believe that the meaning is the aptitude for death, borrowed from the animal world, which was subsequently given to man in a providential design, but not forever. It covers him outwardly, but does not extend to his inwardness; it penetrates the sensory part of man without touching the divine image itself. [Ibid.]

Any Hindu theologian would delight in such an explanation of the distinction between the inner self or *ātman* ("the divine image") and the corporeal self ("sensory part of man").

At another point Gregory uses the image of wings, familiar in symbolic usage, basing his meditation on several scriptural references to the wings of God from the Psalms. Referring to the verse, "Turn away thine eyes from me, for they have given me wings," Gregory argues that since man was created in the image of God, he too has wings (tenor: potential spirituality): "If then the archetype is winged, human nature must be so too." Gregory then expands the image, alluding to birds and, in its special Christian context, to the dove, whose tenor is mystical ecstasy (vehicle: flight). Gregory concludes by moralizing:

> It is evident that the word wings should be interpreted in a metaphoric sense if it is to be applicable to God. The wings of God are power, incorruptibility, and other things of the same kind. . . . Therefore, since these qualities were in man as long as he resembled God in all ways, and since the inclination toward evil has despoiled us of these wings, the grace of God hath appeared in order that, denying ungodliness and worldly desires, we should have wings again

> through piety and justice and that our soul might be winged once more in accordance with primordial grace; that the soul which had lost its wings through the disobedience of the Protoplasts should regain the wings of the dove through virtues. [Ibid., p. 277]

Thus, on the image of wings, Gregory hangs his moralizing tenor of human salvation.

Enigmatizing Images and the Awakening of Insight: *Saṃvega* or Aesthetic Shock

Visited by the wounded stag, Jaques falls into a deeply agitated state of moralizing insight. Coomaraswamy has written that Pali Buddhist texts, which abound in parabolic forms, call such a state of responsive excitation *saṃvega* or aesthetic shock. His definition of the term could well apply to Jaques:

> . . . saṁvega is a state of shock, agitation, fear, awe, wonder or delight induced by some physically or mentally poignant experience. It is a state of feeling, but always more than a merely physical reaction. The "shock" is essentially one of the realization of the implications [i.e., tenor] of what are strictly speaking only the aesthetic surfaces of phenomena that may be liked or disliked as such. The complete experience transcends this condition of "irritability." [Coomaraswamy: 1942-"Saṁvega, Aesthetic Shock," p. 176]

As applied to the literary image,

> The Pali word *saṁvega* is often used to denote the shock or wonder that may be felt when the perception of a work of art becomes a serious experience. [Ibid., p. 174]

The enigmatizing images of Ṛg Vedic speculation functioned in just this way to awaken consciousness to the noumenal implications of experienced phenomenal forms. Sanskrit speculation began in part with the serious contemplation of these shock-producing images that enigmatized ultimate reality, with the institution of the Ṛg Vedic symposium.

The tradition of enigmatizing images, though it did not begin with the Pali texts, can be illumined by considering several examples from this source (which is often linguistically close to Vedic Sanskrit). First, Coomaraswamy explains, quoting from Aṅguttara Nikāya 2.116:

> . . . and as a horse is "cut" by the lash, so may the good man be "troubled" (saṁvijjati) and show agitation (*saṁvega*) at the sight of sickness or death, "because of which agitation he pays close heed, and both physically verifies the ultimate truth (*parama saccam*, the "moral") and presciently penetrates it. . . ." [Ibid.]

Indeed, sickness and death constitute major Buddhist images, enigmatizing the ultimate truths of human mortality and transience. Such truths were often directly contemplated by Buddhist monks at burning grounds.

In a second example, Coomaraswamy quotes the words of the Buddha from *Sutta Nipāta* 935–38:

> "I will proclaim," the Buddha says, "the cause of my dismay (*saṁvegam*), wherefore I trembled (*saṁvijitam mayā*): it was when I saw peoples floundering like fish when ponds dry up, when I beheld man's strife with man, that I felt fear" (or "horror"), and so it went "until I saw the evil barb that festers in mens' hearts." [Coomaraswamy, p. 174]

Paradoxically, insight into the true nature of reality beyond its surface appearance comes from the image projected by reality itself. Though by its very functioning it hides its tenor, the image also reveals it. "Nature loves to hide," as Heraclitus remarked.

In the third example cited by Coomaraswamy, prince Yuvañjaya (Yuvañjaya Jātaka #460, Fausbøll edition, V:120, lines 4–9), mounted on his splendid chariot, proceeds to his pleasure garden to enjoy himself, when,

> seeing dew drops strung like pearl strings on the tips of reeds, as on tree tops, grass spears, tips of branches, and on spider web filaments, asked, "Say companion charioteer, what are those called?," and received the answer, "They are called dew drops; they fall in the cold season."

Unknown to the prince, the dew enigmatizes his worldly pleasures, which are as transient and yet as beautiful as the morning dew. He is "blinded" by phenomenal beauty. In this and in other similar Buddhist motifs, the prince represents ignorant humanity, which protects itself from realizing the true nature of compounded existence. Returning in the evening, Yuvañjaya cannot understand the disappearance of the dew drops (tenor: does not realize the transience of existence):

> "Say, companion charioteer, how is it that I do not now see those dew drops?" "O Lord, as the sun rose all were destroyed without exception, and fell back onto the earth."

The prince experiences *saṃvega* and is transformed thereby:

> Upon hearing this the prince fell into saṃvega and said: "Like the dew drops on the tips of reeds indeed are the life-experiences of living beings. I will no longer be afflicted by sickness, old age and death, I must go to ask permission of my mother and father to wander forth" (as a samaṇa, wandering mendicant). [Ibid., lines 10–15]

The passage clarifies the tenor of the dew image: the life-experiences of living beings, transient like the dew, disappear because of the fierce sun's heat (tenor: time's destruction of transient existence). The text explicitly asserts the prince's usage of the image presented to him by nature to inform his destiny-determining contemplation:

> Thus having taken those dew drops as an image for contemplation ("ussāvabindum eva ārammaṇam katvā") and seeing (thereby) the three existence realms to be as if ablaze [tenor: transient], the prince returned home to become a monk. [Ibid., lines 16–17]

The image's aptness extends beyond the account, for, as Cirlot (1962, p. 77) remarks, dew alludes "also to spiritual illumination, since it is the true forerunner of dawn and of approaching day."

A Speculative, Enigmatizing Image from Archaic China

The use of enigmatizing images has never been confined to a single literature. Images flourish, especially when literature undertakes to speculate about the unknown forms of the reality supposed to underlie phenomenal surfaces.

A report of an actual speculative experience, induced through deliberate attainment of an ecstatic, visionary state, suggests that use of an enigmatizing image can help to enlighten someone in an ordinary state of consciousness about the nature of the visionary experience. In chapter two of the *Chuang Tzu* (Burton Watson, *Chuang Tzu Basic Writings* [New York: Columbia University Press, 1964], pp. 31–32), Tzu-ch'i employs a yoga-like discipline of body (sitting leaning on his armrest), breath (breathing), and mind (staring up at the sky, not making any object the focus of attention), and thereby enters into an ecstatic, visionary consciousness. He then propounds the piping enigma to his companion, Tzu-yu, who has remained unecstatic. When Tzu-yu asks what this preliminary enigma means, Tzu-ch'i follows it with an extended metaphor enigmatizing all of world process.

The image literally astounds with its mystical embracing of all phenomena. It encompasses all the Tao, all the ten-thousand things, in the breadth of a few lines. It encompasses the Taoist understanding of the ordering principle behind the diversity of phenomena, a diversity so confusing to human understanding, which usually skirts only the surface of things:

> Tzu-ch'i of South Wall sat leaning on his armrest, staring up at the sky and breathing—vacant and far away, as though he'd lost his companion. Yen Ch'eng Tzu-yu, who was standing by his side in attendance, said, "What is this? Can you really make the body like a withered tree and the mind like dead ashes? The man leaning on the armrest now is not the one who leaned on it before!"
>
> Tzu-ch'i said, "You do well to ask the question, Yen. Now I have lost myself. Do you understand that? You hear the piping of men, but you haven't heard the piping of earth. Or if you've heard the piping of earth, you haven't heard the piping of Heaven!"
>
> Tzu-yu said, "May I venture to ask what this means?" Tzu-ch'i said, "The Great Clod belches out breath and its name is wind. So long as it doesn't come forth, nothing happens. But when it does, then ten thousand hollows begin crying wildly. Can't you hear them, long drawn out? In the mountain forests that lash and sway, there are huge trees a hundred spans around with hollows and openings like noses, like mouths, like ears, like jugs, like cups, like mortars, like rifts, like ruts. They roar like waves, whistle like arrows, screech, gasp, cry, wail, moan, and howl, those in the lead calling out *yeee*!, those behind calling out *yuuu*! In a gentle breeze they answer faintly, but in a full gale the chorus is gigantic. And when the fierce wind has passed on, then all the hollows are empty again. Have you never seen the tossing and trembling that goes on?"
>
> Tzu-yu said, "By the piping of earth, then, you mean simply [the sound of] these hollows, and by the piping of

> man [the sound of] flutes and whistles. But may I ask about the piping of Heaven?"
>
> Tzu-ch'i said, "Blowing on the ten-thousand things in a different way, so that each can be itself—all take what they want for themselves, but who does the sounding?"

This passage demonstrates the close relationship between ecstasy and speculation. The enigmatizing image mediates between the ecstatic penetration of the undersurfaces of reality and the speculative formulation of what is thereby understood. In the first enigma, Tzu-ch'i tells his companion that there are three levels of insight into phenomena: the human or conventional (piping of men), the natural (piping of earth), and the spiritual (piping of Heaven). This last is the level of the Tao itself, which underlies all phenomena, human or natural. To explicate, Tzu-ch'i offers an extended metaphor enigmatizing world process, in which the Tao's yin and yang (the *yeee*! and *yuuu*!) alternate to produce all phenomena (vehicle: the sounds from the ten-thousand hollows).

The whole speculative endeavor depends upon Tzu-ch'i's ability to achieve a visionary state of consciousness Tzu-yu notes his mentor's transforming ecstasy, saying, "The man leaning on the armrest now is not the one who leaned on it before!" Tzu-chi has transformed himself, enabling himself to attain special insight, even into the highest level of reality.

The poets of the Ṛg Vedic symposium undertook a similar self-transformation. They hoped thereby to gain access to what they considered the ultimate level of reality. They also speculated about the unknown, using enigmatizing images to communicate enlightenment to the unecstatic. The ensuing chapters will focus upon various usages of enigmatic and archetypal imagery in the speculative poetry of the Ṛg Veda.

PART I

The Ṛg Vedic Symposium and Enigmatizing Images in Early Sanskrit Speculation

It is a stupendous fact about nature that the territorial disputes of thousands of species [of birds] are something like artistic contests—song duels. The struggle is mainly musical (counter-singing), not pugilistic.

—Charles Hartshorne: *Born To Sing, An Interpretation and World Survey of Bird Song*

1.
The Sacrificial Symposium as Context of Ṛg Vedic Speculative Uses of Enigmatizing Images

One of the most striking phenomena to the student of Sanskrit symbolism is the explicit presence of a special, figurative sublanguage in the Ṛg Veda (circa 1,500 B.C. to 1,000 B.C.), Sanskrit's first recorded literature. This specialized, sacerdotal language clothed and hid its meanings in images, deliberately employing an esoteric style to conform to its esoteric context, the sacrifice. In the belief that images gave life to language, the Vedic poets used complex figures to portray their visions and to accompany the rites with sacred speech.

Commentators have studied this metaphorical language from the earliest times (see the Nirukta and Brāhmaṇas and, to a much greater extent, the Sāyaṇa). The works of modern translators and exegetes have furthered the task. One need only glance through the footnotes of Geldner's translation (1951), which summarizes the interpretations of its predecessors, to find numerous examples of this special language and its interpretive commentaries. For example, the sisters symbolize the ten figures that perform the ritual operation (Grassmann: 1873, p. 1643, "bildlich von den Fingern"), either (as in 1.71.1) when they kindle and serve the sacrificial fire (Agni), or when they press the juice from the sóma plant (as in 9.65.1 or 9.93.1).

This figurative style participates in all realms of Ṛg Vedic discourse, in the language of rite and its supporting myth, in the laudatory hymn, and in speculative and cosmological thought. Much of the explicit imagery of the Ṛg Veda (the simile, using the semantic markers *ná, iva,* and *yáthā*) is poetic decoration, which has been amply described and studied in a voluminous literature.[1] In addition, many scholars have discussed and attempted to fathom the meanings of the images of Ṛg Vedic symbolism, despite the uncertainties involved.[2] Further study is needed, not only of the possible meanings of this fascinating figurative language, but also of its form and function in various contexts, ritualistic, mythic, speculative, and cosmological. The following study explores the use of enigmatizing images in Ṛg Vedic speculative-ritual contexts, seeking to discern how and why images of this character were favored over the more explicit, nonfigurative language expected in such contexts. I will argue that the use of enigmatizing images was deliberate and intentional, and that their enigmatic form was as important as their speculative content.

Since the time of Bergaigne and the earliest translators of the Ṛg Veda, it has been customary to dismiss enigmatic portions of Vedic language, whether in individual verses or whole poems, as obscure or hopelessly unintelligible. Bergaigne considered such passages to be Vedic balderdash ("galimatias," cf. Renou: 1960, p. 35). More than once he referred to the "mystical incoherences" of the verses.[3] In more recent times, notably in Geldner's translation (1951) and the critical studies of Renou (cited below), some scholars have tentatively argued that this dismissal was premature, based on a fundamental misconception of the function of figurative speculative language. However, not all recent commentators have agreed. Kunhan Raja (1963, p. 1) claims that many Ṛg Vedic passages are obscure or even unintelligible because the meanings of their symbols have been forgotten and lost. In his last translations from Sanskrit, Edgerton called the *asyá vāmásya* hymn (1.164, see chapter 5) a series of "disconnected riddles, the answers to which are mostly unknown or at best conjectural" (1965, p. 51). Since scholars continue to disagree with one another on the possibility of interpreting these passages aright, it is important to come to an understanding and evaluation of the semantic form and function involved. The task calls because those passages considered most obscure or unintelligible occur in contexts where we would least expect poetic triviality.

Operating on the interpretive principle that explicit statements, either from the text itself or from the time period in which it was composed, are the primary authority in establishing the meaning and use of its particular modes of thought and language, we must seek our evidence within the Ṛg Veda. Such internal evidence fortunately exists in the text. Several complete poems describe sacrificial symposia at which enigmatizing images or *bráhmans* were composed and responded to by poet-priests, much as poets in later classical times would vie before their royal patrons for victory in the composition of extemporaneous *kāvya*.[4]

In the older Vedic symposia, contestants preparing for the performance of a ritual would compose and attempt to respond to bráhmans. Those bráhman verses, which several such poems preserve, are the very passages that have confounded previous translators with their apparent obscurity. Speculative enigmatizing images constituted a specialized language form in the Ṛg Veda, used only in the context of sacrificial symposia or the oratorical contests preceding the performance of some sacrifices. These specialized enigmatic verses were given the ancient, most sacred name of *bráhman*.

As it is used in the Ṛg Veda, the term *bráhman* (neuter, accented on the first syllable) usually means a hymn or incantation (also *mántra*), spoken or chanted, expressing through sacred articulation a holy knowledge or wisdom. It thus gives man access to that power or potency considered inherent in the sacred word.[5] Behind this notion lies the idea that the power or potency, also called *bráhman*,[6] can be made manifest or immanent through special sacred verbal formulations. Such a manifestation requires an adequate vehicle, of which the form is as important as the content.[7] In the case of the two hymns in the Ṛg Veda which apply the term *bráhman* to such verbal manifestations of the sacred, the language form referred to is the enigmatic bráhman, considered the most effective verbal vehicle to manifest bráhman-potency. In other words, the enigmatic image was both vehicle and tenor, embodying and implying the bráhman reality articulated in sacred speech.

The first of these hymns, Ṛg Veda 10.61, describes its enigmatizing images as a 'raúdram . . . bráhma' (v. 1)[8]—"formidable" or "dazzling" bráhman. Needless to say, translators have always considered this hymn as belonging to the most difficult or hopeless portion of the entire text. The second hymn, RV 1.152 (studied by Renou: 1949*b*), twice refers to its enigmatic images (vv. 2–5) as a bráhman, and once, recalling the *raúdram* of 10.61.1, as a "powerful" mántra ('mántraḥ . . . ṛ́ghāvān,' v. 2b). Particularly significant is its phrase, 'acíttam bráhma' (v. 5c), applied to the enigmatic structure of the preceding verses. Literally, this translates as "incomprehensible bráhman-enigma." Should translators be so vexed, then, as to consider them hopeless when even their original authors considered them unintelligible, at least to ordinary perception? In these contexts, *bráhman* translates as verse of enigmatic or enigmatizing images, specially designed to be *acítta*[9] in form, semantically concealing its meaning from ordinary modes of comprehension.

What is of interest is the reason why such incomprehensible mántras were composed. To ascertain this, first consideration must be given to the Ṛg Vedic evidence concerning their use and the context of their composition. In both hymns cited, *bráhman* designates verses featured in special oratorical contests. RV 10.61 figuratively calls such a contest a "race" (*ājí*),[10] chariot racing being a favorite form of contest during those times. The "formidable bráhman" of the hymn is placed in the race-contest by one whose speech is "prepared" (*gūrtávacas*) with poetic inspiration (*krátvā*).[11] Another figurative expression *pŕ̥tanā* (normally "battle"), symbolizes the oratorical contest in the final invocatory verse of 1.152, when the poet-contestants ask: "May our bráhman-enigma prevail in contests! / May our rains be divine and prosperous!" (v. 7cd). For further insight into this specialized type of enigmatic mántra, we must examine the poems describing these priestly oratorical contests or symposia.

One such description occurs in a hymn to Agni Vaiśvānara, RV 10.88. Agni in the form of Vaiśvānara ("of all men"), is the patron of contestants seeking divine inspiration. In effect, his title means "inner inspirer of all men." The analogy between the blazing sacrificial fire and the inner light of divine inspiration dwelling in the heart (6.9.6) is the source of this identification. Remarkable, too, is the presence of Agni in many of the hymns describing the bráhman symposium. The poet often describes himself as sitting before the fire (as in 1.164, 6.9, 10.88). The mysterious presence of the god incarnate in the dancing flames seems to be the immediate source of his inspiration. We are here in the presence of an ancient nexus where the fire, the enigmatic sacred word, and divine poetic inspiration mingle in what is surely a major source of the speculative core of the Brāhmaṇas, the great

Agnicayana of the Śatapatha.[12] This particular hymn (10.88) is an Agni laud introducing his Vaiśvānara form in v. 12. After several verses (13–16) recalling Agni's creation and nature and several cosmic mysteries, the hymn calls the oratorical contest a *sadhamā́da* or symposium (v. 17c), describes it in several verses (17, 18cd, 19), and states the bráhman, which is the object of contention among the participants (18ab, in italics):

13.
The gods, poet-seers worthy of worship,
generated undecaying Agni of all men (Vaiśvānara),
The ancient aster, unaltering though mobile,
surveyor of mystery, powerful, high.[13]

14.
Vaiśvānara always shining with mántras we
address you, poet-seer Agni.
You who with greatness encompasses the broad
two worlds—god from above and below.

15.
Two, I have heard say, are the paths of the
fathers, the one of the gods, the other of mortals;
To the two goes all this moving world which
is between the father and the mother.

16.
These two united bear the wandering one, from the
head-born, (and thus) reflected on by mind,
He who above all creatures abides, never
careless, benevolent, and shining brightly.[14]

17.
Of these (subjects/mysteries) two (priest-
contestants) dispute ($\sqrt{vad}$), sitting at the
prior and later (positions), wondering,
"Which of us who conduct the sacrifice will
discern (*ví* $\sqrt{vid}$, i.e., the meaning of the
bráhman in 18*ab*)?"

The companions (of the brotherhood of priest-contestants) brought the two to the sacrificial symposium (*sadhamā́da*);
(Now) they approach the sacrifice (after the bráhman contest)—Who has explained (*ví* $\sqrt{vac}$, aorist) this (enigma)?

18.
"How many are the Agnis (fires), how many are the suns? How many are the dawns, and how many really (svid) are the waters?"
Not to vex you do I dispute ($\sqrt{vad}$) O fathers! I question ($\sqrt{prach}$) you, O poet-seers, to truly know ($\sqrt{vid}$).

19.
As long as the winged (flames of Agni) grow bright (on the altar), as they do on the orb of dawn,
So long does the brāhmaṇá-priest pose (the bráhman), approaching the sacrifice, (then) is sitting below the *hótṛ*.

According to the last three verses, two priests contest the bráhman, or dispute ($\sqrt{vad}$, synonymous with *ví* $\sqrt{vad}$; for other synonymns, cf. Kuiper: 1960, pp. 268–74), sitting in two distinct positions, the prior and the later (repeated in 10.71.9a), attempting to discern (*ví* $\sqrt{vid}$) a proper response to the questions posed by the brāhmaṇá priest before they enter into the performance of the morning ritual.

The brāhmaṇá is the priest who silently oversees the proper performance (its "health") of the sacrifice (Gonda: 1950, pp. 56–57). His role is to comprehend, he is (to use the earlier term for this office) the *brahmán* (masculine, note accent), the one who understands or bears the potent *bráhman* (ibid., p. 61). As the sacrifice is prepared (the flames grow on the altar as the sun rises, v. 19), he poses it to other participants in the sacrificial oeuvre, thus preparing them for their role in its enactment. Two participants are described as disputing (v. 17), wondering naturally which one of them will discern the meaning of the enigmatic questions posed by the brāhmaṇá, and then are described (v.17d) as having completed the contest and as approaching the sacrifice. The narrator himself wonders which contestant has prevailed in the encounter ("aorist" indicating an event, newly occurred, which the speaker has witnessed, Whitney 928).

In verse 18, some participants claim sincerity in disputing over such enigmatic questions, saying that it is not to "vex" ('ná-upaspíjam', hapax) but to know truly ('vidmáne kám'). This indicates that the questions are indeed taken seriously in intent and that their form is deliberate, designed to produce not annoyance but a transformed understanding. On the surface the questions seem nugatory, but in actuality they place before the inquiring mind of the participant the mystical paradox of the one and the many, of perceived diversity and hidden, to-be-perceived, underlying unity.

The form of the questions is precisely identical with the Brāhmaṇa-period ritual disputation form, the *brahmodya* ("dispute [*udya,* from $\sqrt{vad}$] about brahman [initiated in enigmatic questions]"), which descended directly from this Ṛg Vedic sacrificial symposium (on which see Renou: 1949*a*, part B). This form also appears in disputations in the early speculative Upaniṣads.[15]

In the symposium contest, priests prepared for the sacrifice by mentally grappling with verbal formulations evocative of bráhman. The peculiar, enigmatic formulations deliberately attempted to force them to leave ordinary modes of consciousness to reach other, enhanced, paranormal modes that would permit full visionary participation[16] in the sacrifice, thus guaranteeing its total effectiveness. This hypothesis conforms to the phrase *acíttam bráhma,* indicating that the bráhman was not open to ordinary modes of understanding (see chapter two).

The particle *svid* ("really," 18b), occurs often in bráhman and brahmodya verses, underlining their enigmatic force. In such instances, the particle emphasizes the requirement that the participant attain to an inspired state of visionary consciousness, seeing things "as they *really* are," an ideal common to later Indian speculative and soteriological traditions.[17] Many verses describing members of the brotherhoods of disputants (including 10.71.4–9, 4.5.5 and 12, and even 9.37, a sóma hymn, whose v. 6c, *anakṣā́so badhirā́ḥ,* is parallel to 10.71.7a and 9) deal with those who fail to achieve the level of vision which transcends ordinary awareness (the prefix *ví* in *ví* $\sqrt{vid}$, v. 17b indicating vision gone beyond ordinary levels of consciousness) and who thus fail really to understand.

Proper participation in the sacrifice presumes a prepared state of consciousness achieved partially as a result of the bráhman contest. That this disputation-contest receives the name *sadhamā́da* (symposium in 17c, where *sadha-saha* = *sy(n)m),* further indicates its function of providing inspiration to be achieved before the rite, for most surely the participants were drinking sóma. Their Greek counterparts substituted Attic wine, but the two drinks ultimately served similar purposes. *Máda (mā́da* only in *sadha-)* indicates a state of transformed, prepared (cf. 'áram hitó . . . vā́jināya,' 10.71.10d), visionary consciousness, full of the imaginative transport essential to ritual participation and produced in conjunction with drinking the sacred sóma and disputing over bráhmans. The term *vípra* for inspired priest indicates the state of oratorical "trembling"[18] (cf. *vipaścít,* 1.164.36) that accompanies such moments of inspiration. This state seems essential not only to the composition and recitation of mántras but to the statement and response to bráhmans preparatory to full participation in the sacrifice. Sóma, the poet reports, puts the mind in motion (9.21.7, note that those who fail in the contest do not prepare or partake in the sóma, 10.71.9b) and acts as an eye to the tongue (1.87.5). The entire ninth maṇḍala might be read in terms of the poet's search for divine inspiration (note particularly hymns like 9.73), occasionally experienced as the "immortality" that becomes the goal of spiritual inspiration in later ages, as in 8.43.3ab:

> We have drunk sóma, immortal have we become
> We have found the light and the gods![19]

In Ṛg Vedic sacrificial symposia, contestant-priests prepared themselves for the drama of the sacrifice, attaining through sóma and sacred disputation the transcendent form of consciousness essential for mystical participation in the cosmic reality evoked by the ritual. During the symposium, contestants were brought to the special contest area by their companions (*sákhi*), members of brotherhoods of disputants (*sakhyá*). Several hymns describe these brotherhoods, adding substantially to our understanding of the context of bráhman verses used in their contests. Two praise Agni Vaiśvānara, the patron of poet-contestants. One (4.5) gives a report of a contest made by a poet who participates successfully, while another (6.9) is a rare, intensely personal account of one poet's experience of the contest and the exaltation he attains as a result of Agni's inspiration. A third, 10.71, addresses itself to the feminine form of bráhman[20] (*Vā́c*, Holy Word), evoking a bhakti-like eulogy to bráhman personified as a female goddess. All three poems exhibit the particular personal devotion of each contestant for his patron deity in the contest. So remarkable is 10.71 that it is worthy of translation in full.[21]

1.

O Bṛhaspati the first beginning of Vā́c was
when they came forth giving names,

What (before) was their best, what was
spotless, placed hidden in mystery,

Was manifested because of love right before
the eyes!

2.
It has been like (farmers) winnowing grain
with a basket,[22] when the wise with mind have
made Vā́c.

Then the companions (*sákhi*), recognize (others
of the) brotherhood (*sakhyá*), for they place
their auspicious mark in Vā́c.

3.
Through sacrifice they followed the tracks of
Vā́c; they discovered her inhabiting the
ancient seers (*ṛ́ṣis*).

Having brought her here they placed her in
many places—(Now) seven laudators praise
her in unison.[23]

4.
Many a one seeing Vā́c does not (really) see
Vā́c, and many a one hearing does not (really)
hear her.

But also to many does she reveal her body,
like a beautifully clothed bride desiring
her husband.

5.
Indeed they say many in the brotherhood are
intoxicated into immobility, these they do
not urge into oratorical contests (*vā́jina*);

Such a person competes with a milkless *māyā́*,
hearing Vā́c (for him) is without fruit and
without flower.[24]

6.
He who abandons a comrade, his fellow in
knowledge, shares not even a portion of Vā́c;

If he hears her, in vain he hears; surely he
does not fathom (*pra* $\sqrt{vid}$) the way of the well done.

7.
Though (each) possesses eyes and ears,
companions are unequal in swiftness of mind. . . . [25]

8.
When brāhmaṇá companions sacrifice together,
fashioning with the heart mental flashes,

Then surely many a one is left behind (*ví*$\sqrt{hā}$)
because of (lack of) insights, while many
others far beyond go (*ví* $\sqrt{car}$) having solved
the bráhman-enigma.

9.
Those who do not take the prior and later
(contest positions), are not brāhmaṇás, nor
do they participate in the (accompanying)
sóma rites;

They evilly approach (*abhi* $\sqrt{pad}$)[26] Vā́c, and
unenlightened they weave on the loom (of
sacrifice) with gossamer.[27]

10.
All the companions rejoice with a companion
returned with glory, victorious in the
assembly contest (*sabhā́*),

For he removes their faults and bestows
nourishment (on them), and he is well prepared
for (future) contest.

The power of sacred word (bráhman-Vāc) to reveal what is mysterious and beyond normal comprehension bases itself, the hymn says, on the original vision that occurred when the first seers, by giving names to what was shrouded in mystery, brought it "right before the eyes." Even so do the companions when they fashion sacred speech; but the reality which bráhman-Vā́c makes immanent is only potentially revealed, since not all men truly understand what they hear of sacred word and, consequently, what they "see." The reasons (for all the companions have ears and eyes, 7ab) are several. Some do not participate in the contest (not taking up the disputing positions 9a) and do not partake of the sóma in rites accompanying the symposium (9b); they are thus not "true" brāhmaṇá priests, able to understand beyond levels of ordinary comprehension. They have not (by responding properly to contest bráhmans) already attained to required visionary levels of consciousness before taking part in the sacrifice. Thereby unprepared to sacrifice, their approach to Vā́c being wrongful (*pāpáyā*), they are unenlightened (*áprajajñayaḥ*) and not visionary. To take part in the sacrifice would be in vain (superficial, without knowledge of its true meaning). For this, the poet adopts the image of weaving with gossamer! Other verses specify additional reasons for exclusion or failure. One cause for exclusion, v. 6 reports, arises when a member of the oratorical brotherhood has abandoned fellow contestants. His hearing becomes in vain (*álakam*, 6c), and he fails to understand the path of the properly performed (*sukṛtá*) sacrifice. Others drink sóma to excess, becoming intoxicated into immobility (5a) so that their brothers do not even urge them to participate in contests. Their hearing of the sacred word has neither flower (attainment) nor fruit (reward). If such persons do compete, they lack sufficiently powerful *māyā́* to succeed, *māyā́* being the power or ability to create sacred word in imitation of the first seers and thus to reveal the mysterious hidden reality for all their fellows to envision "right before the eyes."[28]

The preponderance of verses dealing with comrades who fail to understand indicates that their desire to achieve a special state of consciousness motivates the members of the brotherhood to compose and contend over bráhmans. Whether contestants fail or succeed depends on whether they move from the level of ordinary understanding to the level of visionary realization—or, to use the terms of later visionaries and philosophers, from the relative to the absolute: "Many a one seeing Vā́c does not (really) see Vā́c, and many a one hearing does not (really) hear her . . . " (4ab).[29] For the sacrifice to be effective, full participation in its visionary level must be reached; otherwise it is only an external performance of superficial ritual acts. Through the sacrifice, participation in cosmic process is sought, the sacrifice itself being only the means or vehicle.[30] Were it to remain mere ritualistic performance, as it would be perceived by a casual observer, it would be pointless. Any dramatic performance reveals two sides: one can see it as a "play," or by imaginatively participating in it, as a created reality.

The reason for the sacrificial symposium-contest now becomes apparent. Sóma drinking and other acts, such as the preparatory contest, helped prospective participants in the sacrificial drama to transform their consciousness. The form of the bráhman required this shift in understanding, because no ordinary level of consciousness could produce a proper response. To succeed in the contest, participants had to attain visionary status, hearing the enigma or Vā́c "truly." To do so meant seeing her embodied in the bráhman, in a vision right before the eyes (*āvíḥ, 1d*).

The contest required surviving the trial or ritual ordeal of the enigma. The image which completes v. 4 shows the poet's meaning. Vā́c reveals her body to successful contestants "like a beautifully clothed bride desiring her husband." The beautiful clothes represent the phenomenal reality of the bráhman. Perhaps some contestants failed by becoming entranced with this surface reality of the verses.[31] The clothes of the bride, like bráhman-enigmas, both reveal and conceal;[32] though they suggest superficially her underlying beauty, if they are not removed, the groom (contestant) surely will not participate amorously in the fullness of his bride's beauty. So too the poet, for he understands Vā́c in vain unless he goes below surface appearances and participates in the depth of her revelation. Then the sacrifice can be meaningful because he has achieved the level of visionary consciousness.

Comrades who achieve success in the contest receive honor from their companions because they bring glory to themselves and their fellows (v. 10). Some find themselves left behind because they lack insight when the companions compete (v. 8c), calling upon the source of inspiration in the heart. Others, victors who had responded properly to the bráhman-enigmas (8d), go far beyond to experience consciousness transcending its ordinary bounds, seeing and anticipating 6.9.3b, *ṛtuthā́* (according to reality as it is). The use in several verses of the verb $\sqrt{car}$ (to wander) (*manasā*, passim, imaginatively, in consciousness) with the prefix *ví*, means to go far beyond ordinary modes of thought, to attain visionary consciousness. The prefix *vi* does not function negatively, as it does in later usage in such terms as *vikāra*, *vikṛti*, and even *vijñāna*.

A remarkable *sūkta* addressed to Agni Vaiśvānara, 6.9, confirms this meaning of *vi* and gives a rare, autobiographical account of the experience of transcending consciousness. Though autobiography is not a Vedic genre, the poet recounts his actual experience of the contest and describes the inspiration he receives from Agni, his divine patron and the poet's muse. The poet fills his poem with Agni's presence. He sits before the fire (4a) and honors Agni as the king who overcomes the darknesses (1cd, and, by analogy, the poet's lack of inspiration, his initial ignorance). Again, mystical participation in the fire focuses the poet's awareness, and through it he attempts to attain the divine inspiration to carry him successfully through the contest (*samará*, 2b, another term for battle applied figuratively), prepared for the mysteries of the actual sacrifice:

1.
Both the dark and the clear day turn on
themselves, along with the two spaces,
according to the ordinations.

When once born Agni Vaiśvānara like a king,
overcomes with (his) light the darkness.

2.
I do not really understand it (*ví* $\sqrt{\textit{jñā}}$), the
thread nor how to weave, nor what they
weave as they (other contestants) enter onto
the contest ground.

Indeed whose (companion) will be the "son"
to respond (correctly to the bráhmans) which
are to be explained here at the prior position
(placed into competition) by the "father"
(sitting) at the later position?[33]

3.
Only he (Agni) truly understands the thread
and how to weave; he should solve (the bráhmans)
which are to be explained according to reality
as it is (*ṛtuthā́*),

He is who (really) sees it (the level of reality
the enigma intends), he is the protector
of the immortal, moving here below and
above observing through another.[34]

4.
Right here is the original *hótṛ*, look at him,
this light, the immortal among all those mortal![35]

Here he is, generated (on the altar) firmly
seated, undying, growing bodily.

5.
A firm light placed for vision—a mind (*mánas*)
most fleet of all that fly!

All the gods, one-minded, single-intentioned,
go directly beyond (*ví yanti sādhú*) to this
one inspiration (*krátu*)!

6.
Far beyond soar (*ví* $\sqrt{\textit{pat}}$) my ears, far beyond
my eyes, far away to this light which is
set in my heart!

Far beyond wanders (*ví* $\sqrt{car}$) my mind, its
spirit (goes) to remote distances.[36]
What really (*svid*) shall I say? What indeed
shall I even think?

7.
All the gods honored you, O Agni, fearing
when you stayed in the darknesses.

Vaiśvānara bring us help! Immortal bring
us help!

This poem undoubtedly marks one of the earliest recorded milestones of Indian mysticism. The poet awaits his turn in the bráhman contest, watching others entering onto the contest ground (2b). He admits to not having attained the level of visionary consciousness, saying that he does not truly understand anything of the sacrifice or the contest which precedes it. He uses weaving imagery to apply both to the contest and the sacrifice.[37] He thus claims neither to understand the thread from which the contestants weave the sacred mysteries nor to understand how to weave. In order to participate meaningfully in the weaving of the sacrifice he must achieve visionary consciousness, he must know the process and its meanings. He wonders whether he or other of his companions will be able to respond properly to the contest bráhmans, taking up the prior position on the contest ground. There, as the "son" in the contest, he will try to answer the "father," who at the later position poses the sacred enigmas to him.

Imagine the total scene, where tension and drama build as fires light for the holy rites, as the dawn grows, as the symposium proceeds, and as others take their respective positions as sons and fathers on the contest ground and then go on to the sacrifice. The poet sits near a fire already blazing, seeking inspiration to compete successfully in the contest when his turn arrives. He addresses his longings to Agni Vaiśvānara, the Agni who incarnates his divine light in his fiery immortal body (4b), serving as the unique single inspiration whom poets and even the gods seek for enlightenment. Agni's mythology encourages him, for it is Agni (as sun) who, when born of the dawn, overcomes the dark unknowns of night (v. 1). Even the gods were fearful when, before his manifestation, Agni hid in the darkness, concealed in the waters (as in 10.51.3, "We (gods) searched manifoldly for you, O Agni, when you had entered the waters. . . . ").

The poet's personal experience follows this mythic structure: because he lacks inspiration adequate to visionary consciousness, he must seek Agni as the gods did in the beginning. Further, Agni is light, inspiration, illumination, enlightenment, which the poet has right before him. Only Agni, he says, understands the process of the sacrifice and the contest; only Agni understands the thread and how to weave (3a), so only he can respond properly to the bráhmans. The poet further knows that this power really to understand gives access to the immortal (3d), to the divine. Thus he addresses Agni, asking for visionary inspiration, for "light" to see (5a, *dṛ́śaye kám*). Agni incarnates this light (with analogy to the sun, which lights up the entire world after night); Agni, a "mind" most swift of all, hence the brightest, most intelligent one, whose gift of vision the poet needs to be successful.

The climax comes in the sixth verse. The poet receives from Agni the inspiration he so desired. The light, in fact, he finds set in his own heart (6b)! Away soar his now visionary senses, his hearing and sight, away from their phenomenal objects to noumenal mysteries; far beyond wanders his mind to remote, cosmic mysteries (cf. note 36). His senses no longer link him to the phenomenal world but have undergone a mystical transformation. He prepares to take part in the transcendent meanings of the bráhmans and the sacrifice, indicating his absorption in a state of speechless wonder: "What really shall I say? What indeed shall I even think?"

For the mystic, ordinary speech and thought during certain moments are left behind, as part of lesser, worldly concerns. Mystical selflessness transcends these vehicles of phenomenal being. We can surmise that one proper response to the bráhman could be that silence indicating genuine transcendence. The particle *svid* recurs, indicating not the inability to answer but rather the realization that what might be said in such a state would fall short of what is being experienced. In the contest, his wonder would be noticed by the "father." His success in achieving such a silence of realization would be recognized as a sign of achievement, even as the guru of later ages recognized the breakthroughs of realization by his disciples not only by what they said but by what they did not say.

The poet thus reports his achievement of that visionary consciousness required of him for both contest and sacrifice. He has discovered the Agni of "all men" in his own heart. When the poet reaches a state of mind equal to the challenge of the enigmatic bráhman, the special reality of the sacrifice opens to him "as it really is." It reveals itself not as a limited human endeavor, a vain imitation of the mysterious cosmos, but as the process of reality itself. In this sacrificial reality, the poet gains entrance into the otherwise hidden mystery (*gúhā hitám*, 4.5.8b), experiencing the *ṛtá* (that order uniting the diverse appearances of the ordinary world into a creation), not a chaos but a divine order. Kunhan Raja (1963, pp. 34–5) reconstructs Dīrghatamas's experience of the sacrifice and the world following the contest. Sitting before Agni, meditating on bráhmans stated in the course of the poem (1.164), the poet passes into the visionary state when the question, posed in brahmodya form, is put to him by another: "I ask you: 'What is the farthest end of the earth?' " (1.164.34a).

The poet responds, indicating that he directly experiences the sacrifice as identical with the cosmos: "This altar is the farthest end of the earth" (35a). Kunhan Raja comments on the implications of Dīrghatamas's answer:

> He (Dīrghatamas) had been participating in the rituals of worship before, and now he is sitting before the altar at a similar ritual. The ritual itself has taken *a new form* in his eyes. He finds some sort of unity between the world and the ritual. It is not something within the world; it has become, for him, the entire world itself. . . . Till then he had been seeing the altar as a small piece within the immense world; now he finds the altar as forming the entire universe itself. However far he may be able to view, he sees only the altar. It is even in the farthest distance. . . . Dīrghatamas *is seeing the entire world force and world activity within that ritual* at which he was sitting, when he has become a poet. [italics added]

Still another complete *sūkta,* 4.5, directly reports the poet's experience of the contest.[38] As before, Agni Vaiśvānara serves as his patron. The first three verses contain the poet's praise for Agni following the contest. He says that even though he was *pā́ka* (2c, also 1.164.5a, juxtaposed with *ávijānan*), "unrealized, sincere but as yet artless (in the contest)," Agni blessed him with special insight (*rātí,* 2a) and revealed (*prá* $\sqrt{vac}$) to him the deep meaning of the enigma (*manīṣā́,* 3d) so that he succeeded in the contest. The poet honors Agni as the guardian of the contest against evil (v. 4) and remarks that those who participate falsely in it are brazen like brotherless maidens and act maliciously like husband-deceiving spouses (5ab).

The remaining verses return in time to describe the contest. Faced with the difficult bráhman, the poet at first paranoically thinks that such evil competitors (*pāpā́saḥ sánto anṛtā́ asatyā́*) have posed the enigma (5cd), the *padáṃ . . . gabhīrám* (profound phrase), so that it will be impossible for him to understand. He is only discouraged

(v. 6) and he asks "clarifying" Agni why he has placed on him "like a heavy burden" this enigma (*mánman*, 6b) also called the *pṛṣṭá* (question, 6d), described (6cd) as being lofty, profound, new, and "seven-leveled" (*saptádhātu*, meaning very complex).

Immersed in the contest, the poet confronts the bráhman (first stated in 7cd, then 8cd, 9ab, and 10), continuing to address Agni so that through his inspiration (*krátu*) he might achieve a clarified spirit (*punatī́ dhītíḥ*, 7b). But, in the following verse the poet again hesitates and becomes discouraged, asking about the enigma posed to him in 7cd, "What part of it should I explain? (what part is *pravā́cya*, 8a), noting that, "They explain (*úpa* $\sqrt{vad}$, *hapax* but equivalent to $\sqrt{vad}$) in secret what is hidden in mystery."[39]

With this realization, the poet as contestant begins to approach in a proper frame of mind the revelation of the bráhman. His attitude toward the world shifts away from his ordinary presuppositions to those which are more in keeping with the visionary, mystical approach to its reality.[40] The enigma series resumes (in 8cd, 9ab), but the poet relates to it in a new manner. He says,

> At the place of reality as it is (*ṛtásya padé*)
> I discover (*ví* $\sqrt{vid}$) (the face of the divine, referred
> to in the enigma) shining brilliantly in the mysterious
> (*gúhā*[41]), moving rapidly, rapidly (disappearing).
>
> [v. 9cd]

He begins imaginatively to enter into the mystery revealed by the bráhman, which has spoken mysteriously of the face (*ánīka*) of the divine (9a). The poet responds with a cry of mystic exaltation when he sees the face "right before his eyes" (see note 1.41).

He has reached the goal of participatory insight into transcendent reality through his contemplation of the enigmatic images of the bráhman. Their revelation returns to be stated again in v. 10, at the climax of the poem where presumably the poet can fully understand their import. In the remaining verses the poet looks back on his achievement of visionary consciousness, saying first to Agni (Jātavedas) that when he was questioned ($\sqrt{\textit{prach}}$, in the contest by the "father" or enigma-posing priest), he spoke ($\sqrt{\textit{vac}}$) reverentially (*námasā*) of reality as it is (*ṛtá*, 11ab). He then asks Agni, upon whom he has relied and who is master of all this cosmos and its riches, what he will obtain (what fruit he should expect) for his devotion and proper action in the contest (11cd, 12ab). This request for the reward (the *phala-śruti*) closes the description of the contest.

Renou and Geldner see many references in this poem to what may be technical terms pertaining to the contest. In v. 4, *dhā́man* may refer to the rules governing poetic creation in the contest, which, with *prá* $\sqrt{\textit{mī}}$, may mean "infringing upon the rules." Perhaps *ṛtáṃ voce námasā* (11a) means "to explain reverentially according to the rule (*ṛtá*) of the contest, responding properly to the bráhman." Here the rules would function so as to ensure a proper, visionary response to the enigma. The limits or speculative bounds of the contest may be the meaning in v. 13 of *maryā́dā*, and *vayúna*, the means or proper ways of responding to an enigma. Of note also is the poet's concern in v. 14 with inadequate competitors (as in 10.71) who constantly threaten the success of the contest.

These terms, haphazardly preserved in chance survivals, remain outside the main focus of this investigation. Unhappily, the full details of the ancient Vedic ritual symposium will never be available. Kuiper (1960, p. 217) rightly warns against the tendency, which he attributes to Geldner and Renou, "to overemphasize the importance of literary contests." Indeed, how often such speculative symposia were held is unknown, nor does the evidence allow any statements about the particular circumstances in which they would be performed. This discussion has merely allowed us to determine the context of Ṛg Vedic speculative enigmas. Doubtless, this very symposium-contest is the first recorded context of Sanskrit speculative thought. What we do know about it can now lead to new insights into bráhmans previously little understood.

2.
The Bráhman as Object for Speculative Vision

Of the first bráhman introduced in Ṛg Veda 4.5, Louis Renou wrote:

> Voici, donc, brusquement introduite (comme dans I.152,3 et suiv.) l'Énigme formant le thème de la joute: "le gracieux (ici un substantif neutre ellipsé) de Pṛśni, (celui qui siège) dans la peau du breuvage (?), le disque-solaire (?) hissé au haut de la montée (?)." On ne peut imaginer, en quelques mots, plus redoutable accumulation d'obscurités. [EVP II (1956), p. 58]

Can anything truly meaningful be said about such formidable accumulations of obscurities? Certainly nothing in paraphrase could duplicate the effect of verses designed explicitly to catapult imagination into far, undreamed of distances. Something irreducible inhabits the enigmatic that finally serves as its source of power to transform. Still, we can say something not only about the images used in these speculative bráhmans but about these bráhman language forms as the first recorded, specialized objects for speculative vision in Sanskrit literature.

When poet-contestants entered the contest ground to contend over bráhman enigmas, they hoped to achieve visionary consciousness. These figurative expressions sought to direct awareness to a relatively lesser-known level of reality presumed to lie hidden beyond the surface appearance of things, being unavailable to the senses. Speculation and metaphysics both tried to apprehend this reality underlying the surface forms of things. The sacrifice, as an instrument, tried to ascertain such underlying structures of reality in order to influence them decisively in favor of human, empirical concerns. By being the vehicles for preparing participants to become visionary in the sacrifice, bráhmans functioned as speculative objects. Their images helped to found Sanskrit speculation, and their poet-creators became the originators of primal images that helped to establish the meaning of the cosmos informing the Sanskrit world view. The authority of the Veda guaranteed that its images of the cosmos were heard for centuries in Sanskrit literature. In discussing these bráhmans, what can we say first about their special language form, and then (in the second part of this study) what can we say about their images?

In any nonliteral, figurative usage of language we may separate vehicle from tenor, to use the terms of I. A. Richards. This distinguishes between the figurative expression itself, the vehicle, and the referend or meaning, its tenor. In the bráhman contest, the vehicle is the enigmatic bráhman, its tenor is the mystery that each contestant desires to experience directly, the beyond that eludes ordinary perception, language, and thought. Further, we may call this bráhman vehicle an object to focus a kind of disciplined, meditative thought, in short, a support for speculative vision. To be speculative means to further the apprehension of unperceived features of reality, a frequent concern of archaic speculation.[1] It is meditative since it brings consciousness to focus on such levels of reality in a special, visionary state.

Visionaries have selected any of several speculative language forms to pursue their goals and to express themselves. The fact that the creators of this earliest speculative language of the Sanskritic tradition chose to use an enigmatic language based on images should interest readers of the Veda. Speculative statements, after all, can use (as in philosophical systems) literal, nonfigurative, propositional language, with or without specialized technical terms and rules for making proper assertions; or they can use figurative language (characteristic of prephilosophical, archaic speculation); or they can use specialized language forms, such as the enigma, riddle, and paradox. The bráhman contest poets of the Ṛg Veda chose the enigmatic, combining it with the figurative.

Study of the language forms that have been used in Indian speculative thought remains largely neglected. Renou has been one of the few scholars to deal with the subject. At the end of his seminal article on the powers of language in the Ṛg Veda (1955), he entertained the thesis that the "entire Ṛgveda is an allegory" (p. 26). This recalls the medieval Western assertion that scriptural style is parabolic (cf. Coomaraswamy: 1946, p. 188 ff.). In any case, Ṛg Vedic speculative imagery has often been interpreted, but its language form has been overlooked. Indeed, after suggesting that the entire Ṛg Veda be read allegorically, Renou himself came to an even more striking conclusion about its language which, perhaps because it was too daring, has received little attention. Speaking of both Ṛg Vedic language and that of Sanskrit literature in general, he wrote, "*the manner in which things are said bears* (comporter) a *didactic* value almost as great as the matter" (Renou: 1955, p. 27; italics added). Though a case for such an assertion can rather easily be made for the styles of Sanskrit grammarians, poets, and *sūtra* writers, Renou's observation applies equally well to the creators of the bráhman form. His comment can illumine these difficult verses and serves as the basis for the discussion to follow.

Jan Gonda, another student of Vedic figurative language and figures of speech (Gonda: 1939, used by Coomaraswamy: 1939, on the same topic, and Gonda: 1949) commented on the form of such language in connection with his studies on the meaning of the term *alaṃkāra*. He asked, does *alamkāra* mean merely "stylistic embellishment," or does it have another function as well in the scriptural Vedic style? Dealing specifically with stylistic peculiarities of the language of Atharva Veda I–VII[2] (alliteration, anaphoric repetition, paronomastic juxtaposition, rhyme, and homoioteleuton, Gonda: 1949, p. 3), Gonda concluded that these figures were not mere ornaments. Rather, as special scriptural language, they served to intensify and hallow the religious value of the text, to make it solemn, thereby "rendering it suitable for its purpose" (ibid.). He proposed this as the original meaning of the term *alaṃkāra* (cf. also Gonda: 1939, especially pp. 109–11). At their origin such figures, essentially types of *yamaka* or figures based on repetition of sounds, were not primarily ornamental figures of speech or aesthetic embellishments. Rather, they contributed to a nonaesthetic level of the text associated with its sacral or magical power, its ability to evoke the mysterious. Gonda proposed an interesting hypothesis:

> In my opinion there is reason enough for contending that the simile in the earliest Indian literature was a phenomenon that might be considered as an "alaṃkāra," i.e., as a stylistic "Ausdrukswert," which added strength to the text, made it such as is required, made it fit, prepared, which contributed to giving it the correct form of style. [Gonda: 1949, p. 4][3]

Gonda's argument that the *yamaka* and even the *upamā* figures function nonaesthetically, as more than mere embellishments (a meaning of *alaṃkāra* more relevant to the *kāvya* style), applies as well to figures of speech occurring in speculative contexts, though Gonda in his own remarks on similes in Sanskrit literature (1949) barely deals with such figures.[4] In fact, Ṛg Vedic bráhmans contain paradigm cases of such speculative imagery. The bráhman was a speculative *alaṃkāra* of the Vedic scriptural-speculative style. Its significance goes beyond even the stylistic level, into the semantic realm. Stylistically, it gives added strength to the revelations made by these special mantras about brahman. Semantically, its enigmatic figures make possible the special revelation of the bráhman by conveying meanings impossible to convey in nonfigurative, nonenigmatic linguistic vehicles. These techniques created effective, powerful mantras for visionary contemplation.

This Ṛg Vedic bráhman form bears out Renou's claim that the manner in which something is said can be as didactic as what is said itself. The study of this speculative *alaṃkāra* holds the key to understanding many verses previously considered beyond the ken of translators. A similar approach has unlocked the meaning of other "enigmatical" authors,[5] as Wheelwright's masterful translation of the oft-studied aphorisms of Heraclitus (1964) demonstrates. Heraclitus's ancient translators considered him obscure, dark, and riddling (Wheelwright: 1964, pp. 12, 116) in much the same way that translators have regarded bráhman verses. Wheelwright's approach to Heraclitus's often enigmatical, figurative aphorisms avoids such conclusions by considering the form of the language itself to be semantically significant. He approaches the aphorisms as conscious vehicles whose tenor requires a special form adequate to its profound or mysterious meaning:

> In the case of a writer like Heraclitus, who employs figures of speech not for prettification but as a means of exploring and adumbrating some of the more hidden aspects of reality, it is helpful to examine the ways in which those

> figures of speech function semantically. [Wheelwright: 1964, p. 94]

Rather than comdemn the bráhman form for obscurity, we should view that obscurity as essential to its special attempt to communicate about brahman, the mysterious. When representing the mysterious, as the *Tao Te Ching's* author has claimed, "Straightforward words/ Seem paradoxical."[6]

The deliberate enigmatic character of bráhmans means that the contest poets were conscious enigmatographers. Most commentators have ignored this possibility, arguing instead that the bráhmans have become obscure for the contemporary reader for philological or other reasons. Even those who have recognized the presence of "riddles" in such verses have ignored its implications by not considering the nature and function of intentionally obscure language. Kunhan Raja (1956) translates the many "puzzling" bráhman verses of 1.164 without dismissing them as hopelessly unintelligible, claiming instead that they are a "mystery" in many places. Unfortunately he argues that the hymn was not a mystery to those who composed it, denying its deliberate enigmatic character. The mystery, he says, arises because we no longer understand its "symbols" as the Ṛg Vedic poet did when he composed its verses:

> The whole poem (1.164) must have been quite plain to the people of those days. They knew the entire set of symbols. [Kunhan Raja: 1963, p. 46]

> We have completely lost the meaning of the symbols that he (Dirghatamas, author of 1.164) makes use of in expressing his philosophical ideas, *and for this* reason, his poetry *becomes a mystery* in many places; it is a riddle, an enigma. [Ibid., p. 1; italics added]

Thus, Kunhan Raja contends that these verses are enigmatic not because of the form of their composition but because we have lost the key to their symbolic meaning.[7] Such a view hardly accords with the evidence of their language form or context. Rather, the enigma originally stated a mystery, being so designed to express a meaning instrinsically enigmatic. Bráhman verses were intentionally allusive, deliberately obscure language sets using special means to suggest understandings of reality not ordinarily perceived or experienced. The enigma conceals its meaning in or by its own formulation, and must be contemplated to have its full effect. It creates new meanings by altering ordinary usages and expected meanings of words, forcing those who confront it to question ordinary conclusions in favor of some new, more comprehensive apprehensions of truth. As the classical Greek writers knew, the enigma is a "dark saying"[8] that deliberately uses the suggestive, multivalent, plurisignative potentialities of language to communicate a meaning otherwise impossible to express. For the Ṛg Vedic speculative poet these enigmatic verses did not refer to ordinary world realities but to a sacred beyond, experienced only in visionary states, for which only special, visionary forms of language were appropriate.

Two other specialized language forms, the *paradox* and the *riddle*, at times contribute to the bráhman. However, they should be technically defined and distinguished from *enigma*, as the two terms often function falsely as its synonymns. *Paradox* presents a claim that appears to be inconsistent with common sense or logical thought, or that seems self-contradictory or lacking somehow in self-consistency, but that all the while contains truth, which upon closer examination or contemplation becomes evident or acceptable despite its paradoxical vehicle. Paradoxes can be more or less enigmatic, possessing degrees of paradoxicality. Some paradoxes express trivial truth, based on verbal play, as in the case of the claim that Freud was not a Freudian. Other paradoxes, more enigmatic, resist restatement or explaining away in nonenigmatic terms,[9] but need to be contemplated to see the truth within their surface inconsistencies or disharmonies. Such paradox achieves ontological significance by saying something that transcends ordinary expression. It performs its essential function in producing a new view of its subject. Heraclitus's paradoxical aphorism, "The name of the bow is life, but its work is death" (Wheelwright: 1964, p. 91) says something unique about life, something we do not ordinarily realize. To effect this paradoxical understanding, it uses as its image vehicle an object, the bow, unambiguous and concrete, to shed light on life, highly mysterious. It reminds us of the two-sided process of life which we ordinarily experience only unidimensionally. Wheelwright comments:

> To him [Heraclitus] nothing is exclusively this or that; in various ways he affirms something to be *both* of two disparates or two contraries, *leaving the reader to contemplate the paradox,* the full semantic possibilities of which can never be exhausted by plain prose statements. [Wheelwright: 1964, pp. 91–2; second italics added]

Though *riddle* implies something dark or puzzling, it is formally distinct from *enigma* and *paradox*. The riddle expresses a question or verbal puzzle. It usually contains its own answer in a series of clues that, when correctly perceived, often in terms of an underlying image, will give its solution. The Ṛg Veda contains explicit riddles (cf. note 2.7). The riddle of the Sphinx is easily solved when the image of one who walks on three legs in the evening is "seen" to be man in his advanced age, walking with a stick or cane, contrasted to man walking on twos or crawling on all fours, in the noon and morning times of life. Still the riddle retains a measure of the enigmatic to be contemplated since it condenses the entire mortal day of man into a single image, seeing the unity in temporal diversity. Some riddles employ surface or verbal paradox ("A man and not a man": a eunuch; "A stone and not a stone": pumice), while others approach much closer to the enigma. The famous inscription at Apollo's oracle in Delphi, "Know thyself," asks us to contemplate the mystery of being mortal. As with paradox, riddle can either be superficial, as those propounded in games of wit, solved merely by putting together the subtle clues it contains, or more profound. The latter require a response that transcends the bounds of ordinary comprehension, resembling more closely the bráhmans of the Ṛg Veda.[10]

Bráhmans used unconventional language to refer to unconventional realities. Ordinary conceptual language functions denotatively. In the language of the market, *apple* refers only to apples and not to oranges or bananas. Enigmatic language, by contrast, uses images and other allusive techniques to point by indirection to reality rarely as tangible as apples and oranges. Unlike marketplace reality, such depths conceal themselves in the process of revealing themselves; they appear and disappear and re-appear only after sustained effort to reach them. As opposed to language tied to its referent by the single, explicit string of concrete denotation, enigmatic language implies levels of meaning, being allied with its referent through the techniques of allusion and suggestion.

Contemplating the images of such language, Ṛg Vedic enigmatographer visionary poets apprehended the mysterious depths of reality, the "face" of the divine "shining brilliantly in the mysterious," "moving rapidly, rapidly disappearing" (4.5.9cd). What enigma did this poet contemplate to receive such a vision? In Renou's translation, its first statement reads:[11]

> The gracious (here ellipsis of a neuter substantive) of Pṛśni (the one who is located) in the drinking skin (?) the solar-disk (?) hoisted to the top of the slope (?). [*sasásya*

> *cármann ádhi cāru pŕśner ágre rupá ārupitaṃ jábāru* 4.5.7cd]
> [Renou: EVP II (1956), p. 58]

Even Renou's later, less tentative translation of this bráhman sustains its enigmatic impact:

> The precious (milk) of (the Cow) Pṛśni (is) in the Skin of food, the solar-disk (is) risen to the summit of the earth.
> [Renou: EVP XIII (1964), p. 9]

Quite apart, indeed, from our ability to understand this verse in the sense of being able to paraphrase or restate it, no leap of the imagination is required to see it as a visionary, meditative object whose porous, figurative suggestivity is essential to the contemplation. One might even go along with Renou, who suggests that this bráhman's theme is proto-Vedāntic! (EVP XII, 1964, p. 97). It involves the identity of Agni, his basic nature, in short the underlying unity of diverse sacred phenomena, whether it be Agni enclosed in the skin of food, or the precious milk of the Cow, or Agni as the solar disk risen high above the earth. The meditation gains in complexity as we elaborate the possible tenors of each image in the vehicle—and all can simultaneously be intended. Monier-Williams lists Pṛśni as figurative for milk, the earth, a cloud, and the starry sky (p. 647), expanding several-fold the dimensions of only one of the bráhman's components. These images function in the ambiguous half-light of the enigma, providing for the contestant a meditative support adequate to the vision he sought and soon attained.

The second enigma of this particular contest opens up even broader speculative horizons by introducing mythological allusions, avian imagery, and mention of the entrance to the mysterious realm, which is Agni's special domain and charge:

> If (humans) open (this mystery) as (one opens) the door (?) of Cows [allusion to the familiar myth of the imprisoned

cows] (the procedure is in vain, because it is Agni himself who) guards the top of the slope [cf. X.127,7 asyá mūrdhán "at the cranium of this (world)"], the region of the bird. [Renou: EVP (1956), p. 58] [all this to translate, *yád usríyāṇām ápa vā̆r iva vrán pā̆ti priyáṃ rupó ágram padám véḥ*!]

Renou comments that he intends this to be as adequate a translation of the verse as is possible, since its enigmatic quality belongs essentially to the bráhman:

Thus do we propose to understand this part of the verse, where, as in the preceding one (i.e., v. 7cd), *the obscurity is, so to say, essential.* [Ibid., italics added]

The bráhman, then, reveals something and at the same time approximates its ineffability through its own linguistic ambiguity. Its proper enigmatic form approaches more closely than any other linguistic vehicle its intended level of reality (*ṛta,* the real, cosmos, order, *satya,* unqualified truth). By contemplating the bráhman's extended meditative image, reports the poet, he becomes a visionary participant in the hidden brilliance of Agni's divine revelation. Renou's later translation of the entire bráhman sequence includes the poet's autobiographical report of his attainment of visionary participation in the mystery (in 9cd):

7.
The precious (milk) of (the Cow) Pṛśni (is) in the Skin of food, the solar-disk (is) risen to the summit of the earth. (padas cd)

8.
When one has discovered (it, this mystery) of the auroral cows, like an opening, (one has found Agni who) watches over the beloved summit of the earth, over the track of the Bird. (padas cd)

9.
Such is the illustrious grand face of the great (gods), the one which accompanied at the beginning

> the auroral cow. In the region of the Order I have found (this face), shining there hidden, moving itself in a rapid (flow), rapid(ly disappeared). (autobiographical final sentence, padas cd, not part of enigma)
>
> 10.
> So, as he shines with his mouth (open), next to the two (rubbing sticks, his) parents, (Agni) in thought evokes the precious (milk), secret, of Pṛśni. In the supreme region of (his) Mother, facing towards the cow, the tongue of the male (Agni manifests itself), of the flame extended in front.
>
> [Renou: EVP XIII (1964), pp. 9–10]

Though attempts to understand these verses must be relatively frustrating, their dismissal would relegate to meaninglessness an entire class of verses scattered throughout the Ṛg Veda. These verses occur in speculative contexts in definable bráhman form. Their frustrating obscurity serves, in fact, as a marker of their distinctive class. Were one to encounter someone in a foreign land (and this is what the speculative realm is) speaking an exotic tongue, it would be foolish to consider the foreign language meaningless. One would rather grant the legitimacy of the stranger's language. In the same way, the seemingly incomprehensible Ṛg Vedic speculative bráhman form is a specialized, exotic language designed to further the processes of visionary experience. It never did need to conform to the ordinary ways of language, nor did it ever intend to be explicit and denotative. Rather, to be speculative, it originated a novel language form to achieve special insights into the mysterious. Considered in this light, its obscurity takes on new meaning, and our efforts to understand find new avenues.

Bráhmans use images imbedded in enigma as elements of a figurative visionary language. This language only superficially resembles denotative language. Its terms do not designate their literal referent but have a tenor. While in ordinary use, *cow* points to a specific referent, but in such language it has a second level of reference. Often difficulties arise in specifying the tenor or tenors of these figurative expressions, but none need be a candidate for the category of "Vedic balderdash." Translators and interpreters have a responsibility to seek understanding in terms of the criteria of reasonableness assumed by the original authors of these verses. None should fall into the fault of censure when further attempts at understanding are in order.[12]

The later development of the bráhman leads us too far afield for consideration here. An interesting transitional Ṛg Vedic example marks the development from the earlier bráhman, which generally was not put in the question form at all, to the later brahmodya. This later form occurs in post Ṛg Vedic ritual texts (cf. particularly Renou: 1949*a*, part B, pp. 22–41),[13] especially the White Yajurveda, for use in such rites as the Aśvamedha, Rājasūya, and Vājapeya. It involved the posing and answering of set questions and answers. This Ṛg Vedic enigma is transitional because it adopts the brahmodya question form but has no answer immediately following:

> How many are the Agnis (fires), how many are the suns?
> How many are the dawns, and how many really (*svid*)
> are the waters?
>
> [10.88.18ab]

The text provides no answers for these questions, as was the rule later. Perhaps this was meant to preserve the enigmatic nature of the question in order to enhance its speculative force, or perhaps it was considered that the answer could not be explicitly stated in verbal form. Concrete evidence exists that such bráhmans were already becoming brahmodyas in the Ṛg Veda, because we have recorded answers. Traditions must have built up around answers to questions repeatedly used in the contest until one or another became popular enough to supersede its competitors. In this way the force of tradition would begin to accumulate, giving after some time the sanction of orthodoxy to a particular answer.

Renou (1955, pp. 11–12) considers that the Vālakhilya verse 8.58.2 is actually the accepted response to the bráhman questions of 10.88.18ab, particularly since tradition usually inserts this verse after 10.88.[14] Since there is almost complete correspondence between questions and answers, this suggestion appeals to common sense:

> One only is Agni, though kindled many times; one
> is the sun though it rises forth for all;
>
> One only is dawn, though all this she illumines;
> one indeed is this, which produced all.

The only change occurs in pada d, where the more archaic *waters* image becomes abstract. Both *waters* and *this* refer to the creative source of the cosmos, and so are equivalent. The change probably indicates that answers of this sort were added later, with the archaic, figurative formulation being replaced by more sophisticated abstraction, common in later times. That they did receive such answers indicates as well that such enigmatic questions were considered meaningful and did participate in speculative endeavor. Hidden in this simple set of four questions we find what, to Sanskrit speculation, became one of the most profound mysteries: whether that which is diverse and many can ultimately be one and unified? In short, these verses state the speculative theme of unity in diversity, using a form that some would consider to be fumbling, archaic questioning. Analysis reveals them on the contrary to be sophisticated, figurative contemplations of a mystery that remained fundamental to the entire history of later speculation.

If what appears to be a nonsensical riddle turns out to be an early posing of the mystery of unity in multiplicity, involving the metaphysics of appearance and reality, then perhaps other bráhmans also conceal more than their surface reveals. Another bráhman based on the early brahmodya question form shows how fundamental speculative issues were stated in incomplete riddling questions. These riddles contain insufficient internal clues to provide adequate bases for answers, which must rather be stipulated; in this respect they function enigmatically:

> I ask you: what is the farthest end (limit) of the earth?
> I ask: where is the navel of the world?
> I ask you: what is the semen of the powerful horse?
> I ask: what is the highest sky of speech?
> [1.164.34]

Each image provides a support for contemplation of what the poet considers significant speculative ultimates (farthest end, navel, semen, highest sky), but gives no indication of their proper tenor. The answers, given in the following verse in brahmodya style, reveal that their tenor is the sacrifice. Each answer shows the primary, sacrificial tenor of the bráhman:

> This altar is the farthest end of the earth.
> This sacrifice is the navel of the world.
> This soma is the semen of the powerful horse.
> This brahman-priest is the farthest sky of speech.
> [1.164.35]

Each image supports the contemplation of various aspects of the sacrifice. The bráhman facilitates the focusing of awareness on the deepest comprehension of the transcendental meanings of the sacrifice. In the first two *padas*, sacrifice is experienced as simulacrum of cosmos, relating sacrifice and cosmos not through abstract doctrine but through the more fluid terms of a meditative image.[15]

The task before interpreters of Ṛg Vedic speculative language now opens onto new horizons. We have yet to dig below this puzzling landscape's surface to discover some of the beginnings of Sanskrit speculation.

3.
The Enigma of the Two Birds in the Fig Tree

One of the most dramatic Ṛg Vedic collections of bráhmans was recorded in Dīrghatamas's famous account (1.164) of a symposium he experienced. All the elements occur in his account to mark this as a symposium: Agni, the contestant's patron and source of inspiration; perplexing bráhman verses; and the poet's own autobiographical report of receiving inspired visionary consciousness. The total effect of the bráhmans reminds one of Gaston Bachelard's observation, "Tout s'active quand s'accumulent les contradictions." This seems to have happened to Dīrghatamas, by his own account.

Several powerful images have come down to Indian speculative traditions from that great contest, including the metaphor of the wheel of life (see chapter 5) and the image of the two birds in the fig tree. This latter enigma, stated over three verses, is remarkable. It actually is an enigmatographer's enigma. We should have expected such verses somewhere in the Ṛg Veda, since enigmatographers relate quite consciously to their craft and have fun with it. Surprisingly no one, neither the ancient commentators on the Veda nor any of the western translators and interpreters of this verse, has ever found out Dīrghatamas's original tenor. The primary Ṛg Vedic tenor of this enigma was not some mysterious aspect of cosmic reality or power, but the symposium itself. In this rare case, Dīrghatamas chose to enigmatize what was happening around him during a symposium, and he even parenthetically mentioned his own attainment of visionary awareness.

As Vedic goes, the language of this bráhman is not overly difficult:

20.
dvā́ suparṇā́ sayújā sákhāyā samānáṃ vṛkṣám pári ṣasvajāte/
táyor anyáḥ píppalaṃ svādv átty ánaśnann anyó abhí cākaṣīti//

21.
yátrā suparṇā́ amṛ́tasya bhāgám ánimeṣaṃ vidáthā-abhisváranti/
inó víśvasya bhúvanasya gopā́ḥ sá mā dhī́raḥ pā́kam átra-ā́-viveśa//

22.
yásmin vṛkṣé madhvádaḥ suparṇā́ niviśánte súvate ca-ádhi víśve/
tásyéd āhuḥ píppalaṃ svādv ágre tán nón naśad yáḥ pitáraṃ ná véda//

[1.164.20–22]

Recent translators, beginning with Geldner,[1] followed closely by Thieme's critique,[2] and then by Kunhan Raja,[3] Renou,[4] and Brown[5] agree to a great extent on the translation of this bráhman. Differences arise in identifying allusions made by the verses and even more in interpreting the tenors of their images. If we take Geldner (G) as a standard contemporary translation, and take into account Thieme's (T) improvements, a consensus on its translation is possible. One need only make a few modifications of Thieme's corrections of Geldner. (T) is undoubtedly correct (1949, p. 63, #5) in revising (G)'s translation of *píppala* from "Berre" to "Feige," and "fig" is more appropriate than either Kunhan Raja's (KR) "berry" or Brown's (B) "fruit," as Renou's (R) translation "figue" concurs.

For the phrase *amṛ́tasya bhāgá* (T) substitutes for (G)'s "Anteil an der Unsterblichkeit" (followed as well by KR, R, and B) the more proper "Anteil am Leben," offering convincing parallels from other passages. In most Ṛg Vedic contexts, it is preferable to translate *amṛ́ta* as "life,"[6] and in this case the cautious approach is to do the same, even though we can presume that in such a speculative context, if anywhere, it might have a connotation more like its later meaning of immortality.

Furthermore (T) disagrees with (G) on the identification of the allusions made by *mádhu (madhvádaḥ,* 22a) and *bhúvanasya gopā́ḥ* (21c). Geldner (1951, p. 65, followed by R and B) supplies "Frucht," making the *mádhu* refer to the *píppala* of 20c, but the parallel is not justified since *svadú* was previously used, not *mádhu*. As (T) notes, *mádhu* is "honey" (KR agrees), and this must refer to *sóma*, which the symposiasts would be drinking on the occasion of the sadhamā́da. This leads to (T)'s further identification of the "protector of the world" also as *sóma* (p. 66), especially considering the use of *ā* $\sqrt{\textit{viś}}$ as the verb in 21d. Certainly this identification is superior to (G)'s "der Allvater." However, here (B)'s suggestion that it is Agni is probably best, since Agni is the patron of the contest and the poet's inspirer. Since Dīrghatamas is speaking of his attainment of inspiration, the reference must be to Agni entering him. Furthermore (T) is not correct when he claims, counter to all other translators, that *suparṇá* should not be translated as "birds" but "eagles" (p. 59). The reason is purely ornithological; in fact, eagles are not frugivorous and probably would not be nesting in a fig tree but in some lofty deodar or on a towering cliff. It is also probably better to agree with (G) over (T) on the correlative construction of *átra* with *yátra* in v. 21 (see T, p. 66, fn. 3).

By far the most vexed problem in the triplet, however, is offered by *vidáthā* in 21b. Translators disagree both as to its grammar and its meaning. (G), (T), and (R) take it as it stands, a neuter accusative plural, while (KR) and (B) translate it as a Vedic neuter locative singular, which is admittedly counter to the word's form.[7] It must therefore be taken as an accusative plural. As to its meaning (G) translates "Weisheit," (T) "Verteilungen," (R) "cénacles (rituels)," (KR) "before the learned assembly," and (B) "in conclave." In this case, given the context of the verses, "contest" seems most appropriate, despite Thieme's[8] survey with convincing arguments for other contexts, and Kuiper's agreement[9] with him. J. P. Sharma,[10] criticizing the previous discussion of R. S. Sharma,[11] more recently has concluded that (T)'s interpretation is too limited for all contexts of the word and favors for a greater number of occurrences the meaning "assembly":

> Vedic literature shows that the *vidatha* was a local congregation performing mainly religious rites and ceremonies for the good luck and prosperity of the settlement. . . . In short, it was a local assembly meeting mainly for religious purposes. [Pp. 79–80]

In the context of these verses, it is safe to conclude that *vidátha* means "enigma contest."

A reasonable translation of the triplet would be:

20.
Two birds, paired companions, occupy the same tree.
Of the two, one eats the sweet fig,
The other, not (yet) eating, looks on.

21.
Where birds unwinkingly celebrate contests, their
life's bounty,
There he, the splendid herdsman of all creation,
Wise (Agni) entered me, unrealizing (before that).

22.
Onto that tree honey-eating birds all alight and mature,
At the top of it alone, they say, is the sweet fig—
No one reaches up to it who knows not the father!

If we can fairly well agree on the translation of this bráhman, what of its interpretation? Thieme surveys earlier interpretations (1949, p. 56 ff.), which need not be repeated here, and takes cues from them for his own, somewhat naturalistic interpretation. He argues strongly against Geldner, whose interpretation admittedly is cursory, developed only in footnotes to the verses. Brown tends to follow Geldner, and both rightly avoid using the later interpretation (developed by Vedānta interpreters and others), which identifies the two types of birds (or knowers) as two types of self. Kunhan Raja (1956, p. 37) introduces part of the later understanding in rejecting Geldner's interpretation of the tenor of the tree image, but agrees with Geldner and Brown in the main.

Since Geldner's interpretation resembles all these short attempts, his may be quoted as representative:

> 20–22. Der Erkenntnisbaum, ein schönes Gleichnis. Die Auflösung wird durch 22d nahe gelegt. Der Baum ist das Wissen, dessen höchste Frucht die Erkenntnis des Allvaters ist. Die beiden Vögel repräsentieren die zwei Arten der Wissbegierigen mit verschiedener Fassungsgabe. Nur den einen, zu denen sich der Dichter selbst rechnet, offenbart sich diese höchste Erkenntnis (21cd), während die anderen, die Nichtspekulativen, leer ausgehen . . . 21a *amṛ́tasya bhāgám* ist die Frucht der höheren Erkenntnis, wie aus 22*d* erhellt . . . 22b führt das Bild von den Vögeln weiter aus. Dies wird noch mehr verständlich, wenn man bedenkt, dass sich die Gelehrsamkeit vom Vater auf den Sohn vererbte . . . 22d. Der Vater ist wieder der Allvater, in dem viele der vorangehended Str. (vgl. bes. 21) gipfeln. [1951, I: 231]

Brown's interpretation (pp. 208, 214) is much like Geldner's. He calls the triplet "a parable dealing with the attainment of immortality, which is represented by the sweet fruit of a tree, presumably the tree of knowledge" (p. 214). All disagree on the allusion made to "father" in 22d, along with *bhúvanasya gopā́ḥ* in 21c, (G)'s solution of "Allvater" being countered by (B)'s reading of Agni, while (KR) equivocates by referring 22d to "references to a father in earlier verses" (p. 41). By way of contrast (KR) rejects (G) (p. 37), arguing that only the "tasty berry" (p. 36) has the tenor of wisdom, which the wise (birds, in 22) partake of, becoming inspired. Apparently because of the tree image at Kaṭha Upaniṣad 3.1, possibly an ectype of the Ṛg Vedic image, and because of evidence from Vedānta, (KR) only allows that the tree's tenor is the universe itself,[12] and, like the others, considers the two birds to be two types of people in it.

Renou also offers only a footnote level interpretation in the course of the Veda selections in his *Anthologie Sanskrite*. There he writes:

> 13. on a interprété le vers (et les deux suivants) spéculativement: l'arbre de la connaissance, dont le fruit est la participation du divin au Père, les deux oiseaux représentant deux types d'aspirants, dont l'un seul accède à la connaissance. Mais l'interprétation naturaliste doit être primitive: les étoiles = les Pères se hâtant vers la lune, leur séjour, pour avoir part à l'ambroisie. [P. 23]

Hardly very helpful, Renou does bring up the possibility of an "interprétation naturaliste [qui] doit être primitive," and this leads directly to Thieme's attempt, perhaps based on the same sources to which Renou was vaguely referring.

Of the recent interpretations, Thieme's is not only the most carefully thought out and presented but also the longest. Essentially, Thieme argues that the overall tenor of the entire image is the nighttime sky.[13] The "Rätselallegorie" represents the drama of the night, with the two birds of v. 20 symbolizing the waxing and waning moon.

In turn, when the number of the birds switches from dual to plural (in v. 21 and 22), the stars are represented which "alight and increase," that is, appear in the sky, first a few and then in ever greater multitudes. The birds (stars) contrast with the moon since they do not close their eyes (stay out all night), as opposed to the moon which "sleeps" or disappears for three nights in each lunar cycle. Furthermore, the waxing and waning moon is the tenor of the bird that eats, distinct from the others that only look on and stay the same. Completing the analysis of the extended metaphor's tenor, Thieme concludes that the sweet fig and honey refer to "light" and "life" (p. 66), which are none other than the heavenly sóma juice. Both the moon and the stars have the same relation to the "lebendigen Himmelslicht" or the sóma. This allows Thieme to interpret 21d as referring to the inspiration the poet receives from drinking sóma.[14]

Much recommends this analysis. It accounts for all elements of the compound image, its tenor exhibits an internal consistency, and parallel passages support its interpretations. It also has a satisfying literalness, reminding one of "naturalistic" interpretations of Vedic symbolism of other scholars. As Thieme notes (p. 60) the opposing concave positions of the moon in its first and fourth quarters could well be represented by the two birds in the tree, separately and alternately eating the sweet fig at the top. Unfortunately, nothing in Thieme's interpretation decisively rules out the possibility of the other shorter interpretations already noted.

It is also unfortunate that Thieme apparently did not have the interesting article on this bráhman image by K. N. Dave, "The Golden Eagle and the Golden Oriole in the Vedas and *Purāṇas*."[15] While Thieme dismisses the importance of achieving zoological accuracy,[16] Dave approaches the problem of this riddle by seeking a solution that makes an ornithologically precise determination of the image vehicle. In fact, this may suggest a resolution of the hermeneutical dilemma in that it offers some basis for deciding among the available interpretations. Dave clearly thinks it necessary to establish the image vehicle before interpreting its tenor (moral).[17]

Making first some general observations about the Himālayan Golden Eagle and Golden Oriole, Dave begins by translating the phrase *dvā́ suparṇā́ sayújā* (two birds, paired companions, v. 20a) as a "pair of Golden or other Eagles" and "a pair of beautiful little orioles" (p. 85). The former pair nests at the top of the tree from which, Dave says, the female Golden Eagle surveys the surroundings defiantly, thus providing protection for the latter. The orioles, nesting below, enjoy this protection of the larger and more impressive birds above. The oriole pair, being frugivorous, feeds in the tree, while the other merely looks on. Dave considers v. 21 then to state the point of view of the orioles, who express their gratitude for the protection with sweet notes. He offers the following paraphrase:

> There in the fig tree each discerning (*vidathā*) Oriole ceaselessly sings his grateful acknowledgement of his share of good things . . . in these words . . . "weak as I am, the wise Lord and strong (*inah*) Protector of the world (of birds) has (graciously) admitted me into this (safe) tree (*atrāviveśa*)." [P. 86]

Dave finds the moralizing tenor of this image in v. 22:

> The "suparṇā" (plural) in this verse stands for the people, the fig-tree for the Tree of Life or the mundane world, the heavenly Pitā or protector for the Sun. What the sage, therefore, means to say is that those who live, multiply, and prosper on the Tree of Life but do not know (i.e., gratefully acknowledge) the protector, cannot really enjoy the sweet fruit growing on the tree (i.e., the gifts of the pitā). By implication, they are worse than the Orioles who know the truth. The idea is that a gift is fully appreciated

> only when you know the giver and are duly grateful to him for it. There can be no feeling of gratefulness and no true enjoyment of an anonymous gift. We are told in a word, that gifts of life are enjoyed all the better for the grateful knowledge that they are a boon from the Heavenly-father. [Pp. 86–87]

On the whole, this interpretation is at least as satisfying as Thieme's, but it suffers structurally from a failure to distinguish vehicle from tenor, tending to confuse the two. While advancing the discussion ornithologically, Dave's interpretation still makes no decisive move toward certainty. He makes no convincing analysis of the image vehicle, a desideratum for any adequate interpretation.

Dave's ornithological identifications, further, leave some doubt as to their appropriateness. Professor Carl Naether, an ornithologist, doubts that an oriole would build its nest below that of an eagle.[18] In fact, Salim Ali and S. Dillon Ripley's standard *Handbook of the Birds of India and Pakistan*[19] states that the Golden Eagle's nest is "a huge platform of sticks on a ledge of a cliff, but more usually in a deodar, juniper, or such-like tree overhanging a steep precipice or growing out of a cliff-face in difficult and fearsome situations" (1: 274). This is hardly where orioles live, for while both birds may have frequented the same general area where the Ṛg Veda was composed[20] and even today occasionally frequent similar altitudes (the zone around 2,000 meters), it does not sound likely that the oriole would be nesting in the type of tree favored by the eagle. Ali and Ripley (vol. 5) describe orioles as being "chiefly arboreal and frugivorous" (p. 103), as feeding upon wild figs (Ficus spp.), lantana and other berries, "flower-nectar," insects and caterpillars (p. 104). They nest commonly in chenar, willow, poplar, and catalpa, the nests being "built in trees between 6 and 20 metres from the ground, usually under 12 m."

Dave probably knew of these considerations but also noted the curious fact that the Indian Oriole deliberately nests below a "king-crow's nest" (p. 84), and this must have led him to his eagle-oriole identification. But Ali and Ripley say nothing of eagles, recording instead, the "nest [of oriole] often built in same tree, even in same branch, as holds a drongo's [King Crow's] nest for the protection from marauders afforded by these intrepid 'guardians' " (5: 104). Given this evidence, to preserve Dave's reading of *sayújā* as two pairs, it would be better to substitute drongo or King Crow[21] for his identification of Golden Eagle. On the other hand, the term's grammar (dual) probably means just one pair of birds, and this opens a whole new possibility. Following Dave's suggestion, this pair could be orioles, which are striking birds of melodious voice and bright yellow or ochre plumage. This allows a different reading of the image vehicle, focusing on the possible behavior of two orioles. Professor Naether observes,

> I do not think the one was an eagle, since eagles do not live on fruit. They could be orioles . . . or bulbuls, robins, or other of the numerous fruiteaters resident in that country.
>
> Moreover, they could be a pair, with the one eating fruit, perhaps a male, soon to feed it to his mate, awaiting this "service." Or the fruit-eater might be the parent of the other bird, who, still fairly young, seems to disregard the available fruit (food) round-about him, and is simply waiting to be fed [as is quite common for young birds to do]. Incidentally, I doubt very much that an oriole or similar bird would settle in a tree haboring an eagle or other bird of prey. The two birds being the only ones in the tree might suggest that they are of the same kind or species, and somehow belong together, especially since the one seems to be in a state of expectation.[22]

These comments describe the behavior of orioles, either when the male eats fruit and then feeds it (in regurgitated form) to its mate, or when an adult bird eats fruit and then feeds it to an immature bird, which, though out of the nest, still requires some feeding. Whichever moment was in the mind of the poet, both explain how one bird eats and the other looks on with the full realism of the actual behavior of orioles. The image is of one bird eating or participating in the sweet fig and then feeding it to another as a service. There is nothing inconsistent in this understanding of the vehicle image with ornithological data. Further, it makes good sense of the crucial enigmatic reference made by v. 20 to two birds, somehow "paired companions," one of which eats the sweet fig, the other not.

To interpret adequately the tenor of parabolic language one must start with a complete account of the image vehicle, especially when the image consists of an extended metaphor. Each element of the complex vehicle must be distinguished and then interpreted in the reading of its tenor. This first requires an adequate translation and understanding of the vehicle language, which necessitates a review of prior translations and interpretations of the vehicle and its allusions. In this case, pertinent ornithological evidence must also be considered. Without this evidence, nothing in previous works allows a precise determination of the primary Ṛg Vedic tenor of this image. With Dave's start and Naether's improvements, one can attempt to solve the scholarly riddle of this enigma and to emerge from the impasse created by competing interpretations of its tenor present in the literature.

Some compelling evidence must first be brought to bear. Given as background the information presented in chapter one, such evidence presents itself in the verses themselves. Combined with a proper ornithologically based reading of the vehicle, this can lead to an almost certain interpretation of its tenor. Dīrghatamas's account of the symposium throughout 1.164 provides important information and frames the entire poem. Verses 1–7ab describe the symposium as it begins. The fire is set out before the poet (referred to by the beginning phrase, verse 1a, *asyá vāmásya*). He portrays the sacrifice in familiar chariot symbolism and admits his lack of inspiration, asking for understanding. Verses 21, 37, and 52 are similarly autobiographical. The remainder of the hymn's verses are bráhmans, collected either from that particular symposium or, more likely, from among the most popular bráhmans of the age. Dīrghatamas's description and autobiographical insertions thus provide a framework for a diverse collection of bráhmans.

What, then, of this particular bráhman of the two birds in the fig tree which became so immensely popular in later literature, especially in philosophy? In verses 20 and 22, Dīrghatamas creates an enigmatographer's enigma. The bráhman's primary tenor is not the usual mysterious or cosmic reality, but the symposium itself. In this rare case, the poet has chosen to enigmatize his own experience of the symposium. The compelling evidence for this conclusion consists of three technical symposium terms, heretofore unrecognized in their technical import, one in each verse, along with two other terms that should be considered technical in this context.

First, in 20a, the term for the two birds is *sákhāyā*. The *sákhi* is a companion or member of a brotherhood (*sakhyá*) of speculative symposiasts. Second, in 21d, Dīrghatamas describes himself as *pā́kam* (unrealized, uninspired). With the parallel use in 4.5.2c and 1.164.5a, this qualifies as an attested, self-descriptive technical term in contest language.[23] Then, in the third verse, 22d uses the term *pitáram* (father), which 6.9.2d shows to be the technical term for one of the two antagonists' positions in the contest. Further, two other terms point to the symposium tenor of the triplet. The first, *vidátha,* in this context means symposium contest, being parallel to other terms that similarly refer to the "battle" or "contest" of the symposium. These include *pṛ́tanā* at 1.152.7c, *vā́jina,* used in

10.71.5b and 10d, and *samará*, at 6.9.2b, all of which refer metaphorically to the symposium contest as a battle in poems clearly describing symposia.[24] The second, *sayúja* (paired), modifying companions in 20a, must be parallel to the attested contest term *sajóṣas*,[25] which in 4.5.1a also means "symposiasts united or paired, ready for speculative dialogue."

Still other circumstantial evidence suggests that these verses refer enigmatically to the symposium of their poet-speculator author. In effect, it is not correct to consider all three verses to be the bráhman, since verse 21 is an autobiographical insert. While autobiography is rare in the Ṛg Veda, reports of symposia characteristically are interrupted by frequent autobiographical exclamations, lamenting the poet's lack of inspiration or, conversely, celebrating his achievement of it (compare 6.9.6 and 7). In verse 21, the poet steps out of the metaphorical mode of the bráhman (with the exception of "birds" or contestants in 21a) to describe his inspiration, which he attributes to Agni.

Given this accumulation of evidence linking the triplet to the symposium, a complete expansion of the vehicle image, along with its corresponding tenor, should be:

VEHICLE	TENOR
20.	
two birds	two symposiasts or contestants, antagonists who take two positions, the prior or son's position and the later or father's position, corresponding respectively to the candidate-for-vision's position and the accomplished-in-vision or master's position

paired	of the same brotherhood of speculative symposiasts; or "joined" together at the two opposed positions, ready for the contest's dialogue
companions	symposium brotherhood members
occupy the same tree	take their positions on the contest ground
one eats	participates already in inspired vision (i.e., is at the later, father's position)
the sweet fig	the goal of the contest, speculative, inspired visionary participation in the mystery stated by the bráhman enigma proposed by the father
the other, not (yet) eating, looks on	does not participate in, has not (yet) attained speculative vision (i.e., is at the former or son's position, having just entered the contest ground as a candidate for initiation), as yet not realizing and not inspired to speculative vision (*pā́ka*)

22.

onto that tree	onto the contest ground
honey-eating	sóma-drinking
birds	symposiasts (as above)
all alight	enter to take their contest position
and mature[26]	and are initiated, transformed, achieving the inspired state

at the top of it (the tree)	as the contest's culmination or goal
the sweet fig	inspired speculative vision (as above), the victor's goal
the father	the initiator or master who already has achieved the visionary state, and strives to impart it to initiates.

This structural analysis of the complex extended image into vehicle and tenor allows an interpretation both precise and complete, solving the scholarly puzzle presented by the bráhman. Surprisingly, it is an enigmatographer's enigma! Dīrghatamas, whose name (Deep Gloom) fits a master enigmatographer, includes one bráhman in his collection enigmatizing the symposium contest, thereby clarifying the institution itself and also the deliberateness of its principle speculative device, the bráhman enigma. Once analysis makes the vehicle components of the image explicit, a tenor can be supplied that accords with the facts of the symposium contest as well as with the most plausible ornithological suppositions about the image of the two birds in a fig tree. What Dave had read as a protective relationship between eagle and oriole is better interpreted as a feeding relationship between a pair of birds, either two adults or an adult and an immature individual. Birds often engage in such behavior, as the poet could easily have observed. In just the same way—and this is the most revealing feature—in the symposium, a father-companion symposiast already participating in the desired level of inspired vision initiates unrealized sons into the mysteries of bráhman (cosmic power, the *mysterium tremendum*) by posing enigmas and soliciting responses. The metaphor involves an initiatory feeding of an unrealized, uninitiated symposiast. Much like the *kung-an* or *kōan* given to a student of meditative Buddhism by a Ch'an or Zen master, the bráhman relies upon the literary potential of enigmatic density to transform consciousness.

This reading of the primary Ṛg Vedic tenor finds further confirmation in verse 22a, which describes the birds or symposiasts as "honey-eating." The tenor of this epithet must be sóma-drinking. In earlier descriptions of symposia (chapter 1) we have noticed the role of sóma as an active placebo,[27] not producing but facilitating the shift in consciousness from the unrealized (*pā́ka*) state to that of the inspired vision desired by participants in the symposium and sacrifice. Remarkably, in one of the most famous sóma hymns, Rg Veda 8.48, verse 14 uses the term *vidátha* in the technical sense of the symposium contest. The poet asks, after having drunk sóma, that he be protected by the gods, that neither sleep nor idle talk distract him. He states further: "We dear always to sóma, of brave sons, would dispute at contest." Naturally, as an active placebo, the sóma is a stimulus for the desired result, which requires a proper attitude and setting to be realized. Many times, as this reference indicates, poets needed to guard against untoward sóma reactions such as going to sleep or talking idly. To guard against such reactions the symposium was used to catapult consciousness into the inspired visionary state required of sacrifice participants.

If this surmise is correct, the initiatory structure of the contest appears all-important. The bird image stresses the active role of the father or master (later the guru, literally the "heavy" in the relationship) in the initiatory relationship. Just as the bird feeds its mate or child, so the master, after participating in the mystery (the sweet fig at the top of the tree), initiates candidates in the charismatic exchange of "energy" or "inspiration" (note the *śaktipat* exchange of contemporary guru traditions) through the dialogical exchange. The Vedic sacrifice was a simulacrum of the cosmos, intended to be the intermediary in the manipulation by human beings of the whole mechanism of creation for the well-being of all. Participation in such a work required bounteous energy for the performance of detailed, ritually prescribed actions, empathy so that the model of the universe could be participated in as if it actually were the universe, and inspiration to make the activities and sacred speech of the sacrifice truly creative in the cosmogonic sense. Through inspired speech the simulacrum became potentiated with the directing power of its human creators. Essential to all this must have been the initiatory experience, since it brought consciousness out of its ordinary understandings (perceiving fire, altar made of bricks) to enter into another world of meaning, supposed to represent a cosmic dimension of reality. Sóma, as a stimulant and low-level psychoactive (since no hallucinations are mentioned), facilitated this transformation of consciousness while also ensuring the necessary empathy and the production of prodigious energy for the pursuits of the sacrificial performance.

This interpretation of the bráhman of the two birds in the fig tree makes more sense than the vague surmises of Geldner, Kunhan Raja, and Brown. It states its "primary" Ṛg Vedic tenor as close to the Vedic understanding as internal evidence will allow. This does not rule out possible secondary tenors, including some of the suggestions of recent commentators, particularly since bráhman verses, being enigmatic, functioned with deliberate polyvalence. Tenors provided in the contest presumably could have been multiple, their appropriateness being determined situationally by the master according to various criteria, not the least of which would have been the initiate's consciousness as revealed in his response. The tenors suggested by Renou and particularly by Thieme could thus very well have figured in the set of proper responses to the bráhman, but they must be considered secondary. This holds true particularly for such a polyvalent image as birds in a tree, which belongs to the archaic mythic complex of the world tree or tree–of–life myth, well known worldwide. Nevertheless, the Ṛg Vedic tenor of this rare enigmatographer's enigma can be precisely stated.

Since this is so, the image can be treated as a fossil, with its original meaning clearly established for the time of the Ṛg Veda. Later, in popular thought and particularly in philosophical literature, it functioned as a major *dṛṣṭānta* or traditional simile for the doctrine of the two selves, one existential (condemned to transmigration) and the other essential (transcendent), espoused by all major systems including Sāṃkhya and Vedānta. Surprisingly, these later interpretations reversed the valuation of the Ṛg Vedic reading of the image's tenor, thus demonstrating that the doctrine of the two selves, universally attributed in later ages to the scriptural authority of the Ṛg Veda, was not Ṛg Vedic at all. Between the birth of the image in Dīrghatamas's poem and the early Upaniṣads, the most basic features and valuations of the Sanskrit world view shifted 180 degrees, from the life-affirming, physical-world-embracing view of the seminomadic Vedic bands to the transcendence-affirming, modified asceticism of the classical world view.

In the Ṛg Vedic tenor, the eating bird clearly represents the victor in the contest who eats the sweet fig, symbolizing participation in transforming, inspirational knowledge. In the first ectype of this archetypal image, which occurs twice in the early Upaniṣads, the new world view's valuation reverses that of the Ṛg Vedic tenor, for the eating bird is condemned to existentiality and its frustrations, while the observer bird comes to represent the metaphysically uninvolved, non-existential, transcendent spirit. In this way, the image fossil confirms other evidence demonstrating a complete turnabout of valuations of the physical world between the time of the Ṛg Veda and the Upaniṣads.

Many later authors cite this famous image, including

Śaṅkara (Brahmasūtrabhāṣya 1.2.12), Jayanta Bhaṭṭa (Nyāyamañjarī), the Bhāgavata Purāṇa (11.II.6–7), and even the old Hindī poet, Kabīr (Dvivedī edition, # 47). But its two Upaniṣadic citations suffice to demonstrate the fundamental shift in its interpretation. In both Upaniṣadic instances (Muṇḍaka 3.1.1–2 and Śvetāśvatara 4.6–7), only the first verse of the triplet is quoted, followed each time by the same commentarial verse basing its interpretation on the dual structure of the image ("two birds . . . one . . . the other"):

> Two birds, companions closely conjoined,[28] occupy the same tree.
> Of the two, one eats the sweet fig, the other, not eating, looks on.
> [Ṛg Veda 1.164.20, Muṇḍaka 3.1.1, Śvetāśvatara 4.6]

> Immersed in the tree common (to both person and Lord),
> A person sorrows, bewildered by not knowing the Lord;
> (But) when a person realizes the beloved other, the Lord,
> Realizing its glory, he transcends sorrow.
> [Muṇḍaka 3.1.2, Śvetāśvatara 4.7]

Clearly, the Upaniṣadic commentary considers the bird that does not eat the fruit as superior to the one that does, in direct contradiction to the Ṛg Vedic interpretation. The metaphysics of the world view has shifted to place the transcendent, uninvolved, essential self (here archaically called 'the Lord') over that element of personhood which is immersed in existentiality. This latter eats the sweet fig, which no longer symbolizes victorious knowledge but rather bewildered participation in deluding existentiality. Eating the sweet fig in this and later interpretations of the archetype means blindly enjoying physical reality and hence, by being cut off from the divine, becoming bewildered and falling into sorrow. The Ṛg Vedic image recommends the experience of saving knowledge within the fully accepted, empirical world. The Upaniṣadic interpretation, shifting to a metaphysical structure, supports the realization of transcendence through some form of withdrawal from the existential. In Śaṅkara, the observing bird becomes divine in the sense of the essential self (*paramātman*), while the bird participating in the sweet fig represents the karmic or existential selfhood (*jīvātman*). The image never appears in Buddhist texts, possibly indicating the Buddhist rejection of the metaphysics involved. In the Bhāgavata interpretation, the non-eating bird is the element of consciousness (probably, in its metaphysics, the *buddhi* or deep mind) that can know the true self (the goal of *kaivalya,* "uniqueness") when it renounces the sweet fig (reality), as in both the Sāṃkhya and Yoga systems.[29]

Quite apart from later symbolic usages of the two birds image, later thought also manifests deep reflexes of the symposium contest. Long ago, in his work on the play element in culture,[30] Johan Huizinga noted the importance of "ritual riddle-solving competitions" in Vedic literature. He argued that these contests marked the birth of Indian philosophy.[31] To the extent that the Ṛg Vedic speculative symposium influenced both content and form in latter–day India, Huizinga must be judged remarkably insightful in his conclusion of several decades ago. Surely, from what little we know of the symposium, it is the institution closest to the beginnings of archaic speculation in the Indian subcontinent, the first recorded context of speculations concerning the ultimate descriptions of reality. Indeed, speaking of the form of the institution alone, it has had considerable influence on later forms, philosophical and otherwise. In the courts of kings during the classical age of Indian poetries, poets vied like the symposiasts of old to complete verses provided by their royal patrons. Later schools of philosophy adopted the dialectical/dialogical form of the symposium in the writing of technical philosophy, where often the objection came first to be set right in the author's response, and also in the great monastic debates, such as those which Śaṅkara himself carried forth to the four corners of India. Tibetan monasticism continued the form in the Buddhist tradition, as is evidenced in its formalized disputations.[32]

The Greek analogue of the Ṛg Vedic symposium, though social rather than sacral, exercised a similar influence on later Greek philosophy, making this tradition of agonistic knowledge both Ṛg Vedic and Socratic. Robinson's survey of early Greek thought[33] describes the heritage of the Greek symposium form much as we might now describe the heritage of the *sadhamā́da* in Indian thought:

> For the mode of Greek thought is contentious; the *agon* or contest for the prize of victory is central to it; and this spirit has entered into the very texture of the philosophical tradition which is the creature of that impulse.

In the Greek symposia recorded by Plato and Xenophon, we learn how well philosophy was served by the symposium's dialogical structure. In addition, Pollux among others recorded about fifty types of games played at the classical symposium. Among games of wit, he distinguished two principle types, those involving enigmas (*ainigmata*) and those using ruses of all kinds, including riddles.[34] Since Greek symposia also featured some very strong wines probably mixed at times with psychoactive herbs,[35] they more than superficially resembled their Vedic counterparts.

The influence of the Ṛg Vedic symposium can also be traced in literary forms. In later speculative hymns of the Ṛg Veda, questions identical in form to those of symposium enigmas appear, such as the speculative questions in verse 11 of the famous "person hymn" (10.90).[36] In the speculative portions of the early Upaniṣads, brahmodyas are abundant. These are knowledge contests concerning brahman, which meant by then not merely mystery but the one unknown source of all creation.

Surely, too, the phrase from 1.164.22d, "who knows not the father," is an important anticipation of the Upaniṣadic emphasis on knowledge as the source of power (the sweet fig) over death and ignorance. Speaking of the power of the enigmatic in Sanskrit literature, van Buitenen's conclusion that "there is little doubt that the story [of the Mahābhārata] was in part *designed* as a riddle,"[37] indeed strikes a familiar note.

This case for the influence of the symposium's form on later thought can be extended even further. For example, the myth of the Buddha's attainment of inspired knowledge or enlightenment under the bodhi tree probably should be seen as an ectype of the Ṛg Vedic image of the tree in which knowledge (the sweet fig) is won. The sweet fig became in the Buddhist myth the *nirvāṇa* won by Gautama in his contest against Māra (both *eros* and *thanatos*), which was much like Christ's agony in Gethsemane. The initiatory contest structure reappears again a few centuries later in the structure of the Bhagavad Gītā. There, Arjuna initially took the son's position by stating the counterargument, strangely Buddhist in tone and content, to be then refuted by the father, Kṛṣṇa himself. The dialectical form continued to provide the story line of countless moralizing myths, including the Buddhacarita and the Kumārasambhava, both of which oppose *rāga* (passion) and *tyāga* (renunciation). In much the same manner, Indic philosophical traditions dialectically oppose the pulls of *prakṛti* (nature) and *puruṣa* (spirit), *saṃsāra* (the whirling world), and *nirvāṇa* (quiet cessation). *Rāga, prakṛti,* and *saṃsāra* all imply participation in the sweet fig, affirmed by the Ṛg Vedic seers but denied later in favor of *tyāga, puruṣa,* and *nirvāṇa,* all of which seek transcendence of the sweet fig, leading to the goal state of "merely looking on" (*kaivalya, mokṣa, nirvāṇa*).

Finally, the archaic tradition of shamanism stands behind the tree image, which Dīrghatamas used to enigmatize his contest experience, and behind the contest itself, Vedic and Greek. N. Kershaw Chadwick's little book, *Poetry and Prophecy,*[38] amply shows the contest to be an archaic shamanistic institution. "Riddle contests," she writes, "may be said to be universal in oral, as in written literature" (p. 48). She properly sees the contest as an important knowledge-producing institution, stimulating both intellectual and aesthetic skills with its competitive spirit. The "prophecy" or inspired speech so honored in the Ṛg Veda expresses the agonistic spirit of its poets, a spirit that in turn owes its origin to shamanic contests of quick wit and inspired speech intended to produce power-possessing knowledge.[39]

The other branch of shamanic ancestry goes just as deeply into archaic times. When Dīrghatamas chose to enigmatize his contest with the tree image, he used an archetypal myth for the attainment of knowledge. According to Eliade,[40] tree symbolism figures prominently in shamanic initiation, often acted out in a ritualized climbing of a pole. He finds that such ascensional rites continued in the sacrificial post (*yūpa*) of Vedic ritual (p. 403). These symbolisms all replicate the psychic ecstasy entered by the shaman in order to achieve the aims of the vision quest. "To climb the tree" or "to reach the sweet fig at its top" in this discourse realm means to achieve ecstasy, to ascend (Eliade, p. 112). The journey to the top of the tree leads the shaman to the Center, up the Axis of the World (p. 120), equivalent to the consciousness change required for initiation into the realm of the sacred. To reach the sweet fig at the tree's top symbolizes the achieving of ecstasy or inspired vision; the two birds, which recall the ornithological symbolism of the shaman's costume (Eliade, pp. 156–157), represent two ecstatics ready to take flight to the other world's realm of meaning. One, in Dīrghatamas's image, has already journeyed forth into flight and has tasted the sweet fig at the apex. The other, still merely looking on, awaits initiation. All the elements report back to the common ancestry of shamanism: the tree; birds; an ecstatic flight to the top of the tree for the sweet fig; and the initiatory symbolism of reaching the summit, tasting the immortal, sweetest fig that delivers from ignorance and death and gives transforming knowledge. All of these elements place Dīrghatamas's symposium enigma of the two birds in the fig tree squarely in the line of archaic shamanic custom and symbolism.

PART II

Sanskrit World View Bráhmans: Mysteries of Sun and Wheel

The enigma played a large rôle in the development of speculation: it is the condensed, pocket aspect of general mystery. . . .
—Louis Renou, *Hymnes spéculatifs du Véda*

PROLOGUE
Archetypal Images in Tradition, Landscape, and World View

Speculative Philosophy is the endeavour to frame a coherent, logical, necessary system of general ideas in terms of which every element of our experience can be interpreted.
—A. N. Whitehead

Every civilization, world view and all, begins as a tradition in a landscape. India's first recorded tradition comes from the Indus, from a landscape dominated by some profound natural images—the tree, as attested in Dīrghatamas's image as much as on the seals of the Harappā civilization; the sun, as anyone who has ever lived in India knows; and the wheel, which turns endlessly along countless country paths. Surely, even elements of landscape pertain to questions about the origins of a civilization's world view. "All this wealth of visual beauty [that the Mexican landscape presents] served the poets as raw material from which to create their symbolism . . . " writes Irene Nicholson (1959, p. 141). "It was never used for its own sake. . . . Nature [was] used always to illustrate the religious thought." Initial speculations about the invisible order of things, at the beginning of a civilization's literacy, find poets and prophets looking to their natural landscape for images to represent that invisible. Speaking of their God, the nomadic shepherds of the Old Testament said, "The Lord is my Shepherd." Speculation seeks to conceptualize reality in order to provide a frame for a meaningful experience of reality. A civilization's thought is framed by its world view(s), its frame for understanding the facts of life and the givens of human empirical reality. The framers who created the classical Sanskrit world view chose their basic images of the invisible, spiritual order of things from the familiar landscape of everyday experience.

For two years as a young man I lived in Madurai, Tamilnadu, hosted by American and Lady Doak Colleges, now part of the University of Madras. For a while my home was on the outskirts of that ancient southern Indian city, in the Tallakulam quarter, on the last street of a modest neighborhood of three-room, cement block tract houses. Beyond my front door, paddy fields stretched to distant mountains, graced during the monsoon season by multi-gray clouds. One day in November, during the time for rice transplating, I walked from my home with an old Agfa 35 mm camera to photograph the bullock carts bringing the transplants into the fields. I came upon some bullocks yoked to a cart laden with bundles of new rice shoots freshly dug from their seedling beds. I sought for the spirit of the place, trying to capture with the camera's objective eye just what was there, the immediate existent, without preconception. I took several frames of the bullock cart and of women transplanting in the flooded fields. The resulting photographs captured the most characteristic moment, linking that time with the great, wooden-spoked cartwheel and the sun setting over the western mountains. Wheel and sunlight fused, symbolizing to my eye the season that comes round again and again when paddy waters reflect towering monsoon clouds. Although I had at that time not studied Sanskrit symbolism, I chose to represent time and earth's recurrent rhythm by the sun and the wheel.

Countless wheels since Harappā times have turned through Indian landscapes, passing the times of countless sunsets. Observers note that Pakistani carts today still use the same Harappā ruts, in which solid wooden wheels turn, supporting carts just like those represented in the little toy clay carts from Harappā finds. Upon entering India for the first time, after one's initial awareness of landscape, the long and pervasive reach of tradition comes sharply to mind. The subcontinent conserves traditions over remarkable periods of time. Vedic recitation forms demonstrate the ability of Sanskrit culture to preserve itself without change for millennia. The same temper resides in the traditions of everyday life. I remember a domestic scene carved in stone bas-relief on a Sanchi pillar, of women winnowing and pounding grain. I photographed an identical scene two thousand miles to the south, two-thousand years later, in a potters' neighborhood of Madurai. The same implements and body positions figured in the work—a flat winnowing basket of horseshoe shape, a heavy stone mortar pinched in the middle used with a long wooden pestle, the lady pounding from a standing position beside the squatting woman winnower. The Indian material culture and ways of doing things form a tradition, attested from Sanchi to contemporary times, as conservative as its Sanskritic high culture.

For the investigations to follow, several terms need defining. *Tradition* means a consistent (though often unconscious) effort to provide to succeeding generations elements of knowledge or ways of acting deemed important enough to be maintained without innovation. Within any tradition, something is *archetypal* or an *archetype* (no Jungian implication intended) when and if it occurs first; whenever it recurs, it is *ectypal*. The Ṛg Veda itself makes this archetype-ectype distinction when (in 10.130.3a) it distinguishes the *pramā* (archetype) from the *pratimā* (ectype). The *archē* (beginning, starting point, ultimate underlying form or impression) establishes a traditional form, the model for many subsequent ectypes or realizations of the original, conforming more or less to it. *World view* means the basic picture assumed by all members of a group or tradition which serves as the frame of meaningful action and of a civilization's various ways of understanding life (its various philosophies or visions of life). World views ground themselves in one or several *root metaphors*, the image models of fundamental forms of reality as they conceive it. A root metaphor, for instance, of the early Chinese world view involved seeing reality as a living organism ("organicism"), while science's world view sees nature as a machine made of dead matter. The Judeo-Christian-Islamic root metaphor of the expulsion of primal humanity from the Garden sees reality as the testing place of human allegiance to its Creator.

In the Sanskrit tradition, a preliminary world view, expressed in the Ṛg Veda, changed through natural development and interaction with the indigenous, Harappā world view. It became the classical Sanskrit world view first assumed by early Buddhism, Jainism, and early Hinduism (as in the Upaniṣads, Manu, and the Gītā), and then by all later major schools of thought. Clearly, all the texts of these various visions of life assume a view of the world which never doubted certain fundamental ideas about reality. Other world view elements, particularly in the early stages of developing tradition (roughly between the seventh and third centuries B.C.) competed with this dominant view (as Basham's *History and Doctrines of the Ājīvikas* demonstrates) but did not win wide acceptance. I have published one attempt to describe this classical Sanskrit world view (Robinson and Johnson: 1972, pp. 16–17, and see pp. 34–39), and here sketch an alternate set of propositions characteristic of it. These constitute its assumptions, stated particularly from the point of view of its soteriology:

1.
Physical world order, time, and space (*saṃsāra*)
are material, ordered, meaningful, not chaotic;
they are sequential, hierarchical, circular (oppose:
linear) and endless.

2.
Unenlightened personal action within that world order
is consequential, individuality extending endlessly in
time, resulting in continued finite existence, embroiled
in change, suffering, and recurrent death.

3.
Persons wander through *saṃsāra's* endless time,
their course determined by the mechanism of *karman*
(consequentiality).

4.
Creation's appearance (*māyā*) does not exhaust reality;
becoming and being are, respectively, the changing and
permanent forms of reality.

5.
Human material nature is mortal, having no chance
of bodily immortality, but can achieve a heavenly,
though finite and transient, rebirth realm (*svarga*,
heaven).

6.
But transcendence also has an infinite, nonmaterial
side. Humans, though bound to matter, have an
essential, nonaccidental nature that escapes (optimism)
the limiting (pessimism) material rebirth realms.
This soteriology is a pessimistic optimism.

7.
The means whereby this essential nature removes itself
from matter/*māyā* include: nonattachment, renunciation,
self-sacrifice, devotion, and discipline in action and

meditation (both yoga), thereby achieving insight into the difference between one's existential and essential natures.

8.
Ignorance and desire block escape from or transcendence of materiality, or significant insight into its nature.

9.
The experience of creation gives humans the knowledge necessary to promote eventually in them the intention to leave bondage to materiality and to maximize their awareness of their essentially free, transcendent nature.

10.
The greatest good involves this self-transformation, which leads on the long path of multiple rebirths from materiality to spirituality (*mokṣa, nirvāṇa, kaivalya*).

However, world views do not originate in abstractions like these but through concrete images that represent the realities about which speculation asks. Still today, cosmology adopts metaphorical models of postulated events, such as is shown in science's "big bang" and "steady state" models of how creation occurs and continues. The Sanskrit tradition's archetypal images that helped shape its classical world view included the sun, the wheel, and the tree. Art history shows the sacred fig tree already present in visual archetype on Harappā seals. Dīrghatamas's pippala, the lactiferous *ficus religiosa* L., appears clearly on Harappā seals, along with the acacia.[1] By the time of the myth of Siddhārtha's enlightenment (bodhi, hence bodhi tree) under it, the tradition was well established. It was thus an ectype of the archetypal ficus tree of the Harappā priests as well as of the Ṛg Vedic poets. In the tradition of the northwest, the Harappā tree image was the archetype. Dīrghatamas's fig tree was an ectype that became archetypal for the Sanskrit literary tradition.

Not surprisingly, the tree has been studied many times.[2] Bosch's "Prolegomenon to an introduction to the study of Indian symbolism" (as he calls *The Golden Germ*, p. 9) takes the tree as its central image to discuss all Indian symbolism. Inhabitants of the Indian subcontinent have for millennia rested in the shade of trees, under which travelers, scoundrels, and saints have stayed and worshipped. In Harappā seals, we see the fig tree being worshipped, as in the later Buddhist cult of the bodhi tree. A notable Ṛg Vedic tree occurs in an Agni laud (perhaps because both Agni and tree are *vanaspati*, lord of the forest) to enigmatize for the poet's petition Agni's provision of life's full immortality: "We come to you, O Agni, the golden likeness (of immortality), / For refuge, as it were for shade from burning heat" (6.16.38). The tenor of (tree) shade is the spiritual refuge provided by the divinized fire, Agni, as the messenger appointed by the gods to man to bear his oblations. Sacred Agni mediates between sacred and profane as does his namesake, the tree, between sky and earth.

The tree image gained greatest fame in India in an ectype based on the archetype set by both Harappā and Ṛg Vedic civilizations at the beginnings of the tradition. Its ectype portrays the attainment of Buddhahood when Gautama, like Dīrghatamas's bird, tastes the sweet fig at the top of the tree. Here the tree enigmatizes the achievement of transcending knowledge, as in Dīrghatamas's archetypal image, but both sides of its ancestry are integrated into the Buddhist ectypal myth because, as Warren's translation of the *Introduction to the Jātaka Tales*[3] says, the events began at a time when

> there lived in Uruvelā a girl named Sujātā, who had been born in the family of the householder Senāni, in General's Town. On reaching maturity she made a prayer to a certain banyan-tree, saying, "If I get a husband of equal rank with myself, and my first-born is a son, I will make a yearly

> offering to you of the value of a hundred thousand pieces of money." And her prayer had been successful. [P. 71]

This Sujātā had prepared her offering for the full moon day of the month Visākhā, the very day when the Future Buddha sat beneath that tree "to await the hour to go begging." Her servant found him there and, in fine Harappā tradition, believed him to be the spirit of the tree incarnate. Servant and mistress both returned to worship the tree through its genius. Afterward Siddhārtha bathed, ate the offering, rested, and by evening took his fateful place under the bodhi tree.

The myth of Siddhārtha's awakening thus begins by adopting a theme ectypal of the tree veneration evidenced on Harappā seals. The ensuing events under the fig tree adopt ectypal imagery with a dual ancestry. From the Harappā comes the tradition of the sacred fig tree, and from the Ṛg Veda comes the shamanic contest for the cosmic tree's powerful, transcendent knowledge, which is at the same time the refuge it gives from death. Under the fig, Siddhārtha, in proper princely (*kṣatriya* class) fashion, contests with his appointed mortality in the form of Māra. All these ectypes of archetypal images reappear with the tradition's renewal in northern India around the sixth century B.C. in the "awakening myth." Remarkably, in the myth's account (*Jātaka Introduction*, Warren, pp. 75–76) of how Siddhārtha chooses his warrior's spot under the fig tree for his contest with Māra, the symbols of sun, wheel, and tree coincide:

> Just then there came from the opposite direction a grass-cutter named Sotthiya, and he was carrying grass. And when he saw the Great Being, that he was a holy man, he gave him eight handfulls of grass. The Future Buddha took the grass, and ascending the throne of wisdom, stood on the southern side and faced the north. Instantly the southern half of the world sank, until it seemed to touch

the Avīci hell, while the northern half rose to the highest of the heavens.

"Methinks," said the Future Buddha, "this cannot be the place for the attainment of the supreme wisdom"; and walking round the tree with his right side towards it, he came to the western side and faced east. Then the western half of the world sank, until it seemed to touch the Avīci hell, while the eastern half rose to the highest of the heavens. Wherever, indeed, he stood, the broad earth rose and fell, as though it had been a huge cart-wheel lying on its hub, and some one were treading on the rim.

"Methinks," said the Future Buddha, "this also cannot be the place for the attainment of supreme wisdom"; and walking round the tree with his right side towards it, he came to the northern side and faced the south. Then the northern half of the world sank, until it seemed to touch the Avīci hell, while the southern half rose to the highest of the heavens.

"Methinks," said the Future Buddha, "this also cannot be the place for the attainment of supreme wisdom"; and walking round the tree with his right side towards it, he came to the eastern side and faced the west. Now it is on the eastern side of their Bo-trees that all The Buddhas have sat cross-legged, and that side neither trembles nor quakes.

Then the Great Being, saying to himself, "This is the immovable spot on which all The Buddhas have planted themselves! This is the place for destroying passion's net!" took hold of his handful of grass by one end, and shook it out there. And straightway the blades of grass formed themselves into a seat fourteen cubits long, of such symmetry of shape as not even the most skilful painter or carver could design.

Then the Future Buddha turned his back to the trunk of the Bo-tree and faced the east. And making the mighty resolution, "Let my skin, and sinews, and bones become dry, and welcome! and let all the flesh and blood in my

> body dry up! but never from this seat will I stir, until I have attained the supreme and absolute wisdom!" he sat himself down cross-legged in an unconquerable position, from which not even the descent of a hundred thunderbolts at once could have dislodged him.

This extended metaphor combines the tree, the wheel, and, implicitly, the sun, since Gautama maintains a solar orientation to the tree. It is also at the solar orientation's place (facing eastward) that he finds the proper position for his contest against Māra for transcendence and enlightenment. Thus, to describe how Gautama prepares himself for the momentous meditative ecstasy, the myth chooses to describe world reality as a wheel, the center of which is the tree Gautama picks to meditate under. In each case, as he circumambulates the tree, maṇḍala-like, through the four directions, the world sinks or rises "as though it had been a huge cart-wheel lying on its hub, and some one were treading on the rim." The final eastern position facing the rising sun represents the initiatory beginning he is about to experience; Gautama sits aligned symbolically with the Sun, at the place of the World Tree, in the center of the World Wheel. On the night of the full moon, that moment in time when the changing moon becomes whole again, like Dīrghatamas's bird, the Buddha achieves *prajñā,* visionary or ecstatic insight, and the enlightenment it entails.

The same tree in the Kaṭha Upaniṣad (2.3.1) enigmatizes how world creation arises in brahman (the unseen root of the reversed tree invisible in the sky above), but in the Gītā (15.1,3) it enigmatizes *saṃsāra,* the worldly tree that must be felled through nonattachment. Tree symbolism[4] continues to be important in myth, as in the Rādhā-Kṛṣṇa epos, and today the Indian landscape is often dominated by giant trees under which shrines are faithfully served. Bosch (1960, plate 84) found an ectype of this tree archetype in the wrapper picture of a Gandhi biography in Sanskrit verse. The cosmic tree's foliage is shaped into the form of the Indian Republic. Gandhi smiles down from the center of this shaped tree within a sun circle that radiates light in the direction of earth, where silhouetted Indian peasants labor in their fields. Bosch comments:

> The portrait of the Mahātma is here pictured as the radiating sun functioning as the brahmamūla of the Cosmic Tree, and at the same time occupying the place where in the Indian subcontinent the Cosmic Mountain is situated. Tree and India coincide in the picture.

Tree, wheel, and sun—what is the origin of these archetypal images that accounts for their adoption and combination countless times in the tradition's later development? The first extensive evidence of their presence in Sanskrit literature appears in Ṛg Vedic imagery, as Ananda Coomaraswamy ceaselessly demonstrates, especially from enigmas adopted for the symposium. In the following two chapters we will study two image clusters, enigmas of the sun as eternal wanderer and enigmas of the wheel as eternal turner. In doing so, we should remember the landscape that gave birth to this world view and was the natural source of its archetypal images. The words of Nicholson (1959, p. 140) are appropriate here, from another context, when she considers the Mexican landscape of the culture that produced the brilliant enigmatic image of the plumed serpent:

> Today, during the dry season, much of Mexico looks like a barren desert. Yet almost overnight, at the coming of the rains, the landscape can turn from harsh yellow or red sand and dry scrub to a rich and shimmering green. The image of the plumed serpent may have been suggested by the sudden appearance of green, as if a creeping brown reptile had suddenly sprouted wings. Or it may have been

rather the sunset over the Pacific, leaving a phosphorescent trail of light on the water, that created so bright and enduring a paradox. Whatever its origin, the plumed serpent is a natural image, drawn from the rich material to be found on all sides in a continent of extraordinary beauty.

4.
Enigmas of the Sun, the Eternal Wanderer

Aum! Let us mediate on the excellent radiance of the divine creator (Savitṛ, the Sun) that he may inspire our thoughts.
—Ṛg Veda, 3.62.10

Renou thought the sun to be the single most important image contemplated by Ṛg Vedic speculators. He wrote, in his commentary on 1.152 to Mitrā-Varuṇā, "All the enigmas of the Veda gravitate at a certain moment around the forms or the unknown movements of the sun" (1949*b*, p. 270). Archeology and comparative art history attest to the universal presence of sun forms in symbolic materials. The sun, revered as the life force itself and for its light which dispels darkness and night's unknowns, has long been divinized or thought to reveal divine plan or dispensation. Sun has meant light, life, sustained growth in nature below, and divine continuance above. The sun and its sister moon have long been used as symbols revealing hidden dimensions of reality. Of all phenomena, the sun enjoys a rare preeminence in symbolism in literature and in art. In the case of Dante, as Dunbar (1961, p. 23) writes, "Considered in the aspects of life-giving, light-giving, and heat-giving, the sun supplies imagery central in the *Divina Comedia.*" Similarly, in the holiest Sanskrit mantra, the Gāyatrī, translated at the head of this chapter, the sun enigmatizes the divine. This most sacred enunciation of

Brahmanical Hinduism, the secret of secrets, has directed millions to meditate every morning upon the sun.

With such powerful attributes so important to human well-being, the sun was bound to be used by poets, artists, and speculators as an image vehicle to represent what they saw or thought. The sun does not figure prominently in Harappā symbolism, although the solar svastika design appears, as do circular figures, some crossed to indicate a wheel or sun-wheel. Ṛg Vedic poets, however, divinized the sun as Savitṛ and Sūrya. They addressed them exclusively in over twenty hymns, and they enigmatized *ṛta* (truth or order) with solar images. Concern for *ṛta* (the "True" or "Ordered" Creation), preoccupies these Ṛg Vedic poets at all levels, in rite, sacred speech, and cosmos. At its beginnings, between 1,000 to 500 B.C., the Sanskrit world view conceived of world reality as having an inner, unseen order: *ṛta*. To know *ṛta* meant to be in touch with Truth about this Real. According to their understanding, the sun went across the sky with the moon. Fertility of sons and kine depended on the bounty of unseen powers instead of on natural patterns of weather and gynecology, as we now understand them. The ritual of the Indo-Aryans sought direct interaction with this underlying order of reality, the *ṛta*, which guaranteed every day expectations and aspirations. In this effort they were in no way distinct from other human groups who attempted through myth, ritual, and symbol to interact for their well-being with the subtle, "spiritual" level of reality.

The dual divinities, Mitrā-Varuṇā, guarantee *ṛta*. They protect it from infringement, as does the sun (as Savitṛ, in 7.63.3*cd*); the *dhā́man* of Mitrā-Varuṇā (6.61.4*a*) is their dispensation of *ṛta* or settled order. Renou emphasized in interpreting Vedic imagery that it must be seen as interrelating three levels of meaning: ritual, word, and cosmos. The goal of human ritual (cf., *yajñásya dhā́ma*, 10.181.2*b*) and word as sacred speech is to contact and influence divine power and to take the human role in maintaining cosmic *ṛta*. The *dhā́man* (dispensation) of Mitrā-Varuṇā, is equivalent to *dhárman* (manifestation of order).[1] The world view assumes an underlying reality, which, though subtle, nevertheless maintains life's order, the rising of the dawns (cf., *uṣásaḥ . . . ṛtájātasatyāḥ*, 4.51.7ab), and the veracity of truthful statements (10.34.12). Something is *ṛta* when its claims correspond to fact, subtle or ordinary. In the older Indo-European model, *to know* means to see the facts claimed as truth and thus to verify the claim. Agni too, as ritual mediator, protects Truth-Order (1.1.8b, *gopā́m ṛtásya*), and Agni's cosmic counterpart, the sun, is in turn the eye of Mitrā-Varuṇā. Sacred speech unites ritual to cosmic reality, making human action effective in securing divine benefit, maintaining continued order, and assuring protection against disease and misfortune. This manner of conceiving *ṛta*, the Indo-Aryans shared with the Indo-Iranians (cf. Avestan *aša*).

A major Ṛg Vedic bráhman sequence occurs in 1.152, a hymn dedicated to Mitrā-Varuṇā. Renou has published two detailed interpretations of this complex poem.[2] The enigma uses solar imagery to penetrate speculatively the mystery of Mitrā-Varuṇā's dispensation of order. The poem begins amid the ceremonial oblation to the hymn's patrons, celebrating the victory of creation over chaos:

1.

You two are clothed with fatty vestments (the sacrificial oblation),
Your unbreakable thoughts are create things.
You overcame all disorders (*ánṛta*)
You are one with order (*ṛtá*), O Mitrā-Varuṇā!

2.

Many a one (contestant) has not understood this
of them (the symposium fathers),

This Truthful (*satyá*) powerful mántra, proposed (in contest) by the poet-seer:
The fierce four-pointed defeats the three-pointed!
Indeed, the god-mockers aged first.

[1.152.1–2]

The core bráhman (italicized) enigmatizes the victory of ṛta over chaos (*anṛta*) as the defeat of the three-pointed by the fierce four-pointed. The enigmatic abstraction of the four- and the three-pointed is the basic enigmatic vehicle whose tenor is ṛta's victory over chaos. This enigma is the Truthful mantra (i.e., bráhman) that represents symbolically the Truth of established order which prevails over disorder and those who mock the gods. The hymn comes from a primal stage of Sanskrit speculation. The poet reports that this bráhman confounded many contestants when it was proposed in the contest. He wonders which contestants would be able to demonstrate a proper understanding of the Truth-revealing enigma?

Although we cannot presume to suggest what a proper understanding would include in the opinion of a symposium master, we can at least make an accurate interpretation of the enigma.[3] Adopting again the vehicle-tenor mode of analysis, we must distinguish a primary from an intermediary vehicle. The primary image of the four-pointed enigmatizes creation's order, using intermediary solar imagery naturally appropriate to Mitrā-Varuṇā. The basic enigma goes thus:

PRIMARY VEHICLE	INTERMEDIATE VEHICLE	TENOR
powerful four-pointed	sun	creation, dispensation of order
three-pointed	(? trident)	chaos, disorder

Subsequent verses (2–5) extend the enigma through allusions to dawn and sun, making clear that the powerful four-pointed is the sun. But because *caturaśri* (four-pointed) in its only other Ṛg Vedic appearance modifies lightning (*vŕṣandhiṃ cáturaśrim*, 4.22.2a), it is associated first with the term *vajra* (thunderbolt, both the lightning and subsequent thunder, the familiar weapon of Indra) and second as an image with the circular discus shape. Its four-pointed character is later represented in iconography by the vajra and in solar symbolism by the svastika (emblem of well-being). Their numerical symbolism means completeness, wholeness.

If iconography underlies this enigma, it certainly involves the sun and the secondary associations with four-pointed emblems, such as Indra's thunderbolt and the solar svastika. The term *svastika* is not Ṛg Vedic, though its source, *svasti* (well-being), is frequent and is the goal of Vedic religion. Its four-armed symbolism represents the sun on its daily journey, each arm indicating a subsequent position of the sun, turning in the same direction to denote the sun's course. Visually, any of these symbols exhibits the four-pointed:

╳	⊗	⊕	卐
vajra	vajra or sun	vajra or crossed discus	svastika or sun

By distinction, the three-pointed enigmatizes chaos in constant struggle with the dispensation of order. It is incomplete, imperfect, contrasted with the four-wholeness present in the square, the four directions, and the positively valued symbolic fours of Ṛg Vedic symbolism.[4] The forces of the three-pointed assail human aspirations for well-being and mar life with incompleteness—shortness of life, disease, infertility. Demons (god-mockers) rain perpetual hostility on the gods and their order, so necessary to human felicity. If order were not maintained in nature, human life would be futile. Nothing could be relied upon in nature and action would have no meaning or effective power. If an iconographic element underlies this abstract image, perhaps it would be the trident, common in Harappā and later positively valued as Śiva's instrument, or simply anything incomplete:

trident	incomplete svastika

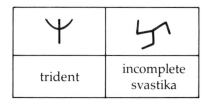

The centrality of solar symbolism in this bráhman becomes apparent when the following three verses enigmatize ṛta with images whose tenors involve the mythology of the dawn and the sun. Each verse adds to the basic bráhman, states its tenor (defeat of disorder by ṛta, v. 3, dispensation of ṛta vv. 4 and 5), and extends the enigma using the intermediate sun vehicle based upon the image of the four-pointed from v. 2. Solar imagery is particularly appropriate to Mitrā-Varuṇā, who are closely related to the sun. The sun is their eye; they appear in glorious light (rays of the sun, glistening garments); they come from shiny heavens. Moreover, it is their dispensation (*dhā́man*) that regulates cosmic phenomena (dawn and sun, cloud and rain), their regularity and beneficence. By their *māyā* (creative power) they hold dominion over beings and things, and they order creation, sending the dawns and causing the sun to traverse the sky daily. No one can infringe or obstruct their dispensation of order; even the gods fall under its sway. From a scientific point of view, Ṛg Vedic poets symbolize nature's regularity through the image of the sun, seeking, as members of the human community, ways of understanding and adapting to their environment. Today science investigates nature through empirical inquiry, whereas Ṛg Vedic speculators explored and mapped cosmos and nature through imagination, proposing images in the symposium contest which shaped the world view of classical Sanskrit.

The enigma extends itself in mythological allusions. Probably the basic enigma of the four-pointed was introduced into the contest, with subsequent elaborations as recorded in these succeeding three verses. Each one recalls and subjects to speculative contemplation the central solar image of the enigma, as if to dazzle with added brilliance. Paradoxically, the enigmatic achieves light by stating darkly, by indirection:

3.
Footless she goes first, before those with feet,
Who understands this of you, O Mitrā-Varuṇā?
The womb bears even his weight,
He (sun) promotes order (*ṛtá*), he has subdued disorder (*ánṛta*).

4.
Traveling all across the lover of maidens we see,
Not his lying down beside (them?),
Wearing the unconstrained, stretched afar.
This is the dispensation (*dhā́man*) beloved of Mitrā-Varuṇā.

5.
Born not a horse, reinless,
A steed neighing, he flies back upraised.
(This) incomprehensible (*acítta*) *bráhman* the young enjoy,
Proclaiming to Mitrā-Varuṇā (their) dispensation (*dhā́man*).
[1.152.3–5]

Here the bráhman (italicized) concludes,[5] so impermeable to mind (*acítta*, beyond thought) but so inspiring to the inner vision. Young initiates, perhaps not yet fully trained in the speculative quest, delight in such verses.

They must have induced powerful experiences. For the purposes not of inspiration but analysis, the extended metaphor needs to be set out, distinguishing vehicle from tenor. The tenor of the three verses is dawn, which develops into sun-dominated day. This tenor of regular dawns and arching sun remains, as in v. 2, the intermediary vehicle enigmatizing the ultimate tenor, the victory of order over chaos.

PRIMARY VEHICLE	INTERMEDIATE VEHICLE	TENOR
3.		
footless, she goes first	dawn	*ṛta*'s promotion of order, subduing chaos
before those with feet	people and animals awaking at light	
the womb	dawn	
bears even his weight	bears the sun	
4.		
traveling all across	visible in the sky during day	dispensation (of order)
the lover of maidens	the sun	
not his lying down beside (them?)	the sun at night, when not seen (them, the dawns?)	
wearing the unconstrained, stretched afar	clothed in light	

5.
born not a horse,
reinless . . . . the sun at dawn . . . dispensation (of order)

a steed,[6] neighing,
he flies back
upraised . . . . the sun arching across the sky

The poet chooses to enigmatize the victory of ṛta in the image of the dawn rising out of the implicit chaos of night, spreading light across the darkened land, being potentially full of danger. The dawns bring the sun, whose steady, regular course across the sky symbolizes the steady, regular course of the natural order of things. Night suggests the disorder prior to creation; dawn suggests the inception of order, with the sun being its visible sign. Without dawn's birth of the sun, and without the sun itself, time, visible space, the seasons, all life and creation would be impossible.

At dawn, too, the beginning of order is ritually celebrated in the sacrifice,[7] coincident with the victory of created order over chaos, the discontinuous, and the anarchical. The extended image proceeds with an order of its own, beginning in dense abstraction (v. 2), achieving a preliminary concreteness in the dawn (v. 3), developing into the sun (vv. 4 and 5). The ultimate tenor of the birth, course, and sleeping of the sun at night is the mystery of creation, which comprises time and space, the passing of the seasons, and the wandering of the years. It is the sun, that "golden germ," that is an image of immortality whose shadow is death itself (10.121.2c).[8] Thus, at an early speculative stratum, Ṛg Vedic poets contemplate an image that broaches the grand concepts of the Sanskrit world view: the divine establishment of order, the defeat of the anarchical, the unity of phenomena, even the paradoxical quality of time that enables death and immortality to proceed from the same order.

All these meanings are possible tenors of the sun enigma of 1.152. This archetypal image provides the basis for multiple facets of the classical world view. Given the occurrence of the sun image in a clearly attested speculative bráhman, and given the abundance of solar imagery in other Ṛg Vedic contexts, it follows that the sun is a major speculative image in the Sanskrit tradition. To show how this image participates in the conceptual formulation of later world views, the following comments trace some of its history in respect to one of the most striking innovations in the world view which supplants the older, Ṛg Vedic understanding. Many commentators have noted this problem and have wondered about the source or sources[9] of the classical idea of recurrent death (*punarmṛtyu*) or rebirth (*jāti*). No religious world view of any other major civilization posits such an idea, though notions of rebirth occur in more archaic and primitive world views. Professor van Buitenen summarizes the puzzle as follows:

> So significant has the philosopheme of transmigration become for Indian thought, Buddhist, Jain as well as Brāhman, that it seems surprising it arrived so late. The Vedic literature is innocent of it until the very last portions of one of the later Brāhmaṇas. And then, astonishingly, it is stated not as "rebirth" but as "redeath." . . . This total absence of the concept in the earlier literature of the Vedas and Brāhmaṇas has led scholars . . . to assume that the doctrine of rebirth has its genesis in non-Vedic circles (which may be true) and therefore in non-Aryan circles (which is impervious to proof). [1970, p. 29]

Indeed, since we have no literary evidence concerning possible non-Aryan sources for this strange, parentless "philosopheme of transmigration," and since we know that it would have been alien to the ordinary Ṛg Vedic understanding of death (see 10, hymns 14–18), could it already have been a subject for speculation in the Ṛg

Veda? In such a case, although it might not have been an accepted element of the world view, it might have been considered speculatively, perhaps in response to non-Aryan stimuli. Zimmer (1964) demonstrates that death and rebirth, in the later world view, are initially conceived of in terms of images provided by the sun and moon. The sun presents to speculative consciousness an unchanging orb giving life and light. Its celestial partner, the moon, waxes, wanes, then disappears from view for three nights, after which it is reborn as a sliver of light on the opposite horizon, no longer rising late at night but setting at evening's dusk. The sun never waxes and never wanes, though, like the moon, it rises and sets. A symbolic contrast presents itself in that they both "die" at the end of their respective spheres of day and night, but the sun's dying is not a true death,[10] but rather is merely an apparent one. Though ordering change and passing through changes, the sun is eternal, unchanging, immutable. It returns from each winter's southward retreat, and throughout the year it unceasingly rises after its nighttime passage, regardless of the season. The moon, by contrast, suffers recurrent transformation, increasing only to decrease, disappearing only to be reborn again and again.[11]

The crucial matter is that such a contrast is drawn in the Ṛg Veda. In 10.85, which is a very late, composite hymn popularly called "Sūrya's Bridal," two verses make this contrast in enigmatic form. They may be bráhman fragments, speculative in character and origin, included in the Ṛg Vedic corpus at its last speculative stratum. This text generally does not accept casual insertions, so someone must have deemed them worthy of being so preserved. Since they use the images of sun and moon, the verses naturally found a home in this hymn to the sun.

Perhaps they were taken from some poet's successful performance in the contest, to be inserted in their present opportune context because they stated some new, radically innovative speculation that had already found some acceptance. The enigma thus became an image fossil, laid down in the very last strata of late Ṛg Vedic speculation, at a time when speculative thinkers were creating new conceptual horizons in the growing civilization, which was by then integrating indigenous thought into its Sanskrit base:

One after another the two turn, by māyā́ (creative power),
Two children playing, going round a sacrifice.
One regards all creatures,
The other establishing the seasons, is born again (jāyate púnaḥ).
Ever anew and anew being born, he comes (repeatedly)
into existence.

[10.85.18–19a]

The enigmas present no difficulty in determining that the sun and moon are the tenors of the two, which turn by *māyā:*

VEHICLE	TENOR
one after another, the two turn	sun and moon, following each other in the natural order of day and night[12]
one regards all creatures	the sun
the other, establishing the seasons, is born again	the moon

However, as in the enigmas of the sun in 1.152, this tenor is but the intermediate vehicle for some other, ultimate tenor containing the real meaning of the speculation. What could this meaning be? Unfortunately, nothing in the context betrays what it may have been, but it is a short way to some speculations of our own which give this enigma an ultimate tenor of considerable importance in the development of the classical Sanskrit world view. Indeed, it can be taken to enigmatize the later fundamental distinction between an eternal and a transient dimension of cosmic order. If the sun has established for the Ṛg Vedic world view the basic philosopheme of world order, could not this sun-moon contrast have done the same in setting the classical view of world order?

This view was first expressed in the archaic Bṛhad-āraṇyaka Upaniṣad (6.2.15 and 16) as the two destinies, solar and lunar, which enigmatize the two possibilities that await human beings at death:

15.
Those who thus know this, and who meditate faithfully
in the forest on the True, (at death) they change into
(crematory)[13] fire, from fire (they go) into day,
from day into waxing moon, from waxing moon into the
six months when the sun goes north, from these months
into the realm of the gods, from the realm of the gods
to the sun, from the sun into lightning-fire. A mental
spirit having come to those lightning fires takes them
to sacred realms, and they dwell at the remote distances[14]
in those sacred realms. For them, there is no return
(to transmigration) again.

16.
But who by sacrifice, donation and austerity win
(phenomenal) realms, (at death) they change into (crematory)
smoke, from smoke (they go) into night, from night
into the waning moon, from the waning moon into the six
months to the realm of the fathers, from the realm
of the fathers to the moon; having reached the moon,
they become food. There the gods, as they address King
Soma, saying "increase, decrease," thus eat them.
When that elapses for them, then just to this ether
do they go, from ether to air, from air to rain, from
rain to earth; having reached earth, they become food;
(then) they again are offered into man's fire, then are
born into woman's fire. Thus rising up into (phenomenal
rebirth) realms, they only transmigrate (repeatedly).[15]

The principles of a just and sober hermeneutics, applied to the enigmas of the Ṛg Veda, require that evidence internal to the text be used in determining their tenors. In this case, the text of 10.85 (or any other hymn) provides no such internal statement of its ultimate tenor, though the context and enigma make clear that sun and moon are its intermediate vehicle. As van Buitenen points out, the new philosopheme of transmigration appears first in the Brāhmaṇa period, not much sooner than the earliest Upaniṣads. These lines from the Bṛhad-āraṇyaka present one of the earliest full-blown, speculative descriptions of bondage to transmigration or of escape from it, the classical goals of achieving *nirvāṇa, mokṣa,* or *kaivalya.* The underlying imagery, solar and lunar, of the Upaniṣadic passages constitutes a clear ectype of the Sūrya's Bridal enigmas, and creates a definite, if ill-attested, link between this late Ṛg Vedic speculation and the still-forming views of transmigration of the Bṛhad-āraṇyaka. Because the two Upaniṣadic passages seem consciously linked to the enigmas of 10.85, it follows that they state the tenor of the prior image, not intrinsically to the Ṛg Veda, but at least squarely from the tradition it fostered.

These two Upaniṣadic passages state the doctrine of recurrent death in imagery that is admittedly archaic and still speculative, with little of the refinement that the idea later achieved.[16] Their style is appropriate to their early formulative nature. They distinguish after death two alternative courses, one which does not lead to return into transmigration and another which leads to repeated "rising up" into phenomenal rebirth realms (*loka*).

The former follows a solar path, after separating (in the Upaniṣadic way) from social and familial ties to meditate in the forest. It leads through the crematory fire to the solar side of phenomena (day, the waxing moon, the sun's northward course) through the realm of the gods to the sun and its mystical lightning fire, which recalls the four-pointed of 1.152.2. This leads to acceptance into the sacred realms, from whence no return to transmigration can occur. Such an end constitutes salvation, the ultimate goal of action within the new world view's assumption of death as eternal recurrence.

The other half of human nature pursues the alternate lunar destiny. Indeed, those who practice the temporal, orthodox religion (village as opposed to forest) involving sacrifice, donation, and austerity, achieve rebirths in phenomenal worlds but suffer at each death repeated transmigration. Like the moon, they rise up again and again into the same set of phenomenal rebirth realms. These realms figure on Buddhist representations of the wheel of life, including hells, the realm of hungry ghosts, animals or humans, and titans or gods. This fate takes them on a lunar path, following the dark side of phenomena through the crematory fire's smoke to night, to the waning moon, to the sun's southward course, to the realm of the fathers (the old destiny of the dead in the Ṛg Vedic view), and finally to the moon. From thence they return as food to the stream of creation to experience rebirth.

This notion of transmigration finds no place in the Ṛg Vedic world view, which considers immortality (*amṛta*, the condition of not being dead) to be a long, fruitful life on earth,[17] terminated sacrificially in the crematory fire leading to the paradise of Yama or the fathers. Nevertheless, a Ṛg Vedic enigma uses images that describe a natural, recurrent death process, images that are fossilized in its latest speculative stratum. This leads to the strong suspicion that speculation on this notion in Ṛg Vedic circles, from whatever source, eventually dignified the concept with inclusion in Ṛg Vedic revelation. The conceptual structure of the transcendent sun and the transmigrant moon provided contrasting destinies for speculative imagination to contemplate as a potential form of creation. It remained for Brāhmaṇa period speculators (on which Heestermann: 1964 is excellent) and early Upaniṣadic sages to apply these images to human nature. They considered human nature to be tied by *karman* (consequences of action) to existential transmigration, according to its lunar nature, and at the same time to be essentially free and transcendent, according to its solar nature. The Upaniṣads conceived of salvation from transmigration (*mokṣa*, release from bondage to recurrent death, or as in Kaṭha 2.3.18, *vimṛtyu*, being free of death) in the image of the sun, the subject presumably of so many Ṛg Vedic symposia.

One need hardly cite the many ectypes of this archetypal image of solar transcendence (such as the vivid example of Chāndogya Upaniṣad 3.11), but, in passing, it can be used to clarify the full-moon symbolism in classical Sanskrit myth. Siddhārtha achieves enlightenment on the night of the full moon and, after the ecstasy of the *rasalīlā* dance, Kṛṣṇa bathes under the full moon in cooling river waters. In both cases, the tenor of the full moon is the paradoxical attainment of and coincidence with solar eternity. Transient, conditioned, "lunar" reality becomes full, infinite, and whole again when, for one night each month, the moon imitates the sun. In much the same way, Siddhārtha transcends his lunar nature to awaken to his true solar nature under the full, "solar" moon, and Kṛṣṇa celebrates the victory of the *gopīs* over separation in the paradoxical solar light of the full moon's arrested transience.

In this context of image fossils caught in the later strata of Ṛg Vedic speculation, note should be made of the image vehicle used for *māyā* (signifying in the Ṛg Veda, divine creative power)[18] from the same Sūrya's Bridal fragment. Later the term came to connote something much more sinister, because the dominant world view shifted its evaluation of phenomenal existence. From its affirmation in the Ṛg Veda, phenomenal existence came, in the classical view, to be evaluated pessimistically as to its ability to fully satisfy human spiritual aspirations, particularly in its notions of transience and *duḥkha* (disease, unsatisfactoriness). In this case, insight comes from focusing on the vehicle chosen by the poet to represent the tenor of the already abstract, technical term, *māyā*. *Māyā* surely ranks as one of the most mysterious of any such terms, including *nirvāṇa*, in Sanskrit. Here, this abstruse term is enigmatized by children playing, and thus, already in late Ṛg Vedic speculation, play[19] is an acceptable image gloss of *māyā*: "One after another the two turn, by *māyā*, / Two children playing (*krīḷantau*), going round a sacrifice."[20] (10.85.18b).

Since it is by *māyā* (divine creative power) that Mitrā-Varuṇā order the dawns and send the sun across the sky, appropriately the term appears here in the enigma of the sun and moon. The *māyā*, or ordered creation, of sun and moon is compared to the image of two playing children who run around a sacrificial ground. What is *māyā*? Why, it is (like) children playing; to understand the mystery of creation as does the Ṛg Vedic poet, we have but to refer to the image. Children playing around ritual performances must have been a common sight to these poets.[21] One day, one of them proposed this familiar scene of innocent, playful action as a striking image of *māyā*, the game or play of cosmic order, so inscrutable in the playing out of its pattern of abundance and decline.

Sun and moon circle earth, one after the other, ordaining the days and nights. The speculative image asserts that the same order holds for all natural phenomena, the fertility of women and cows, plentiful rain, long and disease-free life. It is significant to find this image gloss of *māyā* in late Ṛg Vedic speculation, since the classical tradition repeatedly calls divine action a *līlā* (play).[22] Brahma-sūtra 2.1.32–33 discusses Brahmā's action of creating the world as "not being for any purpose, but as in the world only for play" (*na prayojanatvāt, lokavat tu līlākaivalyam*). This play constitutes the mystery of creation, which reveals and at the same time conceals its source, the divine principle behind it.[23] Or, many times, the actions of divine incarnations are termed a *līlā*, including those of Kṛṣṇa, Śiva, and even the Buddha. Play in the Bhagavad Gītā exemplifies the supreme form of the devotee's worldly actions, which participate in transcendence if performed as a līlā, without concern for result or reward, as in the games children play.[24]

So Mitrā-Varuṇā's sun provides powerful speculative imagery for the development of the classical Sanskrit world view. At every stratum subsequent to the Ṛg Veda, solar imagery supports speculative thought. Coomaraswamy's pioneering article on the beginnings of wandering as a spiritual option in Indian religions, published as "The Pilgrim's Way" in the *Journal of the Bihar and Orissa Research Society* (1937), presents another remarkable early ectype of the sun enigma and comments on the wandering course recommended by the image of the sun. He translates a set of verses from the Aitareya Brāhmaṇa legend of Hariśchandra (Ait. Br. 7.13–18) who, though having a hundred wives, produced no son. Since a son was essential in the Vedic conception of salvation, Hariśchandra prayed to Varuṇa (who, with Mitra, notably ordains such things), promising to sacrifice the son to Varuṇa, should he be born. Rohita, being that son, was by birth thus promised to die (as all humans are), owing to his father's peculiar vow. But each time Varuṇa came to accept the sacrifice, Hariśchandra begged him away from its satisfaction, arguing for a later, more appropriate date. This continued until Rohita became a fully-trained *kṣatriya*, when Hariśchandra was finally ready to assent to Varuṇa's demand for the sacrifice. But then Rohita objected, upon being informed by his father of the vow, and he left him to wander for a year in the forest.

After this first year, Rohita returned to the village because Varuṇa had afflicted his father with disease. He was told on this and on five succeeding occasions, each one year later, to wander in search of a way of avoiding the death appointed to him. Coomaraswamy translates the five yearly exhortations to wander, wondering whether they became a *śramaṇa* chant or pilgrim's song, sung by bands of wandering pilgrims on the road:[25]

> "Manifold fortune is his who wearieth not,"
> Thus we have heard, O Rufus (Rohita):
> 'Tis an evil race that sitteth down;
> Indra companions the traveller.
> Keep on going, keep on going!
>
> Forth-springing are the traveller's shanks
> His person thriveth and beareth fruit:
> All of his ills supine
> Slain by the toil of his progress—
> Keep on going, keep on going!
>
> His weal who sitteth up, up-sitteth too,
> But his who standeth, standeth up:
> His weal who falleth down, lies down
> But his who goeth is itself agoing—
> Keep on going, keep on going!
>
> *Kali* his lot who lieth down,
> *Dvāpara* his who would fain cast off,
> *Tretā* his who standeth up:
> *Kṛta* he reacheth who moveth—
> Keep on going, keep on going!
>
> 'Tis the traveller that findeth the honey,
> The traveller the tasty fig:
> Consider the fortune of the Sun,
> Who never tireth of travelling!
> Keep on going, keep on going!
>
> [Coomaraswamy: 1937, pp. 461–465]

The verses extol wandering, which in the age of the Brāhmaṇa literature (circa 800–600 B.C.) was an innovative spiritual path. Wandering strivers or śramaṇa, first mentioned in the Śatapatha Brāhmaṇa, produced the Upaniṣads, early Buddhism, and Jainism. Rohita and Siddhārtha were kṣatriyas (members of the warrior class)[26] who wandered for six years to search for and gain release from death, Rohita by finding a substitute, Siddhārtha by achieving enlightenment. The Aitareya verses commend Rohita to a course of action that became by preclassical times (circa 600 B.C.) the spiritual path par excellence. Later, *bhakti* and then *tantra* competed with it in their versions of the way to release, along with householder Buddhism. But from the Brāhmaṇic period until the integrative vision of the Bhagavad Gītā resulted in popular, devotional movements that opened salvation to the many classes, the śramaṇa orders formed the spiritual élite.

These śramaṇas resided "in the forest," having renounced "village" life and its commitment to mundane, householder goals (love, gain, and duty). One wonders how such a radical path attracted the finest spirits of the age, since it required that persons cut themselves totally away from society, declaring themselves dead to the world. Surely the new world view's philosopheme of recurrent death influenced many, especially those disaffected kṣatriyas who found new careers as charismatic leaders and followers of the forest dwellers. The fifth verse makes an indubitable learned allusion to the *pippalaṃ svādv* of 1.164.22c, the enigma of the sweet fig of the two birds.[27] This allusion links the growing śramaṇa tradition to the Ṛg Vedic speculative symposium[28] with its archaic goal of knowing through ecstasy.

In the translation style of this essay, this fifth verse reads:[29]

> Only the wanderer finds the honey,
> The wanderer the sweet fig;
> Contemplate the excellence (*śremāṇam*) of the sun—
> Which though always a-wandering, never tires!

This verse directs śramaṇas to meditate on the enigma of the sun eternally wandering across the sky, never changing or altering the solar over the lunar course. By wandering, cut away from all that mutates (the realm of the *grāma*, village or mundane reality), śramaṇas sought to imitate the solar, eternal destiny, thereby escaping from the eternal recurrence of the alternate lunar model.

The excellence of the sun is that, like a Platonic idea or a metaphysical real, it never suffers transmutation. As one of the Sanskrit tradition's sun enigmas, this ectype of the Ṛg Vedic speculative sun enigmatized the śramaṇa way to ultimate salvation. Ritual was no longer considered to give access to ultimate salvation, but only to the same or to other rebirth realms. Wandering as a meta-ritual became the doorway to release from all phenomenality (*saṃsāra*), leading to a destiny not even thought of in the Ṛg Vedic world view. The power of the new way was so great that it created spiritual groups to the left (Jainas), in the center (Buddhists), and on the right (Upaniṣadic circles). It so affected early Buddhism that Horner could write: "One of the more striking features of Early or Pali Buddhism lies in the open or implied stress it constantly lays on movement and motion."[30]

The Aitareya myth of Rohita prefigures the Buddha myth; the latter is the much better-known ectype of the former.[31] Both set a pattern that became a hallmark of Indian spirituality. Centuries later, Śānti Deva, in his *Bodhicaryāvatāra* (Coomaraswamy: 1964, p. 322), recalled the innovation in his vivid description of the wanderer's vision of life:

> Trees are not disdainful, and ask for no toilsome wooing; fain would I consort with those sweet companions! Fain would I dwell in some deserted sanctuary, beneath a tree or in caves, that I might walk without heed, looking never behind! Fain would I abide in nature's own spacious and lordless lands, a homeless wanderer, free of will, my sole wealth a clay bowl, my cloak profitless to robbers, fearless and careless of my body. Fain would I go to my home the

> graveyard, and compare with other skeletons my own frail body! For this my body will become so foul that the very jackals will not approach it because of the stench. The bony members born with this corporeal frame will fall asunder from it, much more so my friends. Alone man is born, alone he dies; no other has a share in his sorrows. What avail friends, but to bar his way? As a wayfarer takes a brief lodging, so he that is travelling through the way of existence finds in each birth but a passing rest.

Though totally different in cultural content, Śānti Deva's wayfaring is not so far from the medieval Christian idea of wandering through life unattached to the world for the sake of salvation, as Gerhart Ladner explains it.[32] He shows that the two principal Christian ideas of alienation involve first, an alienation from God's ordained order (sin) and second, a conception of life as a pilgrim's journey through the world (leading to salvation). "The just, therefore," he writes, "do not settle for good in this world—they know that they are only pilgrims and guests in it. They desire to rejoice where they belong and cannot be happy in a foreign land" (pp. 235–236). Buddhists have shared this conception to the ends of Asia, as the travel sketches of the Japanese poet, Bashō, illustrate,[33] and as the European adaptation of the Buddha myth, the story of Barlaam and Josaphat, attests.[34]

The many enigmas of the sun provided prolific meanings to the Sanskrit speculative tradition, giving to the sun a place equalled perhaps only in Egyptian and native American speculation (Maya, Inca, Aztec). The Ṛg Veda calls that sun a wheel (*sū́ryam . . . cakrám*, 1.175.4, cf. 4.30.4), and refers to "the golden wheel of the sun" (*sū́raś-cakrám̥ hiraṇyáyam*, 6.56.2). The ever-turning wheel, the second of the great symposium enigmas, deserves a separate chapter.

5.
Enigmas of the Wheel, the Eternal Turner

> Fate seems to love the parable of the water buckets on the irrigation wheel: it empties these and fills up those, raises some and lowers others, and others again it keeps in between; and teaching us thus how our life in the world is but an interplay of irreconcilables, it plays its endless games with us.
> —Cārudatta, in Śūdraka's *The Little Clay Cart* (van Buitenen)

Wheel enigmas abound in Sanskrit culture. Literature, art, and speculative metaphysics all used wheel ectypes derived in part from archetypal Ṛg Vedic imagery. Several thousand years before, Harappā toy makers shaped little clay carts like those bringing grain and supplies into the city. Later, when Indo-Aryan tribes migrated across the northwestern mountains down onto the plains, their nobles, the first cowboys, raided local settlements for booty while mounted on fearful war chariots. By the time of Śūdraka (circa A.D. 400), author of the exquisite Sanskrit play, *The Little Clay Cart,* the wheel enigma had permeated world–view thought, based on its powerful Ṛg Vedic archetype from Dīrghatamas's bráhman collection of 1.164. Cārudatta, Śūdraka's hero, with all resolved at the play's end, summarized the ups and downs of the plot using the image vehicle of the water wheel or noria.[1]

As the enigma translated at the head of this chapter explains, all the world's changes produced by its "interplay of irreconcilables" might best be understood by referring to the action of the water wheel. It empties and fills its vessels, turning without end to bring up water and to disgorge it onto forever-parched fields. So too, life fills and empties, due to forces innate in matter, as if the underlying mechanism of change were a wheel, a "wheel of life."

Nothing a priori determined that the wheel be taken as a world image,[2] and nothing in Harappā remains would indicate that it functioned as a major world-view image. Yet by the time of classical India, the wheel[3] was the major weapon and iconographical marker of Viṣṇu.[4] It figured in conceptions of time (as in *kālacakra*), space (as a province or district), creation myth (*bhavacakra*), sovereignty (as in *cakravartin*), sacrifice (*yajñacakra*), in notions of mystical space and order (*maṇḍala* as *cakra*), as theoretical constructs in mystic physiology (the *cakras* of the spine and head), as Tantric temple ground plan or image-model (as at Konarak), and as pattern for Kṛṣṇa's mystic dance, even forming the basis of conceptions of eternal order and truth (*brahmacakra, dharmacakra*). Doubtless, with the sun, the wheel is a major Sanskrit world-view symbol.

Paul Horsch's article, "The Wheel: An Indian Pattern of World-Interpretation"[5] reads like a cinematic history of Sanskrit world image development. Just as the image of the sun enigmatized cosmic order, and sun and moon came to enigmatize the two destinies, the wheel image enigmatized the order of the world in which humans lived. It responded to questions involving the nature of the invisible order as it pertained to daily life. Wheel enigmas revealed the way things are in creation (note parallel, the "uniform wheel" and the "uniform ordination," 7.63., vv. 2 and 3).

The root metaphors that shape whole world views (or "world hypotheses") generally are very few, in any group, tribe, or civilization. Sanskrit literature repeatedly compares phenomenal life (*saṃsāra*) to the wheel, or an ocean, or a lotus; its order follows that of the cosmic tree and creation is conceived after the model of a sacrificial dismembering of the primeval person. Pepper[6] describes the procedure as the "traditional analogical method of generating world theories" (p. 91):

> The method in principle seems to be this: A man desiring to understand the world looks about for a clue to its comprehension. He pitches upon some area of common-sense fact and tries if he cannot understand other areas in terms of this one. This original area becomes then his basic analogy or root metaphor. He describes as best he can the characteristics of this area, or, if you will, discriminates its structure. A list of its structural characteristics becomes his basic concepts of explanation and description.

Students of myth and world view have long observed the use of images that are conceptually productive because of their seminal ambiguity. Scientific theory also recognizes the role of models in understanding complex phenomena. These models often do not duplicate a reality to which they empirically correspond, but they can nevertheless generate accurate predictions about a state of affairs within it. Similarly, a root metaphor acts to create a realm of meaning. In "The Dead Birds," the Peabody Museum's movie of the Dugum Dani, a primitive New Guinea highland community, bird symbolism founds an entire universe of meanings. This includes the forecast of human mortality implicit in their self-descriptive image, likening themselves to dead birds.[7]

Through much the same mechanism, a Ṛg Vedic wheel enigma (1.164.11–15, 48) from Dīrghatamas's symposium influences the classical Sanskrit world view of phenomenal reality. Śūdraka laments its most disturbing characteristic, present already in the Ṛg Vedic archetype, by concluding that the wheel of life "plays its endless games with us." Given recurrent death, the world becomes a realm of what Kees Bolle calls "endless impermanence."[8] These two fundamental assumptions of the classical Sanskrit world view condemn mortal humans to frustration and despair over attaining enduring happiness in any of the impermanent rebirth realms. Māyā, the play of creation, metes out human destinies, life after life, according to human actions and its own principles of order and consequence. Human lives fill and empty like clay (tenor: material) buckets on the water wheel that fills and empties; or the world "turns" like wagon wheels along endless lanes. The immediate motivation for all soteriological action, in the Sanskrit world view, is to escape from just this endlessness.

It had not been so in the Ṛg Vedic view. Though it assumed endlessness, it had not included recurrent death in its list of crucial human attributes. It seems ironic that an attribute of creation, like endlessness, conceived positively at one stratum of speculation, should take on such a different meaning at later, different strata. Without recurrent death and material impermanence, endlessness would have no bite, nor would it entail any bitterness. Regardless, at both strata, the wheel functioned as a basic pattern of intelligibility, imparting a meaning to life otherwise beyond human aspirations for comprehension and some kind of predictability. The archetypal understanding of the wheel as root metaphor came to Dīrghatamas, as recorded in 1.164, which starts with his rare autobiographical account of the beginning of the most famous Ṛg Vedic speculative symposium:

1.
Of this splendid ancient invoker (Agni), the middle brother is the voracious (or the thunderbolt);
His third brother is ghee-back. There (in the *bráhman* symposium) I envisaged the seven-sonned lord of the people (Agni).

2.
The seven yoke the single-wheeled chariot,

Single is the horse that draws it, and seven-named;
Three-naved is the wheel, unaging, unaltered
Where all these world abide.

3.
On this chariot, seven-wheeled, these seven abide,
Seven are the horses which draw it;
Seven sisters sing praise together,
Where the seven names of the cows are placed.

4.
Who saw the first one being born, which (though) boneless[9] bears the boned?
Earth's breath, blood, and soul—what really are they?
Who shall approach the wise one to ask that?[10]

5.
Unrealized (*pā́ka*), unseeing with my mind's eye, I wonder about
The tracks of the gods left at that time (of creation).[11]
Above the yearling (?) calf the poet-seers have stretched
Seven warp threads (ready) for weaving.[12]

6.
Uncomprehending, the truly knowing poet-seers I ask
So that I might understand; (now) I understand not.
Who propped apart these six spaces in the form of the one unborn?
What even really was the one (*ékam*)?

7.
Here (in the bráhman contest) let him explain who really understands,
The track which was left of this splendid bird. . . .

37.
I do not (even) know whether, as it were, I am this; (?)
Enveloped in mystery, absorbed, with my mind's eye, I wander.
When to me has come the first born of order (Agni),
Just then do I attain to a share of his wisdom (*vā́c*).[13]

[1.164.1–7ab, 37]

Following this, Dīrghatamas's description of the symposium frames a collection of loosely connected bráhmans beginning in 7cd. Verse 21, already discussed in chapter 3, is also autobiographical, as is verse 52, where the poet invokes Agni a final time for help. In the first verse, while invoking the three forms of Agni, the poet recalls how he envisaged Agni in the bráhman symposium. He pays tribute to the "lord of the people," Agni, who through the ritual supports life and who, as inspiration and revelation, transforms those who succeed in the contest.

The following two verses immediately begin to describe, in riddling sevens, the symposium-sacrifice. This number seems to denote various aspects of the sacrifice in progress, but it is fruitless to try to specify all of the tenors.[14] The poet observes the sacrifice in the language of enigma, for instance, the seven sons (1d) represent the seven priests who yoke the single-wheeled chariot of the sacrifice.[15] He describes his thoughts as he enters the contest, hoping to achieve participation in the mystery it represents. He sits in front of the fire, which he addresses as the splendid, ancient invoker-priest, carefully preparing for the visionary experience by transforming his consciousness, by nurturing, through enigmatic questioning, his own wondrous sense of the mysterious.

In verses which transport us back to the very beginnings of Sanskrit speculation, the poet first seeks (v. 4) for a witness to Agni's birth, asking about world mysteries in the special question form of the contest. He wonders who is to approach (as a son in the contest) the wise one (a contest father, or perhaps Agni) to ask of its answer. The next two verses each express (5ab, 6ab) the poet's self-admission of ignorance (being *pā́ka*), then formulate in images his wonderment concerning mystery. The first (5cd) describes the sacrifice, the tenor of "yearling calf" perhaps being the unrealized poet, while the second (6cd) poses the basic mysteries of creation and its source, the one. The seventh verse throws the contest open to anyone who can comprehend the "track" (revealed forms) "of this splendid bird," probably Agni, already referred to in similar terms in the hymn's first words. Then, in verse 37 (as in v. 21), the poet reports his inspiration from Agni.

These introductory verses list some of the first Sanskrit speculative questions: "Who witnessed Agni, the first born?" (4a), a question about first principles and whether they arose ex nihilo; "What *really* is the world's breath, blood, and soul?" (4c), a speculation about the nature of that which vivifies matter; "What are the tracks, the traces of the order consubstantially born with creation?" (5b); "Who created space and hence all phenomenal manifestation?" (6c); and, "What really is the source of everything, that mysterious one?" (6d).[16] Despite their archaic age, these questions should not be dismissed. In the case of similar early speculative questions in Chinese literature, Demiéville errs in dismissing them as the "stammerings of a nascent metaphysics."[17] As the first formulations of serious pre-philosophical inquiry, these questions present remarkably sophisticated concepts even while using images and mythological themes, as did Plato, for their articulation.

Dīrghatamas, or an anonymous comrade from a symposium fraternity, provides Sanskrit speculation with a brilliant answer to questions such as those he reports in the first verses of 1.164. He records five verses (11–14, 48) of wheel bráhmans proposing a specific reading of the wheel enigma that became archetypal for Sanskrit speculation. An ever-turning wheel enigmatizes the form of mystery-concealed creation:

11.
The twelve-spoked—that certainly not destined to
age!—wheel
Of order (*ṛtá*) rolls on continually across the sky,
The sons, O Agni, therein abide, paired seven-hundred-
and-twenty.

12.
Five-fold,[18] the father, twelve-formed—
They say he overstretches the higher part of the sky.

Then these others say he is the shining one,
Fixed in the lower part, seven-wheeled, six-spoked.

13.
In that turning, five-spoked wheel, all worlds (or beings) abide,
Its axle does not heat, (though) excessively laden,
Even since the beginning it has not been destroyed, (turning still now) with the same nave.

14.
The felloed, unaging wheel rolls on,
The ten-yoked draw it over her, the outstretched,
The sun's eye travels surrounded by space,
In it are fixed all worlds (or beings).

48.
Twelve are the felloes, the wheel is one, three are the naves—
Who really understands that (*bráhman*)?
In that (wheel) together, like pegs, are set
The three-hundred-and-sixty unaltering.

[1.164.11–14, 48]

Here is the archetypal locus classicus of wheel enigmas for Sanskrit speculation. The bráhman specifies its own tenor: it represents the *cakrám . . . ṛtásya* (the wheel of [world] order), which turns or rolls endlessly across the sky (v. 11). This sun-wheel reveals world order, the comprehensible universe of time, space, and sequence, all taking place within an underlying, unaging order. In spelling out the structural characteristics of the analogy, we see that Dīrghatamas envisions a multiple structure, uniting sacrifice to cosmos. Each attribute of his enigma elaborates on another of that unity's structure. By analyzing each image vehicle into separate tenors, we can outline the poet's speculative vision in technical paraphrase.

First, the bráhman states its primary tenor:

VEHICLE	TENOR
wheel	world order, specifically time (year) and space, creation

Then, it assimilates this wheel to solar imagery, with the sun-wheel stating an intermediate vehicle for the same primary tenor:

VEHICLE	INTERMEDIATE VEHICLE	TENOR
rolls on continually across the sky	the sun-wheel	world order

Finally, the bráhman expands the enigma, through its image vehicle, into a pattern of intelligibility, which is its extended tenor:

VEHICLE	TENOR
11.	
twelve-spoked	twelve months of the year
certainly not destined to age	endlessness of creation's order, unaffected by its own changing
rolls on continually	time (months and half-months, seasons, years) passes endlessly
the sons, paired seven hundred and twenty	days and nights of the year
12.	
five-fold	five seasons of the year
the father	source of creation, order (probably Agni)
twelve-formed	twelve months
he overstretches	he, the father, celestial Agni as sun-wheel in sky

VEHICLE	TENOR
shining one	he, the father, terrestrial Agni
fixed in the lower part	established on the altar, on earth
seven-wheeled	the sacrifice-chariot (see verse 3)
six-spoked	(a) some six aspects of the sacrifice, or (b) six months of half-year, or seasons
13.	
turning five-spoked wheel	five seasons of year
all worlds	the three worlds of Vedic cosmology (earth, atmosphere, heaven), extended space, creation
axle	the order uniting the three realms of creation
(though) excessively laden	with creation's weight
does not heat, since the beginning has not been destroyed, having the same (i.e., original) nave	the unchanging within change, endlessness of world process
14.	
felloed	extended (space)
unaging, rolls on	time passes, endlessly
ten-yoked	ten horses drawing the sun chariot[19] (allusion to mythology of sun-wheel, the intermediate vehicle)
her, the outstretched	the earth
sun's eye	wheel of sun (intermediate vehicle)

VEHICLE	TENOR
in it are fixed all worlds	on the wheel all creation depends
48.	
twelve felloes	twelve months (creation's temporal extension)
one wheel	the unity of time, the year
three naves	the three worlds (as above, verse 13)
pegs (i.e., spokes), three hundred and sixty	days of the year (lunar)
unaltering	participant in endless order

This world-wheel image portrays world order or creation in terms of three discrete sets of attributes, involving time-year, space, and order. These categories progress from the relatively known attributes of the year, its days and seasons, through conceptions of space to the very heart of the enigma, its unknown, mysterious, unaging endlessness. First, the wheel is time, the year of twelve months, or three-hundred-and-sixty days, or seven-hundred-and-twenty days and nights, or five seasons, or six months and seasons. Second the wheel is space, creation, the three levels (earth, atmosphere, heaven), sun, and more abstractly, extension and weight. These two categories have little speculative impact, as they derive from commonsense, empirical observations. Only with the third category, pertaining to the underlying attributes of order, does the wheel become fully speculative, most profoundly enigmatic of the unknown. This distinguishes commonsense observation from speculative vision: speculation seeks beyond the surface orders of time and space to a third, underlying, more comprehensive level in the description of reality, the dimension of the mysterious.

Contemporary metaphysicians, inheritors of the speculative endeavor, no less than symposium contestants, wish somehow to observe and describe the unapparent, subtle, or deep structures and principles of creation, its nature and order. The most fruitful ground for debate and contention has always been the unobservable, the unempirical. This quest has sustained thousands of generations of speculators and metaphysicians, and their most abstruse arguments have provided sustenance for both mind and stomach. The world, speculation assumes, consists of both appearance and reality. In the first two categories, Dīrghatamas's bráhman describes the observable principles of creation; in the third, it describes its underlying reality, through the arts of vision and poetry.

This third level of the enigma articulates the basic Sanskrit understanding of creation. The wheel's order is eternal, its turning endless; its order is numerically sequential and hierarchical, and above all, circular. At the heart of the enigma, this wheel's creation endlessly turns and changes but itself never alters, never fails. The wheel's paradox reveals that, though changing, within itself it does not change. It causes time and eternity, light and dark, heaven and earth to cohabit a single, inexpressible unity.

Speculation at its deepest level perhaps necessarily involves the enigmatic; as Camus remarked, "indulging in metaphysics means accepting paradoxes."[20] To use metaphysical language, the wheel enigmatizes the oneness of being and becoming, the unity of the one and the many, and the coincidence of the changing impermanent and the forever unchanged, the endless. The enigma defines a level of being that transcends what is characteristically observed through the senses. As time passes, things deteriorate, naves overheat, spokes, axles, and felloes wear. All are repaired and eventually must be discarded and replaced. None of this occurs at a deeper level of reality—such is the claim of the wheel image. It posits a realm of being that transcends observed processes.

Paradoxically, the wheel transcends its own nature, which, though turning, never wears, overheats, or perishes. The most striking speculative attribute of the wheel is that it enigmatizes a world which, though turning constantly (*várvarti*, 11b, intensive-frequentive), unlike all individuals and things within it, is not destined to decay (*nahí táj járāya*, 11ab). Thus it escapes death. Somehow, in the totality, though turning, the wheel transcends its turning. Though time endlessly progresses, earnestly creating and devouring its creations, creation itself remains untouched.

Given the Ṛg Vedic world view, none of this threatened dire destinies. In that prior understanding of order, human ritual could always prevail over disorder; through ritual, life could be magnified and death survived. The conclusion that the world wheel turns endlessly did not prevent the people of the Ṛg Veda from aspiring to the hundred autumns allotted them by tradition, fully recognizing themselves to be *mṛtyubandhu* (bound to death, mortal). Should life in the realm of the fathers be endless, all the better, for hymns promised its luxury. Conventional conceptions predicted that dead persons, upon proper ritual cremation, would be taken by Agni to the realm of the fathers and to Yama in the highest heaven, where, reunited with a glorious body, they would enjoy bliss. When, however, speculation replaced these views of death, and when such innovations as the notions of recurrent death and endless, unsatisfying impermanence (for even those who had become gods eventually died) changed the frame of the picture of death, endlessness came to threaten a dire fate, indeed. In the classical world view, saṃsāra's wheel of life portrayed a kind of endless purgatory into which humans were repeatedly born to improve themselves in their ability to transcend it all. Transcendence constituted the only end to endlessness. Salvation meant not ending endlessness, but removing oneself from it, or realizing that one was already beyond it. The prime motivation for undertaking the ways to salvation was the unacceptability of remaining trapped in endless impermanence.

The ancient wheel's archetypal myth of endlessness sent Sanskrit soteriology on a search for ways of transcending time. The unaltering real beyond creation and accident (*māyā*) became the ultimate goal. The tradition reformulated this ultimate human goal hundreds of times, often using wheel ectypes of the Ṛg Vedic original. The most famous such ectype was developed by the Buddhist tradition in textual descriptions and visual images of the wheel of life (*bhavacakra*). Visually, this wheel first survived fragmentarily from Ajaṇṭa[21] and is still recreated today in the tanka art of exiled Tibetan communities. In conception, the wheel of life goes back to the accounts of Siddhārtha's enlightenment visions. He saw first all of his own rebirths, then he saw other beings dying and passing into other rebirths in the five different destinies of existence (*gati*), and finally he saw the chain of interdependent arising (*pratītya-samutpāda*), whose twelve *nidānas* (links) bind beings to continued, recurrent death and rebirth in the wheel's rebirth realms. When this Sidhārthic vision came to be represented visually, it was as the wheel of life.

Divyāvadāna 300 first brings vision and visual wheel archetype together, enigmatizing the Buddha's multiple visions in the single wheel of life. This wheel ectype supplies the Buddhist creation myth, since it accounts for how a person fares in world order. (As world order is endless in the direction of both past and future, no account of creation in the sense of the first moment is required; it is *anādi*, without beginning.) In this passage, following the description of the wheel, two verses moralize upon the image's story of human mortality, recommending that the wheel be utterly abandoned:

> The five-spoked Wheel . . . is to be made with the five destinies (*gati*), the hells, animals, *pretas* (ghosts), gods,

and human beings. Therein the hells are to be made at the bottom, the animals and ghosts above; then gods and human beings; the four continents, Pūrvavideha, Aparagodānīya, Uttarakuru, and Jambudvīpa. In the middle (the nave) passion, hatred, and stupidity are to be represented, passion in the form of a dove, hatred in the form of a snake, and stupidity in the form of a pig. An image of Buddha is to be made pointing out the circle of Nirvāṇa. Apparitional beings are to be represented by means of a windlass as passing away and being reborn. All round is to be represented the twelve-fold Causal Origination in direct and reverse order. The whole is to be represented as swallowed by Impermanence (*anityatā*), and two verses are to be written:

> Make a beginning, renounce your home,
> To the Buddha-teaching apply yourselves;
> Smite away the army of Death,
> As an elephant a house of reeds.
>
> Who in this Law and Discipline
> Shall vigilantly lead his life,
> Abandoning the round of birth,
> Shall verily make an end of pain.[22]

The Buddha instructed that this wheel be "inscribed over the gateway of the Veluvana monastery at Rajagaha."[23] Coomaraswamy reports that such edifying works were even painted on monastery bathroom and sudatoria walls in classical India.[24] Contemporary reports from Tibet before its demise indicate that Tibetan monasteries had similar paintings of the wheel of life for the edification of the junior monks and laity. Waddell reports:

> The avowed object of this picture is to present the causes of rebirth in so vivid a form that they can be readily perceived and overcome; while the realistic pictures of the evils of existence in its varied forms and the tortures of the damned are intended to intimidate evil-doers. The value of this picture for teaching purposes is fully utilized

> by the Lamas. It is placed in a conspicuous position usually in the vestibule, (and usually on the left side as at Ajaṇṭa), and is occasionally, as at Samye, 10 to 15 feet in diameter. Its strange objects and varied scenes strongly excite the curiosity of the junior monks and the laity, whose inquisitiveness is only to be satisfied, or whetted, by a short explanatory sermon. And so great is the belief in the power for good of this picture that Tibetan artists eagerly compete for the execution of so meritorious a work.[25]

The frontispiece represents schematically the traditional image of the wheel of life. The entire wheel is held by the image's tenor of impermanence or death, the fact of material reality from which escape is sought. Impermanence's fangs repeatedly devour beings within the wheel. Saṃsāra or creation is not one but five realms (in later representations, six) into which rebirth takes place according to the law of karman, specifically spelled out in the twelve links of interdependent arising. Within the nave, the reasons for rebirth are symbolized; passion is represented by a dove, hatred by a snake, and ignorance by a pig. According to the Buddha's instructions, some sort of mechanical device showed beings dying and being reborn graphically into the wheel. It must have been quite a sight, with an assistant working the windlass, and a monk working the crowd with moralizing suited to his audience. In the moralizing verses, to "make an end of pain" meant to achieve release from recurrent death and rebirth into endless impermanence.

Though only Buddhists represent such wheels of life, the image epitomizes the classical Sanskrit vision of creation. Within the wheel there exist diverse rebirth realms (five or six) into which rebirth occurs endlessly; each rebirth expresses the consequences (*karman*) of prior actions. Ultimate salvation (*nirvāṇa, mokṣa, kaivalya*) cannot be found within the wheel, even by achieving rebirth in the old Vedic heavens, also plagued by transience. As the Buddha's instructions specify, "An image of Buddha is to be made pointing out the circle of Nirvāṇa." This implies *nirvāṇa* is a wholeness (circle) independent of the wheel of life, an alternate, unchanging (solar) destiny. *Mokṣa*, the usual Hindu term for ultimate salvation, indicates a release from the endless rebirth of continued bondage to the turning wheel of life. *Kaivalya* (uniqueness), the goal of Sāṃkhya metaphysics and yoga, similarly indicates a transcendence of the wheel's ups and downs, its "interplay of irreconcilables," which unbalance the person's equipoise (*samādhi*). This pan-classical world view takes form and authority directly from Dīrghatamas's archetypal enigmas. Their features shaped and colored all Sanskrit literature's world understanding. They provided the agreed-upon basis for contention among the ever-debating schools of philosophy, and in soteriology, gave interpretation and meaning to mystical experiences, authenticating achievements of the ultimate. The diverse parties to Sanskrit soteriology explained the wheel differently, giving it the interpretation convenient to their path, but all accepted the Ṛg Veda's archetypal root metaphor.

The Buddhist wheel, in particular, strikingly returns to its Ṛg Vedic prototype. The twelve links of interdependent arising correspond to the twelve spokes of the wheel of the year.[26] The five or six rebirth realms correspond to the archetype's fives (seasons) and sixes (six months of the half year). The three naves correspond to the three animals symbolizing the motivational causes for a being's rebirth in the wheel's eternal turning. Both images account for the order postulated as the established form of creation. The numerical units chosen for both descriptions of world order coincide with natural lunar units of time, serving to underline their cosmological implications. That such a creation builds on a lunar structure makes it the realm of unsatisfactoriness (*duḥkha*, dis-ease); even those who have by karman become gods eventually cannot satisfy their lust, begin to perspire, their garlands wither and they die a painful death, going to yet another rebirth.

Circularity enters the classical Sanskrit world view as a major consequence of the wheel archetype. Time, once perhaps conceived as linear by the ancestors of the Ṛg Vedic poets, is always circular in later times. Within vast expanses of ordinary world years, creation undergoes long disintegration, winding down to be swept into an equally long period of involution, all subsequently to begin again, like a wheel that starts up anew for the next morning's work. Sanskrit psychology anticipates many of the ideas of twentieth-century psychologies when it analyzes frustration and the sources of anxiety using circular models like those of interdependent arising. Such causal chains occur, for instance, in the Bhagavad Gītā (as at 1.40–44, and 2.62–63). Another wheel ectype concludes the discussion (3.8–15) of the necessity for orthodox Hindus to perform the karman, ritually incumbent upon them by birth into a particular class status. In verse 3.16, the ectype enigmatizes world order as a wheel turned through such human ritual action:[27]

> Who here in this world does not turn the (sacrificial)
> Wheel of life thus set turning (by prior sacrificial action),
> Is injurious (to world order), taking delight only in the
> sensual.
> That person, O Arjuna, lives in vain.

This verse makes its point against those who do not follow the orthodox practice (*yajña*, sacrifice, ritual) by likening the world to a wheel whose circular process is turned or maintained by the countless ritual acts performed by followers of the orthodox way of life. These rites, great and homely, include feeding the ancestors, rarely mentioned in descriptions of "Hinduism," which are prejudiced toward mysticism and doctrine. The second part of the verse moralizes that the person who does not follow duty (turn the sacrificial wheel) injures world order, lives on the sensual surfaces of creation, and exists in vain, being out of touch with the sacred, which gives life its meaning. This ritual orthopraxy is the Vedic religion of ameliorative continuance which seeks to help persons rise in the wheel of creation through proper action into purer and purer rebirth realms. Contemporary evidence from neighboring Burmese Buddhism indicates that even monastic Buddhists follow this mundane soteriology, which sees salvation as being fully within the wheel of life.[28]

In the panorama of Sanskrit soteriology, this religion of continuance remains a distinct minority view, except in its number of followers. In the Bhagavad Gītā, it is cleverly assimilated to the more radical paths of final release innovated by the śramaṇa (*niragni*) traditions. It affirmed the goal of transcending attachment to all one's life and action by considering action free of attachment to consequence as the sacrifice which tradition enjoined. Other wheel ectypes enigmatize the more radical conceptions of salvation as final release from the wheel, conceptions that came into full vogue in the early Upaniṣads and the teachings of the Buddha and Mahāvīra. The early Upaniṣads contain extensive records of speculations deriving from post-Ṛg Vedic speculative institutions similar to symposia. Wheel ectypes apparently were common, as in the example of the Praśna Upaniṣad enigma of 6.6:

> That in which the parts are set, like spokes in the nave of a wheel,
> Know that one as Spirit (puruṣa) which you should experience,
> So that death may not appear to surround you completely.[29]

This likens the Upaniṣadic principle of the inner self (*ātman*) or Spirit (*puruṣa*), which guarantees essential transcendence, to the nave of a wheel, with its motionless, unextended center.[30] This is as opposed to its spokes, which are its extension into space and becoming, into the material aspects of a person. The inner self, the Upaniṣads declare, must be experienced for salvation to occur. To interpret: once individuals experience meditative ecstasy, thus "knowing the Spirit within," they have entered a realm of consciousness not in death's dominion and have cut the bonds to material existence. Once their life terminates, their death will be final, releasing them forever from the wheel's circular recurrence and any further rebirth.

These themes reappear in another example from the speculative beginnings of the Śvetāśvatara Upaniṣad.[31] This section reports the speculators' questions and then proposes images to resolve their quandary about the mysteries. These "propounders of questions about Brahman" (*brahmavādins*) ask:

1. "What is the cause? Brahman. From whence, indeed, are we born? By what do we live? And on what established? Regulated by what, in pleasure and other (states), O propounders of questions about Brahman, do we live out our (worldly) condition?

2. Time, own nature, fate or change, the elements, mother, or a (guiding) spirit—these should be considered. But not a combination of these. Is it because of the inner self (*ātman*)? But the inner self cannot be the causer of pleasure and pain, (so no).

3. Those who practiced yoga and meditation envisioned the power of the divine inner self, hidden behind its own attributes,
Whoever regulates all these (possible) causes, from time through inner self,
He is the One.

4. (We meditate on the image of)[32] That (One), as being single-felloed, three-wheeled, sixteen-ended, fifty-spoked, with twenty counter-spokes;

Which has six consisting of eights, its one binding made of all forms, split on three paths, with one delusion having two grounds.

6. In this huge[33] creation wheel (*brahmacakra*),[34]
wherein both life and rest exist for all,[35]
The goose (*haṃsa*) circles round, confused,
Thinking its inner spirit and the turner (of the wheel) to be different;
Then, inspired by That, it experiences its immortality (*amṛtatva*)."

As is evidenced in this passage, much Upaniṣadic material comes from later forms of speculative symposia. Here, the "propounders of questions about Brahman" ask about the cause, source, basis, and ordaining principles of the worldly human condition. Quite a list of possibilities follows, covering options from the simple passage of time to mother! Or is it, they ask, the inner self? The verse answers no, since metaphysically this self cannot be implicated in any action. Whatever stands behind all phenomena and all possible causes, that is the One (Brahman), the mysterious, unmoved mover behind the world-producing Brahmā, creative demiurge, and his wheel of life.

The third verse also shows that these Upaniṣadic speculators practiced yoga (the śramaṇa system of self-discipline) and meditation, reaching the divine inner self and its power through this means rather than through drinking sóma and engaging in complex ritual actions. Yoga and meditation produce an ecstatic state in which speculative vision becomes possible, as the verb *envisioned* indicates (same verb, Ṛg Veda 6.9, 3, and 4, "to see with the spiritual eye," according to Monier-Williams).

One of the enigmas proposed for the speculative envisioning of the answer to these questions comes in verses 4 and 6, using a wheel ectype (v. 5 proposes an alternate image, that of the rivers of life, a variant of the ocean of life enigma). In verse 4, it undergoes the familiar Upaniṣadic augmenting, providing for more and more separate tenors to the extended metaphor. Verse 6 moralizes on the image, claiming that the goose—the unenlightened (unecstatic) individual—wanders by ignorance through that great creation wheel, which has in it not only life but also rest (recurrent death or salvation) for all. The goose's confusion comes from its error in thinking the inner spirit and eternal turner to be different, when, as the Upaniṣads reveal, they are identical (*ātman* is *brahman*). This holds the key to ultimate salvation from the wheel's vicious recurrence.

The goose symbolizes the mystical potentiality of soaring in ecstasy far beyond material creation. The tenor of the goose's potential for soaring flight is achieving ecstasy. This is the familiar experience in meditation of soaring up, apparently away from one's body, into space. Once inspired, the goose, bird of spirit, soars into space, participant in the wheel's immortality. This is a major speculative vision of Sanskrit literature. As in the example of Tzu-chi'i's ecstasy (Introduction, p. xxvi), in these archaic times speculation and meditative ecstasies went hand in hand.

This understanding of salvation united the radical party to Sanskrit soteriology. Its common bond lay in their shared mystical experience, which diminished differences. The salvation of mystical, as opposed to continuative, religion aimed at an ecstatic participation in the wheel's own self-transcendence, its paradoxical, self-indwelling eternality. The enigma promised transcendence at the center of the wheel, in which Ṛg Vedic speculators posited a mysterious endlessness, permitting and bearing the weight of all creation, but suffering no alteration or attenuation itself.

This opened a whole new stage of development, the inquiry of another age. These Upaniṣadic wheel enigmas only prefigured the elaborate speculations to follow as the

Sanskrit tradition developed. Its major outlines, however, were set by 300 B.C., as Indians entered upon the most expansive upsurge of creative energy the civilization was ever to produce. Finally, after spreading throughout southern and southeastern Asia from Afghanistan to Java, that civilization drifted into eclipse, just as its own metaphor of the turning wheel's lunar nature had itself predicted. Other more aggressive and better-armed peoples plunged the subcontinent into chaos and tragedy, as the Indo-Aryans had centuries before. Today, the "eternal dharma" barely survives in its Ṛg Vedic form, having lasted longer than most. As Frits Staal observes, the sons of the last families who preserve Vedic recitation die now without replacement. One wonders what Dīrghatamas would have moralized, were he able to contemplate the subsequent history of his land. Surely, like Śūdraka, he would have noted life's endless play of irreconcilables framed by the picture of creation's eternal wheel from those great spirits of humanity, Dīrghatamas, Siddhārtha, and Śūdraka.

PART III

The Enigmatic Sense of Reality

But we have learned, far from Paris, that there is a light behind us, that we must turn around and cast off our chains in order to face it directly, and that our task before we die is to seek through any words to identify it.
—CAMUS: 1968

6.
An Auspicious Enigma: In Memory of Albert Camus

> Tombés de la cime du ciel, des flots de soleil rebondissent brutalement sur la campagne autour de nous. Tout se tait devant ce fracas et le Lubéron, là-bas, n'est qu'un énorme bloc de silence que j'écoute sans répit. Je tends l'oreille, on court vers moi dans le lointain, des amis invisibles m'appellent, ma joie grandit, la même qu'il y a des années. De nouveau, une énigme heureuse m'aide à tout comprendre.
> —CAMUS: "L'Enigme," *Essais*

> Fallen from the summit of the sky, floods of sunlight rebound brutally over the countryside around us. Everything silences itself before this uproar, and the Lubéron (mountain) out there is but an enormous block of silence to which I listen without respite. I bend my ear, someone runs toward me in the distance, some unseen friends call me, my joy increases, the same as it was years ago. Once anew, an auspicious enigma helps me to understand everything.

To judge by the passages collected in the *Oxford English Dictionary,*[1] the word *enigma* in English has decidedly negative connotations, particularly when it concerns either a person's religion or his ability to understand something. Only occasionally, as in the sermon passage from Jeremy

Taylor (1667), "A person both God and Man, an aenigma to all Nations, and to all Sciences," does the enigma receive positive valuation. More often, it comes associated with idle godlessness, while "fruitless and aenigmatic questions" create fears as devil-cast bones "among us" (the faithful); a "foe" is darkly referred to as "aenigmatick," and worse, Plato passed on "Jewish Traditions in . . . enigmatic Parables." Two hundred years later the paranoid stereotype of "the enigmatic Jew" appears in G. Eliot. With such an inauspicious side to its history, the word could hardly have a less promising prospectus.

The beginnings of Sanskrit speculation arose in part in the Ṛg Vedic enigmatic sense of reality. The English language, but for the instance of Taylor's sermon, seems ill prepared at the outset to admit and express in the word *enigma* what early Sanskrit speculation meant by the term *bráhman*. Perhaps the presumptions of our language will require revision or augmentation to be able to designate this essential cornerstone of Sanskrit speculation. Certainly the other options present less attractive alternatives: "The Vedic riddling sense of reality," "the Vedic allusive (or obscure) sense of reality," and "the Vedic paradoxical sense of reality" all fail, returning us to *enigmatic*.

The word *enigmatic* seems to function in English with negative connotations because it designates "something hidden or perplexing." Its bad reputation draws strength from common intolerance of ambiguity and the unfamiliar in general. Thus, "plainness" is opposed to "aenigmaticalness" (1684); to conclude enigmatically (1590) means to reason with fault (ambiguously) and to have to conclude with an absurdity;[2] an abrupt end to a romance is called enigmatical; the Nile is an "enigmatical vast river" (because no one knew its source?). Discourses and Sydonius, both called "aenigmatical," were doubtless so remembered because of their own obfuscation, which left the reader "scarse [able to] tell where to finde out his meaning." Berkeley introduces his account of someone's writing, calling it brief and enigmatical, and we suspect the refutation already complete before the exposition has even begun. "In Greeke, Aenigmatists . . . speak riddles" (1621), and elsewhere an author makes claims for his ingenuous account as opposed to what "the abovementioned Enigmatist has done." Generally, then, to be enigmatic meant to be hidden or obscure, most often to the detriment of clarity and common sense. It constitutes the first fault in both ordinary reasoning and philosophy, in the battle of the lucid versus the obtuse. A telling citation comes from 1797: "You speak in enigmas, father."

If, to continue reading the dictionary's account of our language, we are to believe the popular imagination, the enigmatic is the obscure, the "far fetched" metaphor (1781), a "symbole," a riddle. Something is "hidden under darke aenigmas and covert speeches," while something else, presumably much more to the satisfaction of the recipient, is delivered "without any Prophetick Aenigm or Parable," meaning directly in unmetaphorical, plain talk. There is nothing so puzzling as an enigma. "Aenigmas which Oedipus himself could never solve" come attested from 1849, while in 1605 someone sinisterly proposed "to erect a monument . . . A dark enigma to the memory." Four years later when we hear of some "problematique mines" yielding "Obsurde inigmaes," we detect a veritable consternation. All this over the simple potentiality of language for mystery, over the fact that language, like action, can be clear or obscure, direct or allusive. This dictionary-based psychoanalysis of the users of the English language would indicate a negative evaluation of the enigmatic: it is ally to obscurity, the demonic in the midst of our reason. The enigmatic reveals a fault in thought, a confusion on the face of clarity. Some language, like Carlyle's withdrawn person, "being excessively reserved withal . . . becomes not a little enigmatic" (1828).

To begin drawing the enigmatic back from the domination of its dark side, we note that it has admitted some neutral usages, which would complete the dictionary entry but for a few extraordinary cases. In this neutral sense, an enigma is a puzzle or a mystery about the world which we could understand better were the spies more efficient about their work, or were events in the near future or distant past to show themselves truthfully in a magic mirror. We read of Spain that "it certainly has been, and long will be, an enigma" and, seemingly from the same field of diplomacy, we read of war and intrigue, "If the fleet . . . could be supposed to solve this enigma." W. Irving, rather late in this history (1850), uses the word with an ambiguous valuation; it is only sure that he does not use it negatively when, writing of Mohamet, he mentions "the enigmatical career of this extraordinary man." In all these cases, enigmatic refers to the obscure, the dark, the obfuscate, either observing it with neutrality, or, in the greater number of cases, with trepidation and disdain.

Another semantic side of *enigmatic,* devoid of its usual negative valuation, neutral on the continuum from dark to light (negative to positive), enters into English probably because it derives from parlor games of wit and intellect rather than from the disputes of the religious or confounded. Coleridge's own enigmatic pen introduced it into the Oxford dictionary:

> In a complex enigma the greatest ingenuity is not always shown by him who first gives the complete solution. (1809–10)

His observation illumines the process of discovery, or the inspiration that results in seeing with utter originality the first forms of a solution, or the anticipation of a precipitate, no matter how fluid and murky the mixture might appear to the quickened creative imagination. Coleridge allows the first shaft of light into the obscurity of the English notion of the enigmatic, proposing involvement of the creative imagination in the act of discovery while contemplating an enigma. Though he merely observes how a common parlor charade or an intellectual's idle riddle[3] are solved, with a simple shift of tenor it would be possible to state and respond in like manner to the great enigmas of the universe. The novelty is that Coleridge faced the enigmatic with other than distrust and suspicion.

The idleness of the parlor charade and Coleridge's complex enigma comes not from its being contrived but from its lack of a suitably significant or serious tenor. The case against the parlor enigma is simple: it is nugatory, devoid of any reference or allusion to a meaning beyond its charade.[4] Coleridge had inadvertently introduced to the English dictionary a meaning of *enigma*. In fact, it could represent or symbolize something unknown, which, paradoxically, could not exist without being in some degree unknown. In consequence, one might know that unknown after inspiration and creative discovery have illuminated the provisional, transforming darkness of the allusive enigma. In the language of metaphor, the image does not obscure its tenor. If it did, that would be a poor, dark poetry. Rather, the image alludes to its ultimate import, speaking as directly as "metaphorical indirection" (Wheelwright's term, 1968*a*, p. 27) will allow. This simple distinction separates the obscure from the lucid or the allusive meanings of *enigma* and *enigmatic*, as well as from its negative and positive valuations in English. And what is allusive can also be lucid, for English has admitted just such a meaning.

The verb *to enigmatize* is attested in the dictionary entry in two of the three degrees, negative and neutral, but not positive. In Donne (1631) it is a neutral term of literary criticism, meaning to symbolize or to represent a tenor with a vehicle enigma, as in "Acteon pursued by his houndes . . . may aenigmatize a lover chased and Devoured by his Thoughts." Coleridge (1834) uses it identically in, "A poetic tissue of visual symbols . . . by which the Apocalypt enigmatized the Neronian persecutions." A magazine writer, also from the nineteenth century, again uses the verb in this neutral modality: "It is precisely the disregard of details that enigmatizes humanity to Michelet." The remaining instances of the verb present its negative pole. From a distraught magazine editor or reader comes: "Manuscripts . . . so aenigmatised with insertions and repetitions and alterations" (1800), allowing the invention of the hypothetical verb in a phrase such as "Jewish Traditions aenigmatised in Plato's Parables," remarking that both belong to the dark side of the enigmatic sun.

Pope's letter to Sir W. Trumbull, 16 December (1715) introduces into the English dictionary a usage of *enigma* which expands its meaning from a figure that obscures to one that alludes to and thus reveals: "It was one of the Enigma's of Pythagoras, 'When the winds rise, worship the Eccho . . . when popular tumults begin, retire to solitudes." He quotes the enigma and provides its moralizing tenor. It is a lucid, not an obscuring enigma. Is then an allusive, enigmatic sense of reality possible? As soon as the enigma of the parlor game ceases to refer solely to a solution or tenor of its own artificial contrivance, replacing it with a tenor from what is mysterious to human comprehension but not beyond its grasp, the enigma becomes an instrument of insight. It is all a matter of how language is being used, for what purpose, in what context.

The Oxford Dictionary recognizes an allusive, enigmatic usage of language. Strangely enough, this is in an elitist interpretation of the legitimate philosophical prerogative to coin terms and to use language suitably expressive of novelty in specialized realms of discourse: "Philosophers when they wrote any thing too excellent for the vulgar to know, expressed it enigmatically" (1641). Though most philosophers may not be as devious as the author suggests, and though this passage expresses an elitist notion of philosophical sublanguages, it does establish that the enigmatic can allude without obscuring. These supposed philosophers would not wish to obscure their thoughts from each other but only from the vulgar, expressing them somehow to exclude uninitiates. What is light to the users of a sublanguage is dark to outsiders, but this applies equally to the sublanguages of chimney sweeps and undertakers.

A lucid enigma both conceals and reveals, cloaks with an insubstantial obscurity and illumines with a clear, pervading light. Within its dark-seeming veils shines the bright side of the enigmatic sun. It is reassuring that the English dictionary completes the paradigm of the enigma,[5] lucid and allusive, neutral and obscure, even if the latter meanings predominate. Regardless, its obscure and allusive meanings complement each other, not numerically but structurally. The word exhibits symmetrical levels of meaning, having a light and a dark side, a full moon and a moonless night, the sun shining and eclipsed in darkness.

English is still a young language and could develop the paradigm with meanings from Sanskrit, from oral shamanic literatures,[6] and, closer to home, from French. English already possesses the full semantic paradigm from its Greek source, but it has neglected some parts of it and has emphasized others. It could become a transcultural language, expressing humanity's meanings through incorporating the usages of cultures and civilizations now open to it. I do not take its case to the Editors, but only to those who wish a less parochial understanding of basic human reality. I propose, by the pagan authority of the Ṛg Veda and Albert Camus, an enrichment of the English language through an auspicious enigma.[7]

We must first note, however, that there is a jewel in the obscurity, a star in the crown of the meager English recognition of the enigmatic. It is not that enigmatic expression keeps the overly excellent from the vulgar. Rather, the overly excellent cannot be expressed in the vulgar, that is, in ordinary language. This latter functions in an eminently practical manner by devoiding itself of allusion and all ambiguous reference. The enigma seeks to restore a sense of wonder about language and reality, so that men's understanding need not be bound by its own limitations and the hard outlines of words. Some people equate clarity with lack of allusive meanings. They seek to purify their language of allusion, consenting to allow poets and ironists to use it anarchically. In the Oxford Dictionary, the dissenting voices come from religious circles. Not all readers of the Bible can overlook its undeniable enigmas.[8] Being scriptural, they have attracted considerable attention. The result has been that not once but twice in the seventeenth century, Englishmen spoke positively of the enigma, if we accept "Those aenigmata of Joseph's sun, moon, stars and sheaves" (1644–52) as a reference to positively valued scriptural or parabolic images.

In the second affirmation, contrary to expectations entertained at the outset, the English word *enigma* rises to its rightful lucidity. Taylor's apostrophe of Jesus, "A person both God and Man, an aenigma to all Nations, and to all Sciences," identifies for all to see the "light of the world." Jesus enigmatizes divine humanity, neither puzzling nor obscure to anyone, if only the Nations and Sciences would recognize what he represents. Were Jesus not both God and Man, he could be no savior but merely a mortal man or an immortal god, never really involved in creation. Surely, we cannot paraphrase Taylor to mean Jesus, a person both God and Man, as a puzzle or obscurity to people and knowledge. Rather, he proclaims Jesus as a lucid enigma, celebrating his unity of being and becoming. Indeed, despite the contradiction of his nature, Christ for the Christian is an illuminating rather than an obscuring enigma.

If Taylor means this, we can equate *enigma* in this sense

with the Ṛg Vedic term *bráhman*. In the first case, the lucid enigma is that Jesus participates in creation and is its creator; in the second case, to use the example of the wheel bráhmans, it is that the wheel remains essentially still, though eternally turning. This sometimes hazardous excursus on the dictionary's entry offers justification for translating *bráhman* as *enigma*. What makes Ṛg Vedic wheel bráhmans and Jesus both lucid enigmas is their shared expression of mystery. Both take becoming and being as one, envisaging them as conjoined, united, inseparable. Humans wander confusedly for their allotted time through becoming. As sinners or *saṃsārins*, they are mere shadows of the real but are potentially participant in transcendent being. To faithful eyes and hearts, such enigmas[9] can give spiritual inspiration and the possibility of an ultimate lucidity, so that even facing death they need not be fearful but can be unafraid and free.

Logan Pearsall Smith once wrote:[10]

> . . . I shall take this opportunity to point out again how much the origins and adventures of the words we use influence their meaning, and how rich they are in overtones of half-conscious suggestion which confuse us, and which we can only half-comprehend, unless we know their history.

I hope this short history of the English enigma will free it from connotations not intended in the notion of an enigmatic sense of reality. The analysis of the word's history and paradigm allows the Ṛg Vedic term *bráhman* to be situated precisely among its possible English meanings. We are partially misled, when reading metaphorical language, by a meretricious extension of the justifiable assumption that clarity is the first element of style in expression. Communication requires clarity, as much as order requires sanity. F. L. Lucas[11] calls clarity the first

"Courtesy To Readers," boldly quoting Quintilian and Montaigne:

> One should not aim at being possible to understand, but at being impossible to misunderstand.
>
> Obscurité . . . vicieuse affectation.

Lucidity, indeed, is skillful virtue; as the French say, "La clarté est la politesse."[12] However, to extend this practical notion so that it mitigates against special speculative or scriptural styles is unwarranted. These do not function as languages of the marketplace, of vegetables, or of ideas. To consider them obscure betrays their very reason for existence.

The contemporary literary testimony most relevant to the translation of *bráhman* as *enigma* comes from the French of Albert Camus. His phrase, "une énigme heureuse," when heard with all the resonances and associations, spiritual and worldly, of the French "heureuse," provides an excellent translation of bráhman. As to the translation of *heureuse* as *happy* (as in Camus: 1968, p. 155, where the translator is Ellen Conroy Kennedy), I prefer *auspicious*. Though the word commonly means *happy*, Camus is describing the uncommon experience of inspiration, of understanding everything. It requires a better, more expressive word, fit to qualify the enigma that brought Camus the felicitous understanding. As I read his words, quoted at the head of this chapter, I distinctly feel that he is describing the same kind of insight gained when Ṛg Vedic symposiasts contemplated their bráhmans. Aryan and Algerian both experienced comprehensive understanding through the agency of a lucid enigma. Both *bráhman* and *une heureuse énigme* share the unique qualities of being inspired and auspicious, for they both lead, beyond ignorance, to freedom of mind. By such grand enigmas one's understanding faculties become properly inaugurated for insight (note Latin *augurim*,

French *heur*, as in *heureux* and *bonheur*), transformed by the fortunate presence of a lucid, auspicious enigma.

A bráhman in Camus's sense is auspicious precisely because it leads to special understanding. A Ṛg Vedic contestant, flushed with success in responding to a bráhman, might well have thought of it as *une énigme heureuse*. Later in his essay ("L'Enigme," p. 865) Camus gives this contemporary European definition of the lucid enigma:

> . . . l'énigme, c'est-à-dire un sens qu'on déchiffre mal parce qu'il éblouit.
>
> . . . the enigma, that is to say a meaning which one deciphers poorly because it dazzles.

With this contribution to our language from the sunny Mediterranean[13] we can provide an equivalent meaning in English to Sanskrit *bráhman*, one which approximates the Vedic meaning of the term despite our language's history. Direct Ṛg Vedic parallels of Camus's *une énigme heureuse* and his definition of it are *raúdram . . . bráhma* (10.61.1ab) and *acíttam bráhma* (1.152.5c), which can be structurally compared with their French counterparts from Camus's essay as follows:

SANSKRIT	ENGLISH	FRENCH
bráhman	enigma	énigme
(see notes)[14]	auspicious	heureuse
acittam	incomprehensible	un sense qu'on déchiffre mal
raudram	dazzling	qui éblouit

Dazzling is not the usual dictionary translation for *raudra*, but its meaning is vexed; here it could be intended in mixed but predominantly positive valuation, as *bráhman*, which it modifies, requires. The later association of *rudra* with *śiva* (the auspicious) suggests that in this Ṛg Vedic use, *raudra* should be given at least partial positive valuation, paralleling our English word *awe* in structure. In this context, *raudra* means *fierce,* in the sense of something powerfully transforming, like some sudden brilliance or a dazzling light, awesome indeed because initially uncomprehended but eventually seen to possess a transforming clarity, a redeeming light. It is not a matter of obscurity, in any case, or malevolence; this power partakes of the light of inspiration, poetic or spiritual. Both the Ṛg Vedic poets and Camus conceived of lucid enigmas, so that the English words chosen to translate either must use terms of light, not obscurity. *Raudra* could thus mean *dazzling* or *fiercely dazzling,* while *incomprehensible* must be understood as undecipherable to the ordinary sense of reality (to the Nations and Sciences), but light to the enigmatic sense of life which still holds out for understanding everything. Such light, say the accounts, though blinding, confers wisdom upon the visionaries among us. As to its being an auspicious enigma, note two lines from Shakespeare: "The yoke of inauspicious stars," and "Calme seas, auspicious Gales."

What then is this enigmatic sense of reality? Its meaning resides in the texts which speak quite well enough for themselves to sensitive interpreters.[15] Shakespeare just evoked it in his enigmatic image of "auspicious Gales." When language attempts to express this distinct human sense of life in the enigma it becomes most paradoxical; through the enigmatic use of language, humans seek to transcend but in the process affirm it as their ultimate means of knowledge. The poet and the philosopher alike make a similar affirmation.[16] It is mystery enough for mystics to talk of their ultimate knowledge since language, they tell us, runs counter to it and really tells us nothing. This presumably could be said for Sanskrit mysticism but not Sanskrit speculation. Mystical experience goes beyond words, as such things do, whether in

East or West, but I find it even greater mystery that the beginnings of Sanskrit speculation evidence an explicit trust in the powers of language itself. From the very start, Sanskrit speculation did not reject language, but consciously used it with consummate skill, refusing to embrace or compound any obscurity. Vedic poets exalted language as their finest tool for gaining knowledge of self and world. It is not every day that people decide that words, in the mouths of inspired visionaries, can evoke what really is, thus making it possible for them to understand everything, even should this require that they admit into their own language an auspicious enigma.

Notes

1: The Sacrificial Symposium

1. Of this voluminous literature, the following is a selection: H. R. Diwekar, *Les Fleurs De Rhétorique Dans L'Inde* (Paris: Adrien Maisonneuve, 1930), chapters 1 and 2; Bergaigne, Abel, "Syntax of Vedic Comparisons," in *Annals of the Bhandarkar Oriental Research Institute,* 16 (1934–35), 232–261; Bergaigne, "Some Observations on the Figures of Speech in the ṚgVeda," ibid., 17 (1935–36), 61–83 and 259–288; H. D. Velankar, "ṚgVedic Similes," I. Similes of the Vāmadevas (R. V. Maṇḍala IV), *Journal of the Bombay Branch of the Royal Asiatic Society,* 14 (1938), 1–47, and II. Similes of the Atris (R. V. Maṇḍala V), ibid., 16 (1940), 1–42; P. S. Sastri, "The Imagery of Ṛgveda," *Annals of the Bhandarkar Oriental Research Institute,* 29 (1948), 152–196; H. D. Velankar, "Emotional Simile in the Rgveda and the Concept of Bhakti," *Bhāratīya Vidyā,* 25 (1965), 1–43; and K. R. Potdar, *Sacrifice In The Ṛgveda,* Bombay: Bhāratīya Vidyā Bhavan, 1953, chapter 12, "Sacrificial Similes," pp. 248–68. On the Atharva Veda see H. D. Velankar, "Similes in the Atharvaveda," *Journal of the Asiatic Society of Bombay,* 38 (1963), 19–43.

2. The writings of Coomaraswamy, Agrawala, Kunhan Raja, and others fall under this category. A few of their works include: Agrawala, Vasudeva S., *Sparks From the Vedic Fire: A New Approach to Vedic Symbolism* (Varanasi: Banaras Hindu University, 1962) containing a representative selection of his essays; C. Kunhan Raja, *Asya Vamasya Hymn* (Madras: Ganesh & Co., 1963); and Kunhan Raja, *Poet-philosophers of the Rgveda* (Madras: Ganesh & Co., 1963); in Coomaraswamy's

works, references to Vedic symbolism abound, and he devoted specialized articles to the subject, such as "Vedic Exemplarism," in *Harvard Journal of Asiatic Studies,* 1 (1936), 44–64; and "The Darker Side of Dawn," *Smithsonian Miscellaneous Collections,* 94, 1 (1936), 1–18. For a complete bibliography, see "The Writings of Ananda K. Coomaraswamy," *Ars Islamica,* 1 (1942), 125–142, noting especially items # 312–386, which span Coomaraswamy's "Vedic" period.

3. For example, Bergaigne, "Some Observations," op. cit. The entire piece tries to demonstrate the futility of understanding enigmatic images.

4. Renou, in his *Histoire de la Langue Sanskrite* (Lyon: Editions IAC, 1956), chapter 4, describes these *sabhā,* where verses were recited and composed extemporaneously in competitions supported by royal patronage, descendants no doubt of the earlier Ṛg Vedic oratorical contests. In the classical *samasyāpūraṇa* competition, the first portion of the verse was provided to all the competitors, the winner being the poet most successful in completing it. Even this distantly recalls the Vedic bráhman competition, as the structure seen in 1.164.34 and 35 is based on question-and-answer, the answer "completing" or filling in (*-pūraṇa*) the former question, the *samasyā.*

5. The most significant literature on this term for the present discussion is Renou: 1949*a* (A. "Le Mot bráhman dans le Ṛgveda"), and Gonda: 1950. Gonda's monograph is by far the most complete and discusses Renou's previous article in section VI, pp. 57–61, generally agreeing with Renou except as to his proposed etymology of *bráhman* as belonging to a root **brah/*barh* "parler par *énigmes*" (Gonda, p. 58, referring to Renou, p. 21). See also Edgerton: 1965, pp. 23–24. There is no need to cite other literature on the subject, as Renou, p. 7, refers to complete bibliographies.

6. Gonda (1950), p. 58. The later acceptation of *bráhman* as universal principle or absolute, already firmly established in the Atharva Veda, is based on this Ṛg Vedic idea of potency made immanent in sacred word. The grammar of the word's use follows its transformation, a kind of philosophical apotheosis, for the Ṛg Veda uses it often in the plural, while in the Brāhmaṇas and Upaniṣads it always occurs in the singular (Renou: 1959*a*, p. 8).

7. The idea is not at all foreign to Ṛg Vedic reflections on its own language, for example 7.32.13ab, *mántram ákharvam súdhitaṃ supéśasaṃ dádhāta yajñíṣv ā́.* We even find references to what must have been a sacral poetics, which symposia comrades recognize as governing the composition of their bráhman verses (Renou: EVP II, passim). The bráhman is then the supreme verbal formulation which by conforming to the rules of the sacral poetics is capable of manifesting the unseen noumenal power *bráhman.*

8. Geldner agrees (1951, III, 226): "Str. I enthält alles, was in ein Prooemium gehört: den Charakter des Leides. Es ist ein ráudram bráhma. bráhma hier schon in ähnlichem Sinne wie in brahmódya, das Rätselhafte kennzeichnend."

9. The state of consciousness implied by the phrase *acíttam bráhma* resembles the goal of classical yoga, as stated in Patañjali 1.2, *yogaś-citta-vṛtti-nirodhaḥ*, where *nirodha* is equivalent to the negative prefix *a-*.

10. For the *ājí* as figurative for oratorical contest, see Renou: 1955, p. 20. His conclusion strikes to the very heart of the problem of metaphor and reality in Ṛg Vedic figurative language: "The study of the theme of 'horses' in the RV. holds some surprises for those who believe a priori in the realism of Vedic images."

11. This *krátu* is the poetic inspiration or transport which immediately precedes successful competition in the oratorical contest, and presumably then also in the sacrifice. See in a similar context the same use of the instrumental in 4.5.7; and in 6.9.5 it is made clear that this is a divine inspiration which comes from Agni. On inspiration in such contests in general, see Kuiper: 1960 II B, especially p. 248, and the opinion of Kristensen on "eloquence," p. 254, which applies to the bráhman so well that it bears quoting here: "Eloquence had not quite the same meaning for the ancient peoples which it has for us. They did not associate the word with verbal art only, or with an artistic skill. The main thing to them was the authority of the spoken word, its wisdom and power, the success it was attended with. The eloquent word of the popular leader gave his audience the impression of absolute validity; it was authoritative, because one felt that it revealed a law of life. It was as irresistible and valid as the law of life itself. It was no mere beautiful sound, which existed only for a moment. Once pronounced it maintained itself: it created a new situation, it turned itself into reality. Eloquence, therefore, was nothing short of a creative force, a vital energy. Its essence was the mystery of Creation and Life." Indeed, Vedic poets accorded ontological status to sacred word.

12. In fact the Agnicayana *kaṇḍas* of the Śatapatha (6–9) attributed to Śāṇḍilya rather than Yājñavalkya, the authority of the first five, unmistakably point to India's northwest in their geographical references, as opposed to the references to the Gangetic Plain of the first five *kaṇḍas* (Eggeling, *The Śatapatha-Brāhmaṇa,* Sacred Books of the East, part I, p. xxxi). This is where the Ṛg Vedic fire mysticism described herein was most firmly established. The monumental Agnicayana was the speculative peak of the Brāhmaṇa age, and the concrete link between the Ṛg Veda and the Upaniṣadic ātman as brahman doctrine. It stands midstream in this speculative tradition, since eventually Agni Vaiśvānara emerges as the inner ātman identical with brahman. The ancient bráhman enigmas revealed for the first

time in these sacrificial symposia the central mystery of the later tradition.

13. Already we see in this verse the predilection for paradox which prepares the enigma; "generated undecaying Agni" includes a form of *yamaka* (paronomasia, one of the earliest mentioned figures), *ajanayann ajuryám*, which with the paradoxical phrase, *áminac cariṣṇú*, describing Agni as unaltering though mobile gives some idea of the verbal play and conceptual acrobatics which the poets immensely enjoyed, but which served a more serious purpose as well since such phrases and figures participate in the realm of verbal ambiguity wherein the enigma exclusively dwells.

14. We have (in verses 15cd and 16) a form of the esoteric language mentioned at the beginning of this chapter. The father and mother are heaven and earth, which, when united at the eastern horizon at dawn, give birth to the wandering one, the sun, who is "born from the head" of the *puruṣa* (as 10.90.13 specifies, from the eye)—these images being themselves proto-enigmas, since in 1.152.3-5 this theme is the subject of a bráhman. Because man is microcosmically also a *puruṣa*, the sun is reflected on "by mind" (the head corresponds by nature to the sun); and with the implicit suggestion of the correspondence or analogy of Agni-sun-inner light of inspiration, Agni is seen as lighting the mental darkness of the inspirationless poet, just as the sun lights the world. The same image is at the basis of 4.51.1cd, "Now may the dawns, daughters of the sky, afar-radiating, made a path (*gātú*) for man"; as also 6.9.1. For the two paths of the fathers, see 10.2.3 and 7, as well as its familiar descendants in Upaniṣadic speculation, discussed in chapter 4.

15. Again indicating the continuity of this speculative tradition based as it was on fire mysticism, see note 12 above.

16. This accords with the general definition of mysticism, resulting in a form of knowledge in which the knower participates directly in the object of knowledge. In the Vedic sacrifice this means that the mystic participant in the rite seeks to be aware not of its outer form but its inner significance, to see not its surface appearances but its inner reality, which is continuous with cosmic reality itself. It follows that for such participation to be complete there must be a loss of self-reflective consciousness, as clearly appears in later mystical traditions, such as *bhakti*. Even at this level of development, full participation in the sacrifice must have been a "selfless" activity, a primal karma-yoga; by the time of the Brāhmaṇas we may speak of this self, which is an alternative to the ordinary or phenomenal self, as being a ritual self, built up ($\sqrt{ci}$, as in *cayana*, of the Agni-) in the performance of the rite. This alternate self in the Upanisads is called the *ātman*, a term already applied to the Agni altar in the Śatapatha. Indeed the requirement of

selflessness is widespread in Indian mysticism, on which see Coomaraswamy, "Ākiṃcaññā: Self-naughting," *New Indian Antiquary*, vol. III (1940) and "Ātmayajña: Self-sacrifice," *Harvard Journal of Asiatic Studies*, Vol. IV (1942).

17. As the later Buddhist transcendental level of vision, which sees *yathābhūtam*, "as (reality) truly is" (*Pali yathābhūtam pajānāti*), or *paramārtha* as opposed to *vyavahāra* (knowledge); and the Vedāntic *sākṣātkāra*, equivalent to the level of the Tantric Buddhist *saṃpannakrama*, and so forth.

18. Renou:1955, p. 5; also p. 25, for sóma references.

19. See Potdar, K. R., *Sacrifice*, op. cit., p. 99: "Never perhaps has an offering influenced the course of the sacrifice as 'soma' appears to have done in the case of the Ṛgvedic sacrifice. It would be no exaggeration to say that the Ṛgvedic sacrifice is what it is mainly on account of the soma-offering."

20. *yā́vad bráhma viṣṭhitaṃ tā́vatī vā́k*, 10.114.8d. By the time of the Brāhmaṇas, Vā́c was identified with Sarasvatī, appropriately the goddess of eloquence.

21. Translated most recently by Edgerton: 1965, pp. 58–59; the present version offers some revisions and omits the last verse as it is not germane to the present discussion. Renou (1955, p. 23) thinks so much of this hymn that he writes: "All that which the poets left as understood in the form of half-veiled elements, words with double meanings, throughout the hymns, is codified so to say in this poem. *It is in its light* that one must read the RV. if one wants to fully grasp the [understood] intentions, in the appearance which the ChU will call vācārambhaṇaṃ nāmadheyam 'a (substantial) appellation which has a hold (on reality) by language (alone)' " (italics added).

22. The *titaü* can hardly be a sieve or cribble, as translators think, on the strong counterevidence of surviving Indian material culture. Rather than a cribble, a specially shaped flat basket roughly the shape of a horseshoe was probably used (I have seen such represented as early as on Sañchi gate sculpture and such baskets are widely used in India today). The image likening the creation of speech, which is *saṃskṛta* (accomplished, perfected, sacramental), to the winnowing of grain in the wind is interesting. The means of language's purification is the body of rules, implicit or explicit, which govern its creation in proper form, namely grammar and the rules of poetic form. For the bráhman there were special additional rules (referred to in 4.5.13) intended to intensify to the greatest possible extent the effects of the language. The later mantra form exhibits some of the characteristics of this special language use. On purification images, see Renou: 1955, section 22.

23. It is tempting here in pada c, *tā́m ābhṛ́tyā vy àdadhuḥ purutrā́* to

see a reference to the setting up in many places of images or representations of Vā́c for worship (pada d). In any case the solicitous care of Vā́c is reminiscent of bhaktic attitudes, and several other elements in the poem repeat the theme, as note 26 indicates.

24. The imagery of pada d, *aphalā́m apuspā́m* recalls later images of successful spiritual attainment, as in the term *phalaśruti*; also the image of verse 3a, *padavī́*, recalls the notion of the path which one follows to such attainment.

25. The language of cd which illustrates this is quite unclear; according to Edgerton it adds nothing to the idea already expressed.

26. The comrades treat the feminine manifestation of brahman with special holy reverence; their approach (*abhi* $\sqrt{pad}$) should be reverential, not evil (*pāpáyā*) or unprepared; they should be worthy of their membership in the *sakyá* and thus worthy also of her or they will not participate in her bounty (6b, *bhāgá*, from $\sqrt{bhaj}$); also notable is the term *preṇā́* (1d) applied to the motivation of the sages when they reveal the hidden through Vā́c. All these seem strong proto-bhaktic elements in this hymn.

27. *sirī́s*, hapax, ? feminine plural (gossamer) or, in any case, something unfit for weaving (as Edgerton: 1965, p. 59, note 2) figurative for conducting the sacrifice. For the loom as image of the contest and sacrifice, see 6.9.2 and 3, and note 33.

28. This use of *māyā́* is revealing of its earliest meaning, certainly not implying "illuson" but creative power, the ability to manifest—in this case, as in the beginning (v. 1) through verbal means alone. The power is generally ascribed to divine beings in the Ṛg Veda, so that here its attribution to a human being, albeit a divinely inspired poet-seer, is remarkable. Could it be that in the contest the comrade who succeeds possesses the divine power of creation through holy word (the power denoted by the term *nāmadhéya*, lb), based on the ontological status of sacred speech? Such a notion would have far-reaching consequences, for by implication certain inspired images have the power to reveal reality beyond ordinary appearances, literally by creating it, and the person who could understand these images would thereby possess the power of creation. The later Upaniṣadic great sayings (*mahāvākya*) and the Buddhist holy truths (*ariyasacca*) and mantras appear to be statements of this kind, and are often based on images. See Robinson and Johnson: 1977, p. 46.

29. Later seers were equally convinced that people were blind to visionary modes of perceiving reality and only through special means could see and hear at these levels. The image of the eternal drum whose sound is not phenomenal or ordinary exists from Gautama ("In a world become blind, I beat the immortal drum," Majjhima Nikāya) to Kabīr ("The unstruck drum of Eternity is sounded within me").

30. The sacrifice as a vehicle of transcendence and participation is at the basis of the Ṛg Vedic image of the sacrifice as a *ratha* (a chariot or vehicle), see Potdar, *Sacrifice,* op. cit., pp. 250–251. Even more interesting in this connection is 10.135, which describes a young man constructing an imaginary chariot to take him to the realm of Yama, the vehicle being a sacrifice, too. This theme was the basis of the Nachiketas episode of the Kaṭha Upaniṣad, associating the ratha-sacrifice image with a speculative nexus central to Upaniṣadic thought, for the realm of Yama held the secrets of death and hence immortality, too. The Upaniṣad story added an initiatory structure to the ancient story. On this, see Velankar, H. D., "The Ṛgvedic Origin of the Story of Nachiketas," in *Mélanges d'Indianisme* (Paris: 1968, pp. 763–772), and Renou: 1956, pp. 255–256.

31. In later times, traditions regularly had to renew themselves by purging such slavish adherence to surfaces held to be more important than the experience intended. Saraha, in his Dohākośa, wrote: "The paṇḍit fully expounds the śāstras, but does not know the Buddha living in his own body; coming and going are not by that torn asunder, but that fool even says, 'I am wise'."

32. The image of the bride's fine clothes, which both reveal and conceal her body, presents the theme of the paradoxical revealing that also conceals. Applied to the created, phenomenal world, it is repeated throughout the Sanskrit speculative tradition. For the Buddhist, *saṃsāra* reveals its opposite, *nirvāṇa,* while concealing it; *māyā* for the Hindu similarly reveals and conceals. One of the attributes of divinity is this paradoxical action of its concealing revelation in the world.

33. This is an important but difficult verse. It expresses the initial discouragement of the prospective contestant, a common theme in such verses (see 1.164.6, 7, and 37; 4.5.2, 6, and 8).

An alternate translation of padas ab would be: "I do not really understand the warp (*tántum*), nor the woof (*ótum*), nor what they weave. . . ." Renou (1956, p. 37) takes both *tántum* and *ótum* as infinitives (with *na vi jānāmi,* commonly "to know not how to . . ."), but neither Grassman (1873) nor Macdonell (1916) list a $\sqrt{tan}$ infinitive. The present translation takes *tántum* as a masculine accusative substantive and *otum* to be an infinitive parallel to the following present form *váyanti*.

The image describes the contest (weaving as the activity of proposing and responding to bráhmans, the warp and woof being the two contest positions, etc.), and since weaving imagery is commonly also used for the sacrifice itself (same imagery above in 10.71.9d, and see Potdar, *Sacrifice,* op. cit., pp. 249–250), it also applies to the following sacrifice itself as the two are essentially interlocking.

Padas cd have not been adequately handled by previous translators.

This translation is an attempt to account for what appear to be contest technical terms in *putrá ihá váktvāni paró vadāty ávareṇa pitrā*, particularly *parás* and *ávarena*. Renou (EVP XIII [1964] p. 129) argues that *ávareṇa* is redundant, resulting from the Vedic predilection for balanced expression. Quite the opposite! The same pair of terms occurs with the same verb (√*vad*, to dispute in the contest) in 10.88.17a, *yátrā vádete ávaraḥ páraś ca*, describing the positions taken in the contest by the two contestants, and so undoubtedly they describe these two positions also; almost the same terms occur in another description of the contest, 10.71.9a, *ná-arvā̃n ná parā́ś cáranti*. From this evidence the following solution emerges: the terms *pára/parás* and *ávara/ávareṇa/arvā́k* indicate two contest positions, the "prior" and "later"; 6.9.2d further identifies the *pára* position with the *putrá* (the "son" or challenger or initiant's place) and the *ávara* position with the *pitṛ́* ("father," who poses the enigma to the "son" in the prior position); presumably he has attained the later position either by having already solved previous enigmas in the contest as a former son or on the basis of some other attained or ascribed status (such as being a brāhmaṇá priest as is indicated in 10.88.19). When a son solves an enigma he becomes a father, moving to the later position, or he more likely proceeds directly to the sacrifice.

This admittedly is a tentative solution, but one which makes some sense of these apparent technical terms present in several descriptions of the contest, and it gives a better translation than Renou's, "Quel est celui dont le fils dirait ici ce qui est à dire,/ au delà de (ce qu'a fait), en deçà, son propre père?" (1956, p. 37), or Geldner's, "Wessen Sohn könnte hier wohl Worte reden, höher als sein Vater hienieden?" (1951, 2:101). These four technical terms for the positions and participants in the contest form the basis for and are ingeniously used in the series of riddles of 1.164, verses 15–19, where they appear in various forms and are essential to understanding the verses.

34. Apparently the terms in *avā́ś cáran paró anyéna páśyan*, which resemble the technical terms in the previous verse, make no direct reference to the contest, being used rather as part of the parallelism which unites the two verses. The Agni moving here below is his manifestation in earthly and sacrificial fires, while Agni above observes through another of his manifestations, namely the sun.

35. This last phrase, describing the "light," *amṛ́tam mártyeṣu*, perfectly describes the Upaniṣadic *ātman*, of which Agni Vaiśvānara is one ancestor. Many of the attributes of divine Agni, as well as the sun, resemble attributes later applied to the inner self and absolute, not to mention Coomaraswamy's hypothesis of the equivalence of Agni and the Buddha. The heart is the source of divine inspiration in the contest (10.71.8a), for in the heart is fixed this "light" (6.9.6b) of inner divine

inspiration which shines through from within after meditation or other discipline such as drinking sóma. This conception continues in the Upaniṣadic verb *prati* √*bhā* and Pali *paṭibhāti*, as in Kaṭha Upaniṣad 1.2.5, *na sāmparāyaḥ* (i.e., the divine inner light, *ātman*) *pratibhāti bālam*. Similarly, the *ātman* abides in the heart (*sa vā eṣa ātmā hṛdi*, Chāndogya Upaniṣad 8.3.3).

The light (Agni and the inner light of visionary illumination), is a central feature of the fire mysticism of these hymns, and is often associated with mystical experience in India and beyond. In another Ṛg Vedic poem describing mystical experience, an ecstatic *keśin* or *muni* (10.136) flies through the air (mystic flight, a yogic power, Yoga Sūtra 3.41), has knowledge of others' desires (Yoga Sūtra 3.33) and is as later *śramanas* either naked ("wind-grit") or clothed in a soiled yellow robe; in these attributes, light-fire mysticism is a central element, as the first verse indicates: "The keśin carries fire, philtre, heaven and earth / The keśin has heavenly light to see all / The keśin is called, 'This Light.' " Verse 3 of the same hymn acknowledges again the notion that there are phenomenal and supra-phenomenal levels of experience, for the ascetic in mystical flight says that ordinary mortals (who have not attained visionary consciousness or ecstasy) see only their "bodies alone," not their soaring spirits. "Ecstatic with the practice of our munihood/ We ascend to the winds,/ Our bodies alone Ye, O mortals, see!" This contains a possible answer to those who ask of the ecstatic, "Did you really fly?"—body no, spirit yes.

36. This verse, the climax of the poem, describes the visionary exaltation of the poet who has received divine inspiration from Agni. Some sense of the all-encompassing nature of the ecstasy may be gained by explicating the term *dūrá-ādhīḥ* in pada c, "Far beyond wanders my *mánas*, its spirit (*ādhī*) (goes) to remote distances (*dūré*)." The term *dūrá* is conveniently glossed in another hymn, 10.58.1, which describes *mánas* that went to the far distances (*máno jagā̆ma dūrakám*, 1b), these being (vv. 2–12): the sky and earth, the four-cornered earth, the four directions, the foaming seas, the heavenly light, the waters and plants, the sun and dawn, the great mountains, all this which is living, the remote distances (*párāḥ parāváto*, taken up again in Bṛhadāraṇyaka Upaniṣad 6.2.15 as the destiny of those who follow the path of immortality, the *devayāna*, see note 4.-14, below), and finally what has become and what will be (*bhūtáṃ ca bhávyaṃ ca*, thereby embracing the very source of all creation, time and space, recalling the *puruṣa*, see 10.90.2, *púruṣa evédáṃ sárvaṃ yád bhūtáṃ yác ca bhávyam*). From this list it is evident that the ecstatic state attained by the poet at the moment of "going beyond" embraces all of creation including its temporal dimension. Other hymns describe similar exaltations, as for example 10.119,

ostensibly Agni's words but surely a report of sóma-inspired visionary ecstasy; and 10.136, discussed immediately above. The phrase *párāḥ parāváto* as a gloss of *dūrá/dūrakám* recalls the Buddhist goal of going to the other side (*nirvāṇa*), already inherent in Ṛg Vedic boat-crossing imagery, as in 8.42.3, *sutármāṇam . . . nā́vam*, the *satyásya nā́vaḥ* of 9.73.1.

As to the meaning of *vi* $\sqrt{pat}$ (parallel to *vi* $\sqrt{car}$), to soar far beyond, see also 3.55.3, "*ví me purutrā́ patayanti kā́māḥ śámy áchā dīdye pūrvyā́ṇi/ sámiddhe agnā́v ṛtám íd vadema . . .* ," "My desires soar far beyond, away in many directions, I turn towards the ancient divine works. When the fire is kindled let us speak only of the real. . . . " The poem is another enigma piece.

37. The imagery of weaving is familiar in many literatures. Rabelais once used it to describe the cosmic process decreed by the gods: Ballockatso to the devil, my dear friend Panurge, seeing it is so decreed by the gods, wouldst thou invert the course of the planets, and make them retrograde? Wouldst thou disorder all the celestial spheres, blame the intelligences, blunt the spindles, joint the wherves, slander the spinning quills, reproach the bobbins, revile the clew-bottoms, and finally ravel and untwist all the threads of both the warp and the waft of the weird Sister-Parcae? What a pox to thy bones does thou mean, stony cod? (Urquhart and Motteaux edition, London, nd, 2: 69). As to the meaning of the thread (vv. 2 and 3) which the poet seeks, Blake uses the same image to introduce the prologue to the last book of *Jerusalem*: "I give you the end of a golden string / Only wind it into a ball: / It will lead you in at Heaven's gate, / Built in Jerusalem's wall." The symbolism of thread is widespread. For Blake's use of weaving imagery, see Wingfield Digby: 1957, pp. 61–62, 88–90.

38. As a matter of space and convenience (for this is a difficult poem) this hymn is only summarized here, largely from Renou's translation and commentaries. His translation is in EVP XIII (1964), pp. 9–10, with textual notes on pp. 96–97; his more elaborate explication is in EVP II (1956), 55–59.

39. *gūhá hitám úpa niṇíg vadanti*; for *niṇík*, see 1.164.37. This feature of the contest as a speculative endeavor links it directly with the Upaniṣads, which consisted of secret discourses about brahman. The intermediary Vedic rituals were similarly secret, (*āraṇyaka*), for which instruction was given not in the teacher's home in the village but in the *araṇya* outside the village, on a "piece of wasteland between cultivated acres, from where the roof tops of the village cannot be seen" (van Buitenen: 1968*a*, p. 38).

40. Thus the bráhman functions, as do images in other visionary literatures, as vehicles for vision, for imaginative participation in them

as meditative objects. Blake, the creator of visionary books full of graphic images, knew full well their function when he wrote: "If the Spectator could Enter into these Images in his Imagination, approaching them on the Fiery Chariot of his Contemplative Thought . . . then would he arise from his Grave, then would he meet the Lord in the Air." The words apply perfectly to the method which the poet uses in the bráhman contest, even to the result of meeting the Lord in the air.

41. Again *gúhā*, Vedic instrumental indeclinable, often with $\sqrt{dh\bar{a}}$, *ni* $\sqrt{dh\bar{a}}$ (hidden "in the mysterious, in secret"), opposed in meaning to *āvís* (right before the eyes), as in 10.71.1d, *tád eṣā́ṃ níhitaṃ gúhā-āvíḥ*; in imitation of the mythic archetypal action (no Jungian reference) of the first *ṛṣis* (10.71.1), the contestant who achieves vision in the contest sees the hidden, mysterious reality right before his eyes, as in this verse describing his realization, just as did the first *ṛṣis*, when they gave names to the mysteries which were *níhitaṃ gúhā*. The contestant's action is the ectype.

2: The Brahman as Object

1. See for example, H. Frankfort et al., *Before Philosophy* (Middlesex: Penguin Books, 1949), chapter 1, "Myth and Reality." Frankfort's definition of *speculative* is applicable to the present discussion: "We should remember that even for us speculative thought is less rigidly disciplined than any other form. Speculation—as the etymology of the word shows—is an intuitive, an almost visionary, mode of apprehension. This does not mean, of course, that it is mere irresponsible meandering of the mind, which ignores reality or seeks to escape from its problems. Speculative thought transcends experience, but only because it attempts to explain, to unify, to order experience. It achieves this end by means of hypotheses. If we use the word in its original sense, then we may say that speculative thought attempts to *underpin* the chaos of experience so that it may reveal the features of a structure—order, coherence, and meaning" (p. 11). These "features of a structure" already were identified in the Ṛg Vedic notions of *ṛta* and *satya*. Out of figurative and enigmatic poems, such as 10.90 and others (conveniently collected by Renou: 1956) came the impulses for Brāhmaṇa mysticism, followed by the Upaniṣads and early Jainism and Buddhism,. which by the early centuries A.D. had given birth to technical Sanskrit philosophy (Nāgārjuna and others).

2. Gonda refers to his previous article, "Stilistiche Studie over Atharvaveda I–VII," Wageninger, 1938.

3. The same conclusion, Gonda: 1939, p. 111: ". . . When pointing

to material things alaṃkāra- meant things which make alam, which gave the strength required for something > things which bestow a consecrated condition upon a person, amulets, > "ornaments". Now, as the above mentioned characteristics of the Sondersprache of the Vedic mantras made it what it was, made it fit to answer its purpose, because without the typical "figures of speech"—in the manner in which, and with the frequency with which they occur—the prayers and formulas would have no success, would not be "texts" and prayers—these peculiarities of style of the language may have been given the same names as their material counterparts, when the language of the holy texts began to be considered and studied, which was at a very early date. We ought not to forget that the definitions containing the idea "beauty" arise only centuries later and bear on art-poetry. In my opinion the word saṃskāra is something to go by,—we have already pointed out that saṃ-skr- and alaṃ-kr- to an important degree run parallel in semantic. If saṃskāra-a.o. is grammatically the correct form of language which is exclusively effective, alaṃkāra- (for the mantra's) may indicate the correct form of style."

4. Gonda: 1949 devotes a mere ten pages (84–94) to what he calls "didactic and elucidating" similes; furthermore, he takes Atharva Veda 12.4.14, "like a deposited treasure" as the first example of such a simile (p. 86), which hardly does justice to Ṛg Vedic similes, not to mention Ṛg Vedic didactic metaphorical language such as found in the bráhman. If this omission is solely on the grounds that no bráhmans technically have the form of a simile (using *iva, yathā*), then the typology of Vedic metaphorical language is seriously incomplete as it is based on a mechanistic criterion for identifying figurative expressions. Diwekar (*Les Fleurs De Rhétorique,* op.cit., chapitre II, "Les Alaṅkāra dans le Ṛgveda"), though recognizing the presence of figures other than *upamā* (including the *rūpaka*, see # 23, 24), makes no mention of the role which these figures played in Ṛg Vedic speculative thought.

5. To take another example, from quite another culture, compare Irene Nicholson's comments (1959) on paradoxical images and symbols in Nahua poetry, including "burning water," "blossoming war" (pp. 18, 149) and the famous "plumed serpent" image. The Nahua poet represented in a single, bold image man's actual unenlightened existence (he crawls like a serpent on the earth) and his divine potentiality (he may like a bird soar ecstatically into the ineffable). Describing the special enigmatic language of Nahua poetry, she comments on the ability of such language to express, beyond the capabilities of ordinary conceptual language, truths about the mysterious qualities of existence: "The poetry they spoke was not word-juggling or playful image-weaving, but a revelation of the way by

which men might be saved from death. "A firefly in the night," the Nahuas called their songs: a tiny light in a great darkness, a little truth within the ignorance surrounding them. As a vehicle for their wisdom, the Nahuas created a fairy-land which obeys no logical laws. Things change places, turn into one another, can be simultaneously possessed of contradictory characteristics. Gods are at one moment sinister, at another beneficent. Flowers grow in the dark. War and death can blossom into new life. It is a world which at first sight appears utterly fantastic; but as we begin to study it we see that it is really very like life—not the fixed life of man-made rules and regulations, but the life that grows, flowers, procreates, and inexplicably dies" (*Ibid*, p. 17).

6. Lao Tzu, *Tao Te Ching*, translated by D. C. Lau (Baltimore: Penguin Books, 1963), p. 140, # 189. Words which are straightforward to the visionary consciousness of the realized sage seem paradoxical when understood in normal, ordinary modes of consciousness (which expect conceptual exactitude rather than seminal ambiguity); so too those not successful in the bráhman contest—and apparently many translators of the Ṛg Veda—consider the enigmas about bráhman incomprehensible, while in reality from the point of view of visionary realization they are quite "straightforward." Only crooked paths or indirections may lead to such goals as mountain tops and hidden things.

7. His position is basically the same, though also self-contradictory, in the introduction to his translation of the hymn (1956), done some years earlier:

"It [1.164] is full of mysticism. It is obscure. It is mainly in the form of a riddle; it was originally meant as a riddle and it has become a more insoluble riddle for us than for the people of those ancient days" (Kunhan Raja: 1956, p. 1). Up to this point, Kunhan Raja contradicts his position taken in 1963, pp. 1 and 46, that the verses "become" a mystery or riddle because of the loss of symbol meanings; but in the next sentences he reverts to it: "The background is gone. We do not know what the author had in his mind when he composed these lines. He must have presumed that the people of those days understood him, the thinking section of the people. Various notions and symbols current in those days are now lost to us, and so we do not have the necessary apparatus to work up the full and precise meaning of the lines in this poem" (ibid.). If the poem "was originally meant as a riddle," then how would it be possible "to work up the full and precise meaning of the lines of this poem?" The difference between this position of Kunhan Raja and that of the present discussion rests in the understanding of the nature of the original character of the poem. If by riddle one means simply an intentionally designed intellectual puzzle, the answer to which can be stated in nonenigmatic language, then Kunhan Raja's position can be plausibly maintained, given our knowledge of Ṛg Vedic imagery. Genuine riddles of this kind do occur in the Ṛg Veda. For example, in 6.75 several of the early verses in the hymn praising the arms of war are built on riddles that are answered in the same verse, as verse 5 on the quiver: "Of many (daughters) he is the father, / Many are his sons (too); / He rattles having entered onto battlefields: (5ab) / (Answer) The quiver . . . " (padas cd). Furthermore, the brahmodya form, already explicit in the Ṛg Veda, is riddle-like, but since it does not contain in veiled form clues to its own answer, it must be called a visionary riddle, approaching the bráhman's enigmatic nature. It is however not the case that, apart from brahmodyas, Ṛg Vedic bráhman verses are true riddles in this technical sense of the word, as their superficial form alone shows. Kunhan Raja is wrong in calling them riddles, unless by this he means only that they are enigmatic. And if this is the case we should not expect to be able to work out their "full and precise meaning," not because we have lost the meaning of the symbols they employ, but rather because their enigmatic form resists such attempts. As will be apparent shortly, the riddle is a kind of enigmatic language, a special case of it; and only some enigmas are, technically speaking, riddles.

8. Recalling the Tantric Buddhist term *saṃdhyā-bhāṣā* or twilight language, deliberately enigmatic to suggest qualities and aspects of reality or truth not open to ordinary (that is, "daytime") consciousness. For a more complete discussion of suggestive language, see Wheelwright: 1968*a* chapter 5, "Traits of Expressive Language." To say that the enigma or any suggestive language is ontologically significant is to claim that these specialized forms of language are adequate to express or to bring to consciousness facts about certain aspects of reality, as ontology studies 'being' in all its forms.

9. Wheelwright: 1968*a*, p. 97, makes this distinction between surface and depth paradox. The surface paradox "can be cleared up easily enough by anyone who takes the trouble to make the appropriate logical distinctions. . . ." It should be clear that such paradox would weaken the bráhman verse, as it would allow rational solutions to the enigma. What it really requires is a shift of viewpoint in response to the posed enigma, permitting the participant to comprehend (rather than to "solve" by reduction to nonenigmatic language) the truth or revelation expressed through the paradox. There are also cases of apparent surface paradoxes which contain elements of depth paradox, as in Heraclitus's aphorism, "Into the same rivers we step and we do not step" (Wheelwright: 1964, p. 90); contrast the same author's depth paradox, "It is in changing that things find repose" (Ibid., p. 29),

which requires significant, non-ordinary insight into just how there can be quiet and repose in the midst of change. Essentially the same insight is required of the Mahāyāna Buddhist who meditates on the mantra stating that the jewel (*nirvāṇa*, repose) is in the lotus (*saṃsāra*, change), the place of repose being in the unmoving center of the nave, which while turning remains infinitesimally still (see chapter 5).

10. Gonda: 1950, pp. 58–61, discusses the riddle in this function, though he does not distinguish riddle from enigma, using riddle to include enigma. On discussions and contests that feature riddles as objects of contemplation, he writes: "Such discussions, which may strike modern man as a playful asking of more or less difficult questions and as an exercise in acuteness, are (like the Upaniṣads which they resemble) essentially attempts at pushing out into the unknown, at penetrating gradually into an important mystery, at finding the solution of fundamental truths and grasping the meaning of at least part of the great riddle. By doing so these mystics make progress on their path, gain in knowledge and gain in power."

11. In the case of these difficult enigma verses, Renou's translations will be taken as authoritative, as he incorporates the suggestions of previous translators and commentators (Luders, Geldner). Renou: EVP II (1956), "Études Sur Quelques Hymnes Spéculatifs," on 4.5, pp. 55–59, makes a detailed commentary on the poem, translating several of the enigmas; Renou: EVP XIII (1964), pp. 9–10, gives his complete translation with notes on pp. 96–97.

12. Legge, who translated the I Ching out of a sense of duty more than interest or pleasure, made the same methodological error when he criticized the figurative technique of the trigrams and hexagrams, which are linear figures with very definite figurative import. He asks why the lessons of the hexagrams should be "conveyed to us by such an array of lineal figures and in such a farrago of emblematic representations?" (Sacred Books of the East, XVI, 22) This denies a priori the possibility that the figurative technique of the I Ching could itself have significance, and assumes that anything with meaning can be said in words, an assumption reasonable for Legge but not for his original, which assumed the opposite, that words cannot exhaust meanings. Legge's ontological perspective posits the belief that words are entirely sufficient for the communication of all meanings, while a fundamental premise of the I Ching is that knowledge can only partially be communicated by words used in a literal, straightforward manner. Precision in meaning is a technique naturally favored by the scholar-translator, but to require that speculative literature of ancient times espouse the same goals and methods is unfair. All this led Legge to conclude not that his methodology needed revision but that the

original was at fault: "If, after all, they [the readers of his translation of the I Ching] shall conclude that in what is said on the hexagrams there is often "much ado about nothing," it is not the translator who should be deemed accountable for that, but his original" (Ibid., p. xvi).

As for the Indian side of the matter, awareness that symbolism can be a language of speculation based on figurative expression comes in V. S. Agrawala'a article, "Kalpavṛkṣa, the Wish Fulfilling Tree," *Journal of the Indian Society for Oriental Art,* II (1943), 1: "Indian art conveys its meaning in a distinct symbol language. The lotus, the full vase, (*pūrṇaghaṭa*) the Svastika, the wheel (*cakra*), the three jewels (*triratna*), and the Kalpavṛkṣa, part as it were of an alphabet, are being used with perfect mastery as elements of decoration; they have not only invested art, Buddhist and Brahmanic, with endless beauty but also show it as a vehicle of ideas. These symbols formed an integral part of Indian thought for ages serving like pegs for religious and metaphysical ideas." Though Agrawala is describing the symbolic vocabulary of art, his comments apply equally well to the figurative vocabulary of early Sanskrit speculative thought, and as his list of symbols indicates, art may have borrowed many of its "symbols" from previous literatures. The wheel and tree have powerful Ṛg Vedic archetypal presence.

13. It will not be necessary to discuss further the development and nature of this later brahmodya form; Renou discussed the subject in the reference given as well as in 1953*a*, pp. 141 ff. It is interesting that in both articles Renou distinguishes (1949*a*, p. 37, 1953*a*, p. 141) a "brahmodya rigide, réglé d'avance" characteristic of ritual brahmodyas, from those recorded in the speculative books of the Śatapathabrāhmaṇa (10 to 14), which were less rigid and at the "coeur même des controverses religieuses." The distinction is interesting, and seems to indicate that, as the bráhman developed, it split, one form maintaining its more fluid, speculative function, the other being adopted in a rigid form to serve ritualistic functions. This confirms amply that the earlier bráhman was indeed a speculative instrument and participated intimately in speculative milieux, which continued through the Brāhmaṇas to the great Upaniṣads where such speculative brahmodyas appear frequently.

14. Another example of the insertion of a later "answer" in a transitional speculative hymn is 10.121. The first nine verses ask the same question and are answered finally in verse 10, but this is marked as a later addition, since it is not commented upon in the pada text. Obviously the answer, *Prajāpati,* had only later gained enough support to be included as the orthodox answer, despite (and perhaps assisted by) the anticipation of this answer in verse 1, *bhūtásya . . . pátir.*

15. These verses also occur in Vājasaneyi Saṃhitā XXIII.61–62, discussed by Renou: 1949*a*, pp. 32–33 as revealing the conjunction between cosmos and rite.

3: The Enigma of the Two Birds

1. Geldner: 1951, I, 231. For a survey of previous translations, see Thieme *Untersuchungen*, pp. 56–57.
2. P. Thieme, *Untersuchungen zur Wortkunde und Auslegung des Rigveda* (Halle/Salle: Max Niemeyer, 1949), chapter V, "Das Rätsel vom Baum," pp. 55–73.
3. Kunhan Raja: 1956, pp. 36–41.
4. Louis Renou, *Anthologie Sanskrite* (Paris: Payot, 1961, originally published 1949), pp. 22–23; commentary in EVP XVI (1967), pp. 90–91.
5. "Agni, Sun, Sacrifice, and Vāc: A Sacerdotal Ode by Dīrghatamas (Rig Veda 1.164)," *Journal of the American Oriental Society*, 88, 2 (1968), 214.
6. The opinion was expressed long ago by M. A-M. Boyer, "Étude sur l'origine de la Doctrine du Saṃsāra," *Journal Asiatique*, Vol. XVIII (1901).
7. Even though Kunhan Raja (1956, p. 38) says, "This is the alternative form of *vidathe*. Such locative forms are common in the Veda," Whitney *Sanskrit Grammar*, 327*g*, cites no such forms.
8. *Untersuchungen*, III. *vidátha*, pp. 35–49, which opts for Verteilung throughout.
9. F. B. J., Kuiper, "Ví Dayate and Vidátha- ," *Indologica Taurinensia* II (1974), 129–32. Kuiper kindly sent me his article.
10. J. P. Sharma, *Republics in Ancient India* (Leiden: E. J. Brill, 1968), pp. 62–80.
11. Ram Sharan Sharma, *Aspects of Political Ideas and Institutions in Ancient India* (Delhi: Motilal Banarsidass, 1959), pp. 78–95 (originally in *JBRS* 1952).
12. "In *Vedānta*, the tree is the Universe. But Geldner takes it to mean Wisdom. . . . But the tree can be only the Universe" (p. 37).
13. "Dann ist der Baum der Nachthimmel" (p. 60).
14. "Er, "der Weise," [Soma] der in höchsten Himmel wohnt, ist hier, auf Erden, in den Dichter, "den Toren," eingegangen und hat ihm Weisheit und Dichterkraft geschenkt: der Dichter behauptet in heiligen Soma-Rausch zu sprechen" (p. 66).
15. *Proceedings And Transactions of All-India Oriental Conference*, Thirteenth Session: Nagpur University, October 1946 (Nagpur: Nag-

pur University, 1951), part 2, pp. 83–90. Professor Emeneau kindly sent me this article.

16. "Natürlich dürfen wir nun nicht vollständige zoologische Genauigkeit erwarten" (p. 59).

17. ". . . an attempt is made here to offer a purely naturalistic interpretation, leading of course to a spiritual moral" (p. 85).

18. Personal communication, August 3, 1974; this and the following used by permission. Professor Naether is a foremost authority on birds.

19. (Bombay: Oxford University Press, 1968) and ff., vol. I (Divers to Hawks), 1968; vol. 5 (Larks to Grey Hypocolius), 1972; the former includes the Himalayan Golden Eagle (#166), *Aguila chrysaetos daphanea*, the latter the Indian Golden Oriole (#953), *Oriolus oriolus kundoo.*

20. Dave says, "It is thus highly probably that in the pristine forests of the Punjab and the sub-Himalayas the Orioles occasionally shared the 'peepul' or banyan tree with a pair of Eagles on the assurance 'Aguila non capit muscas'—Eagles do not catch flies" (p. 84). However, eagles do not eat figs and peepul is not deodar.

21. Ali and Ripley (vol. 5, # 962, pp. 114–116) say of the North Indian Black Drongo or King Crow: "mild mannered birds such as orioles, doves, green pigeons and bulbuls commonly build in the same tree as holds a Black Drongo's nest, thereby profiting from the bird's vigilance and pugnacity in warding off potential marauders" (p. 116).

22. Personal communication, June 7, 1974.

23. For 4.5.2c, see Renou, "Études sur Quelques Hymnes Spéculatifs," EVP II (1956),54–59; he cites as examples the juxtaposed expressions, *ápracetas* or *ávijānat.*

24. Discussed by Renou: 1955, p. 18 (# 16); F. B. J. Kuiper, "The Ancient Aryan Verbal Contest," *Indo-Iranian Journal,* IV (1969), 217–281, discusses other synonymns, along with the more recent "Ví Dayate and Vidátha," op. cit., especially p. 131. Kuiper accepts *vidátha* as contest but does not associate it with the term *sadhamā́da.*

25. Renou, "Études sur Quelques Hymnes Spéculatifs," p. 55.

26. *Suváte ca-ádhi* (?) might as well mean "and fly off again," which would describe contestants, perhaps just unsuccessful ones (attested in 10.71), leaving the contest ground. Since there probably is here a symbolism involving a maturing transformation or initiatory-type rebirth, the first translation seems preferable.

27. See Andrew Weil, *The Natural Mind* (Boston: Houghton Mifflin, 1972), especially p. 96 where the author defines active placebo as "a substance whose apparent effects on the mind are actually placebo effects in response to minimal physiological action . . . all psychoactive drugs are really active placebos since the psychic effects arise from

consciousness, elicited by set and setting, in response to physiological cues."

28. *Sayúj* is no longer translated in its technical Ṛg Vedic sense, but in accord with the Upaniṣadic understanding of the image's tenor, that the two, the person (existential selfhood) and its essence (the "Lord") are closely conjoined but are no longer companions of the same brotherhood.

29. The Bhāgavata passage says: "These two birds, two companions together, by chance have made their nest in the same tree. Of the two the former eats the pippala food; the latter even without food abounds in strength. And this latter, being wise, knows the Self (ātman), but not the one who eats the pippala. Whoever yokes himself to ignorance (avidyā) certainly is forever bound; whoever is absorbed in wisdom, he certainly is eternally free." This text is quoted in Śrī Swāmī Hariharānand Sarasvatī's article, "The World Tree" (*Journal of the Indian Society of Oriental Art*, II (1943), 201).

30. *Homo Ludens: A Study of the Play Element in Culture* (Boston: Beacon Press, 1955, original edition, 1938), especially chapters 6, "Playing And Knowing," and 9, "Play-Forms in Philosophy."

31. "The enigmatic questions of the Vedic hymns lead up to the profound pronouncements of the Upanisads" (p. 107).

32. F. Sierksma, "rtsod-pa: The Monachal Disputations in Tibet," *Indo-Iranian Journal*, 8 (1964), 130–151.

33. John Mansley Robinson, *An Introduction To Early Greek Philosophy* (Boston: Houghton Mifflin Company, 1968), p. 139.

34. See p. 1581 of the article, "Symposium," in Ch. Daremberg and Saglio, *Dictionnaire des Antiquités Grecques et Romaines* (Paris: Librairie Hachette, 1911) (vol. 4 Part 2, R–S).

35. On which see most recently R. Gordon Wasson et al., *The Road to Eleusis* (New York: Harcourt Brace Jovanovich, 1978), pp. 89–93, especially the following: "Like the wine of most primitive peoples, Greek wine did not contain alcohol as its sole intoxicant but was ordinarily a mixture of various inebriants. . . . At a symposium or social drinking party, the intensity of the inebriation would be ceremoniously determined by the leader or *symposiarchos*, who decided what ratio of dilution would be used. In addition to whatever herbal toxins were already suffused in the wine, the mixing ceremony offered an opportunity to modify the wine's properties further by adding unguents and spices, as was the custom. The ancient testimony about these perfumed unguents indicates their psychotropic nature" (p. 89–90).

36. Compare Demiéville's article, "Énigmes Taoïstes" (see note 5.17), which describes speculative questions from the *Chuang Tzu*

similarly posed in enigmatic fashion at the beginning of that civilization's speculative thought.

37. J. A. B. van Buitenen, *The Mahābhārata* 1. *The Book of the Beginning* (Chicago: Chicago University Press, 1973), p. xvi.

38. Chadwick: 1952, pp. 48–57.

39. Such contests have often been recorded. Recently a native American woman, Delfina Cuero, from what is now San Diego County, California, remembered in her autobiography an example from among the Diegueño Indians. The example included the use of a psychoactive, *toloache*. She recounted, "There would be special witch doctor ceremonies and dances. They used the toloache [Jimson weed, Datura meteloides]. Witch doctors would come from all over. They would try to use their power on each other to see who was the strongest. They would not let ordinary people come near them to watch. The last xu·luy [witch-doctor dance and contest] was held near Campo about twenty-five or thirty years ago. It was on cu·ma· (Tecate Mountain), a special place used only by the witch doctors, high on the mountain." From *The Autobiography of Delfina Cuero, A Diegueño Indian* (Morongo Indian Reservation: Malki Museum Press, 1970), p. 50. My thanks to Gary Snyder for leading me to this source.

40. Mircea Eliade, *Shamanism: Archaic Techniques of Ecstasy* (Princeton: Princeton University Press, 1964).

Prologue: Archetypal Images

1. Cf. especially K. N. Sastri, *New Light on the Indus Civilization* (Delhi: Atma Ram & Sons, 1957), chapters 3 and 4.

2. By far the most complete and important treatment of the tree is Bosch: 1960. Others include: Coomaraswamy: 1935*b*, especially part 1, "Tree of Life, Earth-Lotus, and Word-Wheel." (It may be noted in passing that Coomaraswamy's explication technique appears too loose when he attributes, on p. 9, first paragraph, a long list of characteristics from the Maitrī Upaniṣad to the tree, while the actual passage makes clear no tree referent.) Another very important work is Viennot: 1954—probably the most complete and reliable textual study of the symbol. Also note Sankar Sen Gupta, *Tree Symbol Worship In India* (Calcutta: Indian Publications, 1965), and Agrawala (note 2.12) and Hariharānand Sarasvatī (note 3.29).

3. Henry Clark Warren, *Buddhism in Translations* (New York: Atheneum, 1963).

4. Bosch elaborates the role of tree symbolism in the following apropos manner: "If we now ask once more what Tree-symbolism has

contributed to Indian culture, the chief point to be emphasized is the order that it creates all around it, the order that is inhering in it, just as chaos is inhering in the phenomenal world surrounding primeval man with a fearsome obsession. This order rules supreme in the classification-system sprung from the Tree-motif, and grows into a mighty scheme that holds in its grasp all human ideas about creation, fashioning them into a harmonious whole. . . . Tree-symbolism creates order not only in the macrocosmic and the microcosmic worlds but also in the realm of invisible things, in that of religion and ritual, arts and sciences. . . . Truly, if human culture is characterized by close relation to the idea of order, then Tree-symbolism has been preeminently the factor to establish this order in Indian society" (1960, pp. 238–239).

4: Enigmas of the Sun

1. The translation is van Buitenen's (1970, p. 11); cf. 10.90.16ab, *yajñéna yajñám ayajanta devā́s tā́ni dhármāṇi prathamā́ny āsan*. Here *dhárman* is equivalent to *dhā́man*, both closely associated with the concept of *ṛta*. Note also *dhármaṇā*, 10.16.3b, and so forth (Renou: EVP XIV, 108 has additional references). *Dhā́man*, like *dhárman* (cf. 9.7.1, 9.110.4) is the natural basis of *ṛta*, being consubstantial with creation and the sacrifice, and therefore the basis at death (through the funeral sacrifice/cremation) for the "natural" return of the person to the elements as 10.16.3b shows: in fact, the separate parts being cremated are invoked in this stanza to return to their natural cosmic counterparts. The great importance of knowing the *dhā́man*, the purpose of the bráhman of 1.152, is to know the ordinations, and thus the mysteries of life and death, surely two mysteries for any speculative endeavor. On *dhárman*, see Renou, "Sur Deux Mots du Ṛgveda," *Journal Asiatique*, 252 (1964), 159–163.

2. See 1949*b* and *Bhāratīya Vidyā* 10.133.

3. The interpretation follows Renou's hermeneutics: "The images are to be elucidated on several planes at the same time. . . . From a linguistic point of view, it stands out that the text is to be interpreted in a manner both literal and transcendental; it is situated in language and above it. The *key* to its esoteric meaning is not in arbitrary intuition such as that which such and such mystical thinker of contemporary India aspires to inaugurate. It is in the extensions of a *total* exegesis of Vedic hymnology, *where the thought of the old poets is glossed by itself and for itself*, in a coherent system of cross-references" (Renou: 1949*b*, p. 273; italics added).

4. Though their overall tenor may be surmised—the victory of *ṛta* over chaos—specific meanings of the four- and the three-aspected are difficult to elaborate. Renou: 1949*b* offers some suggestions, calling (p. 269) the "four-pointed" an image on the cosmic level of the totality of the regions, on the sacrificial level of the totality of ritual structures, and on the verbal level of the four parts of speech (eg., 1.164.45); the four-aspected totality or completeness is naturally victorious over the incomplete three-aspected. He also sees other levels of reference based on this simple numerical contrast, including allusion to the slaying of the three-headed demon (10.8.7–9), to the three Nirṛtis (10.114.2, in a hymn full of number symbolism!), to the four *pādas* of the cosmic *puruṣa* (10.90), and so forth. The list of component or sub-tenors could be extended by reference to further passages. The enigma literally explodes with meaning due to its allusive polyvalences.

5. Renou (1949*b*, pp. 271–272) translates the final two verses, not relevant directly to the present discussion, as follows: "Les vaches laitières qui ont aidé le fils de Mamatā [jadis], vont [aujourd'hui] gonfler de lait, à la même mamelle, l'ami du mystère. Celui qui sait les voies cachées, qu'il prenne part à la nourriture! Celui qui veut gagner par sa bouche, qu'il donne libre cours à Aditi! Puissé-je, ô Varuṇa, ô Mitra, vous induire à agréer mon offrande avec mon hommage, avec votre concours! Que notre mystère triomphe dans les compétitions! A nous la Pluie céleste, l'heureuse traversée!"

6. Each component image has its own rich resonances and associations; the image of the sun as a celestial horse recalls the rich Vedic symbolism of the horse, particularly the sacrificial horse, which in 1.163 is speculatively identified with the sun. The image continues by opening the Upaniṣadic opus in Bṛhad-āraṇyaka Upaniṣad 1.1.1, where the sacrificial horse enigmatizes the whole of the cosmos. Meditations on the sun, undertaken in part because it was a stock bráhman image as here in 1.152, probably were formative of much later Sanskrit symbolism. For example, as is demonstrated in Jeannine Auboyer's article, "Some Games in Ancient India," *East and West*, 6 (1955), 123–137, the symbolism of swinging on a swing is based on the image of the sun's course across the sky, northward and southward through the seasons. A hymn similarly dedicated to Varuṇa, 7.87.5d (wrongly cited by Auboyer as 8.87.5, p. 134) calls the sun a "golden swing in the sky," (*diví preṅkháṃ hiraṇyáyam*). From the image, symbolic uses were derived already during the Vedic Age (detailed references in Auboyer, pp. 133–137); symbolic swinging occurs in the *mahāvrata*, where the image is associated with fertility, love, and sexual union (sun meanings), as also in Aitareya-āraṇyaka 1.2.3 ff., from whence developed its classical imagery in Kṛṣṇa mythology (*dolāyātrā*,

cf. the many miniatures showing Kṛṣṇa swinging scenes, which Keith takes to be a fertility-vegetation rite), festivals, marriage ceremonies, and other rituals.

7. Cf. *yajñásya dhā́ma*, 10.181.2b. That symbols have multiple reference levels is discussed by Paul Ricoeur in his article, "The Problem of the Double-Sense as Hermeneutic Problem and as Semantic Problem," in Kitagawa and Long, eds., *Myth And Symbols* (Chicago: University of Chicago Press, 1969, pp. 63–79). He concludes, " . . . the sole philosophic interest in symbolism is that it reveals, by its structure of double-sense, the ambiguity of being: 'Being speaks in many ways'. It is the *raison d'être* of symbolism to disclose the multiplicity of meaning out of the ambiguity of being" (p. 68).

8. The phrase is *yásya chāyā́-amṛ́taṃ yásya mṛtyúḥ*, a paradox built on a *śleṣa*! The hymn, 10.121, clearly indicates a bráhman context since it poses the mystery of the source or lord of creation in terms of a question repeated in the refrain of each of the first nine verses, *kásmai devā́ya havíṣā vidhema*. The answer, *prájāpate*, given in v. 10, was added later, though anticipated in *bhūtásya . . . pátir* of 1b; perhaps this answer became traditional from among those offered in various contests and was successfully inserted. Prajāpati, the lord of beings, evolved as the golden germ (the sun) whose ordinations (*praśís*, equivalent to *dhā́man*) are recognized by all gods (vv. 1–2), is described as being the one who is a likeness of immortality but whose shadow is death. The phrase, based on a *śleṣa* on *chāyā*, meaning both shadow and likeness or reflection (on which see Coomaraswamy: 1935*a*, p. 278) is a striking enigmatic statement of the paradox of time (vehicle: the sun), which brings death but which is also an image of immortality. The tenor is the one lord, paradoxically both the creator and the destroyer, in short time, of life; the vehicle image is the sun, which concretely reveals time. The *chāyā* of time is death, death being the shadow (of the sun) that accompanies human beings through life; but time is also a "likeness" or a "reflection" (*chāyā*) of immortality and nontemporal being, because time is a revelation of its opposite, eternity.

Chāyā has even another meaning, as—and again paradoxically—death is not to be avoided, cannot be avoided, by mortal humanity, but rather is to be embraced, for *chāyā* can mean the shade or refuge from the heat-destruction of the sun (tenor: time), as in 6.16.38, 2.33.6. Here the image anticipates in its structure the basic mystical means of achieving release from time and death recommended in Sanskrit soteriological literature. This happens when mortal beings die (to time and the mortal self or self-concern, by taking refuge in the shadow-shade)—die not a literal death but a symbolic, anticipatory death that renounces attachment to mortal realities in favor of the eternal, nonmortal selfhood.

The image is recombined into its wholeness in 6.16.38, which seems to anticipate this tenet of renunciatory mysticism. Agni (recalling the Agni of the crematory fire) is addressed as the golden likeness whose shade is refuge from burning heat (sun/time). The renunciant sacrifices the mortal self in Agni's symbolic consumption. The verse goes: *úpa chāyā́m iva ghŕ̥ṇer áganma śárma te vayám/ ágne híraṇyasaṃdr̥śaḥ/* "We come to you, O Agni, the golden likeness (of immortality), for refuge, as it were for shade from burning heat." The imagery associated with the paradoxical character of time and life figures prominently in later Sanskrit religious conceptions, particularly in those concerning the characters of Śiva and even more the Goddess; both are divine figures whose manifestation is two-sided. In fact, Zimmer: 1946 quotes Śaṅkara's address to the goddess where this enigmatic structure reappears: "Who art thou, O Fairest One! Auspicious One!/ You whose hands hold both: delight and pain?/ Both: the shade of death and the elixir of immortality,/ Are thy grace, O Mother!" (p. 212). Time as a likeness or image of eternity is the basis of Sanskrit scriptural reports of people who have become enlightened after observing an evanescent phenomenon, as in Jātaka 460 where the evanescence of the morning dew (tenor: transience, *anityatā*) is sufficient to enlighten one who sees it in the morning but not after the sun (tenor: destroying time) has taken it away. The reverse of this would be a dew not subject to the sun's action, nonexistent in the physical world. The conception of time being a reflection of eternity also occurs in Greek philosophy, which considers the visible universe to be the *eikṓn* (image or reflection) of the intelligible, and thus considers time to be an image of eternity (see Peters, F. E., *Greek Philosophical Terms*, New York: New York University Press, 1967, p. 51). Albert Camus, who claimed that at the center of his work "there is an invincible sun," described the enigma of the sun in an interview, recalling much of the Sanskrit speculative appreciation of its dual nature: "What is more complex than the birth of thought? The right explanation is always double, at least. Greece teaches us this, Greece to which we must always return. Greece is both shadow and light. We are well aware, aren't we, if we come from the South, that the sun has its black side?" (Camus: 1968, p. 357).

9. Of course, any complex element of a civilization's world view cannot have a single origin (single effect, single cause fallacy); many influences must have contributed to the notion of transmigration. Van Buitenen: 1970, p. 29 ff., discusses some possible sources, including: the idea of migration of the soul in "primitive" cultures (p. 29), the possible selectivity of Vedic texts representing only the "optimistic"

views of the higher professional classes (while "pessimistic" beliefs in rebirth might have been popularly held), or a spirit of pessimism among the Indo-Aryan peoples deriving from their resettlement in Gangetic India, or from natural disasters, or from the harshness of the Indian climate, and so forth (all p. 33). Significant evidence from the agrarian life-style of the Harappā peoples indicates the sorts of ideas that might be held by an agrarian people who lived close to the natural rhythms of growth, harvest, and the subsequent rebirth of seed in the following season. By contrast, the Indo-Aryans practiced no agriculture until after settling in India, at which time they would have been easily influenced by indigenous ideas. Since Indian religion (Hindu, Buddhist, and Jaina) preserves uniquely among the major historical faiths this philosopheme of transmigration, some special reason for its presence must exist which still escapes us; in this present discussion I seek its speculative sources.

10. Cirlot: 1962, p. 303, similarly reports this aspect of solar symbolism: "The idea of the invincible character of the sun is reinforced by the belief that whereas the Moon must suffer fragmentation (since it wanes) before it can reach its monthly stage of three-day disappearance, the Sun does not need to die in order to descend into hell; it can reach the ocean or the lake of the Lower Waters and cross it without being dissolved. Hence, the death of the Sun necessarily implies the idea of resurrection and actually comes to be regarded as a death which is not a true death."

11. The Sanskrit, especially Hindu, conception of creation similarly likens creation to a dismemberment or a falling away from primal unity into diversity. Thus any fate in material creation is necessarily lunar in nature, hence, ultimately unsatisfactory.

12. Coomaraswamy: 1935*b*, p. 28, incorrectly identifies the "two" in these verses as Heaven and Earth. It is nonsense to say of the earth that "it ordains the seasons and is born again." Such interpretive errors result from a failure to read the images seriously, on their own nonconceptual terms, from a desire perhaps to hold to preconceived conclusions, and from a haste to determine appropriate and proper tenors.

13. The fire is the cremation sacrifice that transports released individuals to their permanent solar destiny, in contrast with those who through its smoke return to mortality (v. 16). The identification of the two paths leading to alternate destinies thus begins in the manner of one's living which determines what the crematory fire does to one's corpse. The passage is admittedly archaic, but the basic ideas appear. It is significant that the solar destiny's cremation leads to fire rather than to smoke, because it thus assimilates into this concept the image

complexes associated with the *ātman* conception. The sources of the *ātman* conception in solar and fire imagery evoke the familiar equivalence of Agni/fire of inner inspiration-Vaiśvānara/sun *ātman*—in short, the "clear," luminous (said of *citta, ātman*), nonmortal destiny. Those who pass into smokiness from the cremation still transmigrate on the path of recurrent death.

14. Radhakrishnan: 1953, p. 314 (plagiarizing R. E. Hume's *The Thirteen Principal Upanishads* almost word for word) renders the phrase, *te teṣu brahma-lokeṣu parāḥ parāvato vasante* incorrectly as, "In those worlds of Brahmā they live *for long periods,*" this last phrase translating *parāḥ parāvato*. Rather than follow Rāmānuja here, it is best to see it as a borrowing from Ṛg Veda 10.58.11, from whence it was probably directly taken due to similarity of context, meaning "remote distances" (*parāvat*, f. "distance"). These are feminine accusative plurals. That *brahma-loka* is plural indicates that this passage is still transitional and quite archaic; the singular will soon be exclusively used, as was the equivalent term in the Bhagavad Gītā, *brahma-nirvāṇa*.

15. These two Upaniṣadic verses use parallelism to structure the distinction between two ontologies of death, the solar leading to *nirvāṇa* or *mokṣa* and the lunar leading to recurrent death. The technique is familiar in many Indic texts, such as Anguttara-nikāya 1.10 on the two types of *citta*. The parallelism is nearly complete, contrasting point by point the two paths to alternate destinies. Those who follow the solar meditate faithfully (*upāsate*, hence *upaniṣad*) on truth in the forest (*araṇye*, cf. van Buitenen: 1968*a*, pp. 1 and 38), while those of the lunar destiny win worlds by *yajña, dāna,* and *tapas,* continuing the orthodox Vedic practice. This contrast continues in the parallels of the cremation fire, which leads to fire (immortality) for those of the solar destiny but to smoke for those of the lunar (in the episode of Godhika's *nirvāṇa*, recounted in Samyutta-nikāya 1.122–23, Māra is described as being a kind of "smokiness" that floats around in the air); to the day versus night; to the waxing half-month versus the waning half-month; to the six months when the sun travels northward versus the six months when the sun travels southward (the direction of death); to the world of the gods (hence the term *deva-yāna*, on which see the following note) versus the world of the fathers (hence *pitṛ-yāṇa*); and finally to the sun versus the moon, the underlying enigma. The symbolism, involving light versus dark, waxing versus waning time, culminating in solar versus lunar, describes the paths leading either to immortality or to recurrent death.

16. Other structures as archaic as the solar/lunar participate in this grand Upaniṣadic synthesis of Ṛg Vedic and post-Ṛg Vedic speculation. In particular the solar path of release (v. 15) is assimilated into the

old Ṛg Vedic *devayāna* or the way of the gods, which originally was closed to mortals ("O Death, take the other path, which is your own, distinct from the way of the gods", 10.18.1ab) but which in the Upaniṣads became the human path to immortality. The Ṛg Vedic *devayāna* was actually the path to immortality but only in the terrestrial sense, attained through proper sacrifice and life's actions (see 10.2.3, where Agni is invoked to establish ritually the sacrifices and seasons, that is terrestrial order; also cf. *samídho devayā́nīḥ*, 10.51.2, and *sugā́n patháḥ kṛṇuhi devayā́nān*, 10.51.5, "make practicable the ways which serve to go to the gods," noting alongside this 10.73.7 where the expression is decomposed into *pathó devatrā́ . . . yā́nān*; references, Renou: EVP XIV (1965), 62, 79). The contrast is with the path of the fathers, which is the only mortal way of dying in the Ṛg Veda. This is the path established by the first man to die, Yama, and the path by which the first fathers departed (10.14.1–2). It is equally served by Agni, but not in his function as bearer of oblations on the *devayāna* (*jātávedā devébhyo havyáṃ vahatu*, 10.16.9cd) but as consumer of the flesh (*kravyā́dam agním*, 10.16.9a), in short, as crematory Agni of the *pánthām . . . pitṛyā́ṇam*, the path leading to the fathers (10.2.7cd, the sole Ṛg Vedic instance of this phrase).

The dual structure of these two paths has been taken over in the Upaniṣadic passages and correlated with the solar and lunar destiny. In v. 15, the solar path reaches the *deva-loka*, and from thence the sun, while in v. 16, the *pitṛ-loka* is reached, leading to the moon. The boldness of the Upaniṣadic transformation stands revealed when we realize that the ancient and exclusivistic Ṛg Vedic way to terrestrial immortality has been opened to all persons via the *ātman* conception (on which see Renou: 1952) as a way of escape from recurrent death. The meaning shift was required because of the new conception of death, seen as leading not to Yama's paradise but rather to new and ever renewed, endless turnings through the cycle of life and death grafted onto the old conception of the *pitṛyāṇa*. This image structure spawned many in its wake; for one example, see Govinda, Anagarika, "Solar & Lunar Symbolism in the Development of Stupa Architecture," *Marg*, 4 (1950), 9–20.

17. As M. A-M. Boyer's little known article, "Étude sur l'origine de la Doctrine du Saṃsāra," *Journal Asiatique*, Vol. XVIII (1901) shows, the Vedic peoples identified a full length of terrestrial life, though it ends in death, with *amṛta*, literally "not dead" (later, "immortality") (p. 464). The author cites particularly passages such as 5.63.2, *vṛṣṭíṃ vāṃ rā́dho amṛtatvám īmahe*, where *amṛtatvam* does not imply immortality but connotes not being dead within the proper span of one-hundred autumns of life. The prayer for rain is interesting because rain later

conveyed an image for bounties not physical but spiritual, as in the Mahāyāna Buddhist Saddharmapuṇḍarīka (5, v. 1–38), where the Tathāgata and his dharma teaching are likened to a great rain cloud. This may in turn be an image derived from the earlier designation of the Buddha as a *nāga* (elephant or serpent) since monsoon clouds, bringers of physical bounty (spiritually, the dharma) are often thought of as sky elephants.

18. See especially Gonda, *Change and Continuity in Indian Religion* (Mouton, 1965), Chapter VI, "Māyā," pp. 164–97; also Gonda, *Four Studies in the Language of the Veda* (Mouton, 1959), Chapter IV, "The 'original' sense and the etymology of Sanskrit Māyā," pp. 119–194, and his remarks (p. 248) on *māyā*, and passim, in "Some Notes on the Study of Ancient-Indian Religious Terminology" in *History of Religions*, 1, 2 (Winter 1962), 243–273. Coomaraswamy's fairly early attempt to define *māyā* (in "On Translation: Maya, Deva, Tapas," *Isis*, 19 (1933), 75–80) may be criticized for not sufficiently distinguishing the various textual and historical contexts in which the term *māyā* has expressed Sanskrit speculations about the mystery of creation. This weakness extends, more or less, throughout Coomaraswamy's work, for he apparently did not think his ahistorical approach to be a critical fault in interpreting Sanskrit texts. Adherence to the first principle of the historical lexicon, temporal sequence, seems far more reliable to deal with such terms, and is the method adopted by Gonda, whose articles are the best contemporary work on the subject.

19. It is interesting to note that "illusion," often resorted to as a translation equivalent for the later meanings of *māyā*, includes a reference to play, from Latin *illudere, ludere* (to play); and note the phrase, "the play of illusion."

20. The image functions as a simile whose explicit comparative particle (*iva* or *ná*) has been elided: *pūrvāparám̥ carato māyáyaitaú śíśū [ná] krīḷantau pári yato adhvarám.*

21. As it is even today. I remember seeing in Huston Smith's movie, *Requiem for a Faith*, a scene depicting some kind of communal Tibetan ritual near Darjeeling, wherein participants, men and women, circled around a smoky fire while children played around them in utter selfless abandon, despite the sacrality of the event—or do Tibetans not oppose sacrality and levity?

22. The St. Petersburg lexicon reports that some consider *līlā* a corruption of the Vedic verb used in this verse, $\sqrt{}$*krīḍ/krīḷ* > *krīḍā, līlā*. Robert Goldman once told me of meeting a man in India who, upon being asked who he was, responded with the question, "Do you mean in the play?" He then specified that in the play (*māyā/līlā*) he was Colonel so–and–so. If the question were to mean, "Who are you

ultimately," he would have answered otherwise, since a major distinction in the classical world view claims that persons have two identities.

23. *Māyā* has been considered both revealing and concealing from Śvetāśvatara Upaniṣad 4.1, where the divine ordains the many colors with a hidden purpose, to Kabīr, who writes (Dvivedi #25, v. 1) "The Lord hides himself, the Lord wonderfully reveals himself . . . " (*hari ne apnā āp chipāyā/hari ne naphiz kar dikhāyā//*); see also note 1.32.

24. The structure that distinguishes binding action versus play was exported with Buddhism, Indian religiosity in its universal form. Jitoku's series of six oxherding pictures (reproduced in Zenkei Shibayama's *The Six Oxherding Pictures*, included in the collection *The Flower Does Not Talk* (Rutland: Tuttle, 1970) ends with the sixth, last picture entitled "Playing"—the action of the enlightened is the tenor of this image. Dumoulin's *History of Zen Buddhism* (Boston: Beacon Press, 1963) gives satori accounts of great Zen masters which similarly describe enlightenment as entrance into the realm of play. One wrote, "In the excess of delight I forgot that my hands were moving in the air and that my feet were dancing" (p. 273). Another, Hakuin, wrote: "Thus I experienced the Great Joy six or seven times and in addition countless lesser enlightenments and delights by which one forgets that one is dancing . . . " (p. 252).

The contemporary northern Indian festival of Holī, as McKim Marriott describes it in his article "The Feast of Love" (in Milton Singer, *Krishna: Myths, Rites and Attitudes* (Chicago: University of Chicago Press, 1968) pp. 200–212, is a way of making concrete the ancient image of play, once again operative as an alternate way of ordering cosmos and action. Fortunately, the festival is held only once a year, since all ordinary *dharma* and action are then reversed, exchanging *karman* and the dictates of duty for play and the delights of playfulness. The world that day, as one informant said, is transformed into "a *līlā*—a divine sport of Lord Krishna!" (p. 201). That all taboos are abrogated on that day indicates how seriously the play image must be taken, for if truly divine activity is mere play (hence what is right? what is wrong? "Oh, it's just a game."), it must be beyond *karman* and the mechanisms which mete out for every action a consequence. Surely in the Indian view, the good woman who doused the beleaguered anthropologist with a pail of urine from her buffalo (p. 203) is thus not condemning herself, since it was Holī day, to the *karman* resultant upon Yankee-anthropologist baiting. Thereby once a year she has a "taste" of divine action, an experience of her own divine play.

25. Coomaraswamy: 1937, pp. 457–458. He concludes that "keep on going" provided a choral response to each verse which would have been sung by a leader. It would seem far more interesting if the verses

were first just such a song of a wandering bardic band, and then were taken into the Brāhmaṇa because of the wider acceptance in that period of its ideas. Since the verses do refer to the Ṛg Vedic two-birds-in-a-fig-tree bráhman, and since the first verse uses the term *sākhā* in the phrase, "Indra is companion to the wanderer," recalling the technical terms *sakhya* and *sakhi,* which describe the symposium brotherhood and a comrade, respectively, it may have been the chant of a brotherhood of speculators who early broke away from their ritualist brethren. Furthermore, the verses are cast in a kind of enigmatic riddling characteristic of speculative verse, again suggesting a source in a wandering brotherhood of the old symposium visionaries.

26. Here may be a way of resolving the incongruity noticed by many (Robinson and Johnson: 1977, p. 20) that Gautama, the name which the tradition preserved for the Buddha, is a *brāhmaṇa* patronymic, but his traditional biography makes him a prince (*kṣatriya*). Perhaps we have taken the myth (an attempt to clothe the personal life of the man in the garb of epic hero myth) too literally. Thus, the personal name can recall Gautama's actual birth as a *brāhmaṇa* (many early Buddhist converts came from this class for obvious reasons), while the myth recalls the same symbolic motif present in the stories of both Rohita and Gautama, that persons who live in houses or palaces may be princes, kings, or queens in the world but still do not escape death (Māra, the true king of the mortal world). Therefore the myth makes Gautama a prince of the world, potentially its king, so that he can reject that destiny by leaving the palace to become a wanderer, symbolically giving up all material aspiration in favor of spirit.

27. Though *pippalam* has been replaced by *udumbaram* (both "fig"), *udumbara* is a fig of another genus, *ficus glomerata* (the switch may merely be for metrical lengthening); regardless, the allusion is doubtless intentional (note also *madhu,* honey, another quote from the bráhman). Coomaraswamy agrees (p. 465, footnote 2) but rather weakly, since he writes, "The 'honey' (madhu) and the 'tasty fig' (svādum udumbaram) are evidently reminiscent of RV 1.164.22."

28. As well as with the few nonconformist ecstatics mentioned in the Ṛg Veda, such as the philtre-drinking *muni* of 10.136, described as wearing long hair and the same "soiled ochre robe" ([*múnayo . . .*] *piśáṅgā vasate málā,* 10.136.2b that Siddhārtha adopted after renouncing his material patrimony.

29. Coomaraswamy: 1937, p. 461, gives the text as follows: "*Caran-vai̯ madhu vindati, carant-svādum udumbaram:/ Sūryasya paśya śrēmāṇaṁ, yō na tandrayatē caraṁś:/Caraiva, caraiva.*" The last phrase reminds one of descriptions of the wheel from the same bráhman collection which 1.164 made, discussed in the following chapter.

30. I. B. Horner, "Some Aspects of Movement in Early Buddhism,"

Artibus Asiae, 10 (1947), 138–141. In the same year she also published the article "Wayfaring" in *Art and Thought*, K. Bharatha Iyer, ed., (London: Luzac & Company, 1947), pp. 202–208. This last volume was a Coomaraswamy festschrift, and in the first paragraph, Horner acknowledges Coomaraswamy's 1937 article. It is interesting to note that Coomaraswamy's general treatment prompted an eminent Buddhologist to write on the theme as it survived in a particular stream of the tradition.

31. Which in fact Buddhism developed, in Saṃyutta 1.61–62 and Anguttara 2.48–49, as Coomaraswamy noted in an addendum to the first article, appearing in *JBORS*, Vol. XXIV, Pt. III, pp. 118–119; the Nikāya Rohita, Rohitassa, had intended "to reach the end of the world by travelling" (p. 118), doing literally as the Aitareya Rohita had, but could not, in terms of the classical world view, succeed in attaining thereby to salvation. He only became a god. To "go beyond" in the classical world view meant to transcend the whole wheel of life, not just to rise to its upper limits (the Heavens, the old realm of the fathers of the Ṛg Vedic world view). All phenomenal realms in the later view are mortal.

32. Gerhart B. Ladner, "*Homo Viator*: Medieval Ideas on Alienation and Order", *Speculum*, 42 (April 1967), 233–259.

33. At the late, frail age of forty, Bashō, by then a famous poet who could have spent his remaining years in comfort, began his wandering journeys, writing, "Following the example of the ancient priest who is said to have travelled thousands of miles caring naught for his provisions and attaining the state of sheer ecstasy under the pure beams of the moon, I left my broken house . . . " (Bashō: 1966, p. 51). So Coomaraswamy writes, "There is, then, a metaphysics of travelling. . . . " (1937, p. 460). Matthew 25:14: "For the kingdom of heaven is as a man travelling into a far country." "We celebrated our start by scribbling on our hats 'Nowhere in this wide universe have we a fixed abode—A party of two wanderers.' (Bashō: 1966, p. 81). "Like pilgrims to th' appointed end we tend;/ The world's an inn, and death the journey's end" Dryden, "*Palamon and Arcite,*" 3 (quoted from Ladner, p. 258).

34. Michael Edwardes, *East-West Passage* (New York: Taplinger Publishing Company, 1971), pp. 159–160.

5: Enigmas of the Wheel

1. P. Masson-Oursel in a short article argues for the noria or waterwheel as the model of the Buddhist wheel of life, discussed below. This is indeed another contributor to the Ṛg Vedic archetype

but appears in literature as an image only much later (cf. Coomaraswamy, "The Persian Wheel," *Journal of the American Oriental Society,* 51 (1931), 283–284, where the author describes a water wheel referred to in Cull. V, 16,2 (Vin II, 122), though I doubt whether *Divyāvadāna* 300 describes, as Coomaraswamy claims, a water wheel, unless this is suggested by the phrase, "by means of a windlass" in that passage; all references after this are later, (e.g., *Rājataraṅginī, Harṣacarita*) so that Masson-Oursel's short discussion dazzlingly touches on the rich symbolism of the water wheel, but does not justify his conclusion (in "La Noria, Prototype Du Saṃsāra, et son Rapport au Dharmacakra," in *Études d'Orientalisme publiées par Le Musée Guimet à la Mémoire de Raymonde Linoissier* (Paris: Librarie Ernest Leroux, 1932) II, 419–421, that Gautama considered the twelve *nidāna* series backward and forward because of the image of the noria ("Les douze termes de ce raisonnement oscillaient dans les deux directions comme tournent alternativement à droite et à gauche les douze palettes multitubulaires d'une noria, cette roue que traverse un courant" p. 421.) This connection sounds farfetched. His general description of the wheel is nonetheless valid, and is one of the first attempts to find image bases for Sanskrit speculative notions, a task this essay takes up enthusiastically.

2. Cirlot: 1962, pp. 350–352, gives a rapid survey of the symbolism of the wheel. He mentions that according to Krappe, "the concept of the sun as a wheel was one of the most widespread notions of antiquity" (p. 350).

3. Wheel, *cakra,* probable etymology "revolving," "moving," according to B. R. Sharma, "Cakra in Brahmanical and Buddhist Scriptures," in *The Journal of the Bihar Research Society,* Buddha Jayanti Special Issue (1956), I, 218–244, particularly 219–220.

4. See W. E. Begley, *Viṣṇu's Flaming Wheel: The Iconography of the Sudarśana-Cakra* (New York: New York University Press, 1973), and Jeannine Auboyer, "Quelques Réflections à Propos du Cakra Arme Offensive," in *Arts Asiatiques,* II (1964), 119–126.

5. Paul Horsch, "The Wheel: An Indian Pattern of World-Interpretation," in Ksitis Roy, ed., *Liebenthal Festschrift* (Santiniketan: Visvabharati, 1957) pp. 62–79. As for the wheel as speculative device, see Coomaraswamy: 1935*b*, pp. 25 ff., and especially "*Kha* and other Words denoting 'Zero' in Connection with the Metaphysics of Space," in *Bulletin of the School of Oriental Studies,* London Institution, 7 (1933–1935), 487–497, particularly 488, 492.

6. Stephen C. Pepper, *World Hypotheses: A Study in Evidence* (Berkeley and Los Angeles: University of California Press, 1961).

7. Also described in Karl G. Heider, *The Dugum Dani, A Papuan Culture in the Highlands of West New Guinea* (Chicago: Aldine Publishing Company, 1970), p. 166.

8. Kees W. Bolle, *The Freedom Of Man In Myth* (Nashville: Vanderbilt University Press, 1968), p. 108.

9. Probably Agni is meant, being the fire (boneless) that supports beings (the boned); most probably, "this splendid bird," 7b, is also Agni.

10. The language of these verses is clearly that which characterizes bráhman contexts; note especially, *kvà svit* 4b, and *kím ápi svid*, 6d, and *pā́kaḥ*, 5a; *upa* $\sqrt{gam}$ in 4d, is used in the sense of approaching a wise man (a "father" in the contest, or is it Agni, the patron of contestants, who is intended?) to learn sacred knowledge.

11. The symbolism of the footprints or tracks left, following which one might find the origin or source again, is pan-Indian in later ages (note the footprints of various deities) and constitutes the basis of path (*mārga*) symbolism in later formulations. Note especially Coomaraswamy: 1935b, pp. 15–17, who rightly sees the Ch'an/Zen Buddhist "ox-herding" pictures as a far-flung ectype of this archetypal imagery. The Upaniṣads explicitly adopted the symbolism, as Bṛhad-āraṇyaka Upaniṣad 1.4.7, "The self is the track of all this, for by it all this is known, just as one finds by footprints one who is lost."

12. The tenor of this image probably is the bráhman symposium at which the poet finds himself, as he prepares to tackle its enigmas. The meaning of the hapax legomenon *baṣkáya* (yearling) is unsure; Brown's suggestion (1968, see footnote 61) is: "ready to be born" (p. 211). The "calf" may be the unrealized cọntestant who speaks in these verses, who sees himself as a "yearling calf" approaching the greater maturing or new birth of inspired eloquence (as he reports in 37cd) so that he might propose and fathom bráhmans in the contest being "stretched" (the image applies to any sacrificial performance) or conducted around him. The verses report the natural feelings of a symposiast at the beginning of a contest.

13. This verse is autobiographical again, and should be read with verses 4–7; in cd, the poet describes the coming of inspiration from Agni, the first born of order. Perhaps the verse appears later in the series because such acquisition of inspiration does not usually follow too closely upon the contestant's entrance into the contest. Through Agni's office, the poet shares (*bhāgám* $\sqrt{aś}$), participates in, has direct knowledge of the mysteries, thus achieving transformed vision, the goal of the symposium.

14. The images repeat familiar themes in Ṛg Vedic sacrificial speculation, such as the mention of the three-naved, unaging wheel (of the chariot-sacrifice), which apparently attempts to recall the sacrificial correlation of the three tiers of creation. The one wheel of the all, the total wheel, has three naves, or levels, these being the "worlds" (earth, atmosphere, and heaven) which are three but one, and thus the

sacrifice is effective in all creation.

15. The tenor of the chariot vehicle image is the sacrifice; the metaphor is amply confirmed in other passages, cf. K. R. Potdar, *Sacrifice in the Rgveda* (Bombay: Bharatiya Vidya Bhavan, 1953), pp. 250–251, "Yajña-ratha."

16. On the One, see especially Renou: 1953*b*, p. 336.

17. Paul Demiéville, "Énigmes Taoïstes," *Zinbun Kagaku Kenkyusyo* (Kyoto University), Silver Jubilee Volume (1954), pp. 54–60, particularly p. 60.

18. "Fivefold" or "quintuple" for *páñcapādam*, rather than the inappropriate "five-footed," its ordinary meaning, as this latter would mix metaphors—a wheel, not an animal, is the subject.

19. Since ten makes no obvious reference to the year, or a familiar Ṛg Vedic conception of space, and since the sun is explicitly mentioned as the tenor (i.e., intermediate vehicle) of the image of c, b also must refer to the sun, thus shifting to the mythological allusions of the intermediate vehicle.

20. Camus: 1968, p. 230; Camus's essay on Brice Paṛain, pp. 228–241, deals with some of the subjects here discussed in a most lucid and inspiring manner.

21. See Jean Przyluski, "La Roue de la vie à Ajanta," in *Journal Asiatique*, 16 (1920), 313–331. Other references include, L. A. Waddell, "The Buddhist Pictorial Wheel of Life," *Journal of the Asiatic Society of Bengal*, 61 (1893), 133–155; Eleanor Olson, "The Wheel of Existence" in *Oriental Art* 9 (1963), 204–209; Theos Bernard, "The Tibetan 'Wheel of Life'," and Gerda Hartmann, "Notes on the 'Wheel of Life'," *Review of Religion*, 3 (1939), 400–415.

22. Quoted from E. J. Thomas, *The History of Buddhist Thought* (London: Routledge & Kegan Paul, 1933), pp. 68–69.

23. Ibid., p. 68.

24. Ananda Coomaraswamy, "An Early Passage On Indian Painting," *Eastern Art*, 3, 219, n. 1.

25. Waddell, op.cit., p. 134.

26. The formal influence of the Ṛg Vedic model may have been quite specific, despite the centuries that separated them. The Pali Text Society's dictionary (p. 394) reports two early chains of causation, one of ten links (which the authors presume to be earlier), the other of twelve (adding *nidānas* one and two). Was the model of twelve chosen over the ten-membered chain on the basis of the Vedic tradition?

27. See also J. Otto Schrader's article, "The Sacrificial Wheel Taught in the Bhagavadgītā," *The Indian Historical Quarterly*, 5, 2 (1929), 173–181.

28. See Melford E. Spiro, *Buddhism and Society* (New York: Harper and Row, 1970).

29. Literally, "not afflict you round," *pari* $\sqrt{vyath}$; the prefix refers to extended becoming, which extends out from the infinitesimal center point of the wheel that transcends becoming's afflictions. Note also *pari* in Ṛg Veda 1.32.15d, *arā́n ná nemíḥ pári tā́ babhūva* (a meaning of *cakravartin* is here).

30. Coomaraswamy notes (in "*Kha* and other Words", op. cit., see footnote 5.5 p. 487) that *kha* in the Ṛg Veda means particularly the emptiness or cavity of the wheel (through which the axle goes) and that *kha* is one of several words denoting "zero" (including *śūnya, ākāśa, ananta, pūrṇa).* All refer to the emptiness or infinitesimal space of the wheel's center, from which extension derives, but which itself has no extension. Interestingly, later Sanskrit conceptions of spirit describe its metaphysics as being empty of extension or extended existence.

31. Presuming the Śvetāśvatara to be a middle-early, nonsectarian Upaniṣad, along with the Kaṭha, Īśā, Muṇḍaka and Mahānārāyaṇa, this passage indicates that the speculative impulse of the old Vedic symposium still was felt in the increasingly sophisticated middle Upaniṣads, and not only in the archaic earliest texts like the Bṛhadāraṇyaka and Chāndogya.

32. This introductory phrase is borrowed from verse 5, omitted here because it shifts metaphors. This verse uses the technique of the extended metaphor, familiar in much later Sanskrit literature. Already present in the Ṛg Veda, as in 10.85, it became a favorite form especially in didactic works; see V. Raghavan's discussion of "sustained metaphor" in *The Great Integrators: The Saint-Singers of India* (Delhi: Publications Division, 1966), pp. 36–43.

33. Huge (*bṛhante*) suggests etymologizing on brahma ($\sqrt{bṛh}$>? *brahman*), in the following brahma-cakra.

34. As a compound, *brahma-cakra* leaves *brahma-* ambiguous, so that it could be read either *brahman* (abstract, absolute Being) or *Brahmā* (concrete god of creation, source of becoming), thus preserving the enigmatic dual reference of the archetypal wheel, and allowing the dual interpretation of *saṃstha* (see following note's discussion).

35. The phrase, "wherein both life and rest exist for all," may be read in two ways; in the first alternative, the wheel is the wheel of Brahmā's creation (becoming, change), and *saṃstha* (rest) means recurrent death; or, in the second, it is the wheel of Brahman, ultimate Being, and *saṃstha* means the permanent rest of release from the wheel's turning. Other Upaniṣadic ectypes exhibit a similar structure. Repeatedly, the nave symbolizes the essence (inner self, *ātman*) of all beings (Bṛhad. 2.5.15) or of the individual (Brhad. 1.5.15), or it is "life" (*prāṇa*, Praśna 2.6, Chāndogya 7.15.1). In the image of Brhad. 1.5.15, the transcendent self (*ātman*) is the nave (*nabhya*) of the wheel,

while the becoming-produced self of acquisition (*vitta*) is defined by the felly (*pradhi*), denoting infinitesimal Being and extended becoming, respectively. The image explicitly states that only because of *vitta* (acquisition, extension of Being into the realm of becoming) does a person fill and empty (*sa vittenaivā ca pūryate apa ca kṣīyate*), which means to suffer the endless transmigrant mutability of becoming. Filling and emptying recall Śūdraka's water wheel, as well as the discussion of lunar and solar destinies of the last chapter.

6: An Auspicious Enigma

1. A check of the French historical dictionaries (Paul Robert, *Dictionnaire alphabétique et analogique de la Langue Française*, and Émile Littré, *Dictionnaire de la Langue Française*) indicates a similar history for the word there.

2. "1590 Greene *Never too late* (1600) 106 "For young men 'tis too soone, for olde men too late to marry; concluding so enigmatically, it were not good to marry at all." All citations are from volume 3 (p. 187) of the *Oxford English Dictionary*.

3. The subject of riddles is a separate topic, having its own dictionary entry and history. A large anthropological and folklorist literature had been devoted to it. There is a regrettable tendency to deal with enigmas under the title of "riddles," as in James Hastings, *Encyclopaedia of Religion and Ethics* (New York: Scribner's, 1961), where the article on riddles (10: 765–770; paradox has a page entry, enigma none) was written by James A. Kelso. He translates Greek *ainigma* as "riddle" (p. 765, col. 2) and uses enigma and riddle as partial synonyms; the article is an interesting survey, though brief, of the history of the enigma and related forms, even mentioning Ṛg Vedic examples.

4. Evidence indicates that the riddle is an ancient human fascination, whether or not provided with a noumenal tenor. For a general survey of its place in world literature, see H. Munro Chadwick and N. Kershaw Chadwick, *The Growth of Literature* (Cambridge: The University Press, 1932), especially III, 834 ff. More interesting and concise is Chadwick: 1952, which notes enigma contests (p. 48) and shamanic notions of inspiration and language resembling those of Ṛg Vedic bráhman contests.

5. I assume that English "enigma" has a potential semantic space or structure, which emanates from its Greek model meaning "to speak a.) allusively or b.) obscurely." These two establish separate poles, correspondingly light and dark. Any enigma, or anything enigmatic, refers to an ultimate tenor that it provisionally "conceals"; that tenor

may be alluded to or obscured. In the first case, it is a lucid enigma, in the second, an obscure. The history of the word in English attests both poles but rarely used the lucid. In using the image of the enigmatic sun, I refer to these two poles of its meaning, since like anything enigmatic, the sun has two aspects, one that creates flesh and the other that destroys it.

6. After reading Chadwick: 1952 it is clear that to understand the enigmatic we must incorporate meanings from shamanic sources to gain a humanistic, transcultural idea of its meaning.

7. I apologize that the enrichment is so meager, offering no sources beyond Indo-European languages; but this is not the place to give a full account of *enigma*.

8. Among many recent accounts, see Sallie TeSelle, *Speaking in Parables* (Philadelphia: Fortress Press, 1975).

9. Agni surely is another such divine, lucid enigma, who consumes everything but is never himself consumed; he hides in the deep, dark waters and is invisible, latent in all that burns, but he also blazes up to dance when ignited by the fire sticks, ever-changing but the same. Then, though hidden to most, Agni radiates in the poet's heart, giving inspiration and light to those who serve him. Aśvaghoṣa also describes the Buddha to be like a sun descended to earth.

10. Logan Pearsall Smith's S. P. E. Tract no. XVIII, *Four Words: Romantic, Originality, Creative, Genius* (Folcroft, Pa.: The Folcroft Press, 1924), p. 35.

11. *Style* (London: Cassell, 1955), p. 67.

12. Brand Blanshard, *On Philosophical Style* (Bloomington: Indiana University Press, 1967), pp. 10–11. Blanshard's argument is a plea for the language prejudices of contemporary analytic philosophy, a good representative of the Anglo-American approach to philosophical clarity.

13. Camus's essay, "L'Enigme" (Camus: 1968, pp. 154–161), written in 1950, is a meditation on the writer's confrontation with the enigma of life, enigmatized as a sun, with both light and dark sides; note as tenors of the sun image, "history" (p. 160), a dark side of the sun, and "peace," "to love and create in silence" (p. 161), its light side. The meditation on the enigmatic sun image framed Camus's eventual subject, the task of the writer, and his own fate as a writer. However, when the essay appeared in *The Atlantic*, 191 (June 1953), 72–73, it was shortened by deletion of the sun meditation so as to deal only with the writer as its English translation title indicated ("What a Writer Seeks"). This was a pity, because the essay frame, its sun-enigma meditation, was totally removed, rendering Camus's eloquent conclusion meaningless to the reader.

14. An appropriate later Sanskrit equivalent might be *śreyas*, from

śrī. The Sanskrit speculative tradition recommended the *śreyas* (the auspicious) over the *preyas* (the merely pleasant), since the first leads to the sacred while the second condemns to recurrent death (as in Kaṭha Upaniṣad 4.1).

15. Some studies have appeared advancing the investigations undertaken in this essay. For example, Robert Goldman sent me his article, "Mortal Man and Immortal Woman: An Interpretation of Three Ākhyāna Hymns of the Ṛgveda," *Journal of the Oriental Institute*, M. S. University of Baroda, 18, 4 (1969), 273–303, which made the following remarks on "covert or indirect representation" in Vedic hymns: "In any case, assuming that the traditional interpretation of the hymn is inadequate, and that we are right in taking it, like X.95, as an example of covert or indirect representation of one of the central mysteries of the Vedic cult, we are still left with some important problems with which we can deal but briefly here. In the first place, one may legitimately ask why the Vedic poets felt it necessary or desirable to speak so indirectly. If they wished to write a hymn about Agni and his 'parents,' why didn't they just do so without recourse to these elaborate dialogues? It is an interesting question and one that is applicable not only to our hymns. Without delving too deeply into the question of why they did, we may just remark that they show themselves to have been fond of riddling speech in many portions and strata of the Veda. All Vedic scholars are familiar with the *brahmodya* type of hymn and the riddling way the gods are so frequently described in hymns to the *viśve devas*. One might also note that Indic poets, at all periods, have been fond of indirection and that the greatest minds of later Sanskrit Aesthetic theory held that *dhvani* or suggestion, was the very soul of poetry."

16. As Bachelard: 1968 remarks, we could learn philosophy from poets! "How much philosophers would learn, if they would consent to read the poets!" (p. 208).

Bibliography

Anderson, Charles R. *The Magic Circle of Walden*. New York: Holt, Rinehart, and Winston, 1968.

Aufrecht, Theodor. *Die Hymnen des Ṛigveda*. Bonn: Adolph Marcus, 1877.

Bachelard, Gaston. *The Psychoanalysis of Fire*. Boston: Beacon Press, 1968.

———. *The Poetics of Space*. Boston: Beacon Press, 1969.

Bashō, Matsuo. *The Narrow Road to the Deep North*, translated by Nobuyuki Yuasa. Baltimore: Penguin Books, 1966.

Bolle, Kees W. *The Freedom of Man in Myth*. Nashville: Vanderbilt University, 1968.

Bosch, F. D. K. *The Golden Germ*. 'S-Gravenhage: Mouton & Co., 1960.

Buitenen, J. A. B. van. *The Pravargya*. Poona: Deccan College, 1968*a*.

———. *Two Plays of Ancient India*. New York: Columbia University Press, 1968*b*.

———. "Vedic and Upaniṣadic Bases of Indian Civilization." In J. W. Elder, *Chapters in Indian Civilization*. Dubuque: Kendall/Hunt, 1970 (vol. I).

Camus, Albert. *Lyrical and Critical Essays*, edited by Philip Thody, translated by Ellen Conroy Kennedy. New York: Vintage Books, 1968.

Chadwick, N. Kershaw. *Poetry & Prophecy*. Cambridge: The University Press, 1952.

Cirlot, J. E. *A Dictionary of Symbols*. New York: Philosophical Library, 1962.

Coomaraswamy, Ananda K. "Chāyā", *Journal of the American Oriental Society*, 55 (1935*a*), 278–283.

———. *Elements of Buddhist Iconography*. Cambridge: Harvard University Press, 1935*b*.
———. "A Note On The Aśvamedha," *Archiv Orientální*, 8 (1936), 306–317.
———. "The Pilgrim's Way," *Journal of the Bihar and Orissa Research Society*, XXIII (1937), pp. 452–471.
———. "Ornament," *The Art Bulletin*, vol. 21 (1939), 375–382.
———. "Līlā," *Journal of the American Oriental Society*, 61 (1941), 98-101.
———. "Saṁvega, 'Aesthetic Shock'," *Harvard Journal of Asiatic Studies*, 7 (1942–43), 174–179.
———. *Figures of Speech or Figures of Thought*. London: Luzac and Co., 1946.
———. *The Transformation of Nature in Art*. New York: Dover Publications, 1956.
———. *Buddha and the Gospel of Buddhism*. New York: Harper and Row, 1964.
Daniélou, Jean. "The Dove and the Darkness in Ancient Byzantine Mysticism," In *Man and Transformation*, papers from the Eranos Yearbooks #5. New York: Pantheon Books, 1964, pp. 270–296.
Day Lewis, C. *The Poetic Image*. London: Jonathan Cape, 1947.
Dunbar, H. Flanders. *Symbolism in Medieval Thought*. New York: Russell and Russell, 1961.
Edgerton, Franklin. *The Beginnings of Indian Philosophy*. Cambridge: Harvard University Press, 1965.
Geldner, Karl Friedrich. *Der Rig-Veda*. Cambridge: Harvard University Press, 1951.
Gonda, Jan. "The Meaning of the Word Alaṃkāra." In Katre and Gode, editors, *A Volume of Eastern and Indian Studies to F. W. Thomas*. Bombay: New Indian Antiquary Extra Series #1, 1939.
———. *Remarks on similes in Sanskrit Literature*. Leiden: E. J. Brill, 1949.
———. *Notes on Brahman*. Utrecht: J. L. Beyers, 1950.
Grassmann, Hermann. *Wörterbuch zum Rig-Veda*. Leipzig: F. A. Brockhaus, 1873.
Griffith, Ralph T. H. *The Hymns Of The Ṛgveda*. Varanasi: Chowkhambha Sanskrit Series Office, 1963.
Guenther, Herbert V. *The Royal Song of Saraha*. Seattle: University of Washington Press, 1969.
Heestermann, J. C. "Brahmin, Ritual And Renouncer," *Wiener Zeitschrift für die Kunde Süd-und Ostasiens*, 8 (1964), 1-31.
Kuiper, F.B.J. "The Ancient Aryan Verbal Contest," *Indo-Iranian Journal* 4 (1960), 217–281.
Kunhan Raja, C. *Asya Vāmasya Hymn*. Madras: Ganesh & Co., 1956.
———. *Poet-Philosophers of the Ṛgveda*. Madras: Ganesh & Co., 1963.

Liebert, Gösta. *Iconographic Dictionary of the Indian Religions*. Leiden: E. J. Brill, 1976.

Nicholson, Irene. *Firefly in the Night*. New York: Grove Press, 1959.

Renou, Louis. "Sur la Notion de Bráhman." *Journal Asiatique*, 236-237 (1948–9*a*), 7–41.

———. "Un Hymne a Énigmes du Rgveda," *Journal de Psychologie Normale et Pathologique*, 1949*b*, pp. 266–273.

———. "On the Word Ātmán," *Vac* #2 (Dec. 1952), pp. 151–157.

———. "Le Passage des Brāhmaṇa aux Upaniṣads," *Journal of the American Oriental Society*, 73 (1953*a*), 138–144.

———. "Les débuts de la spéculation indienne," *Revue philosophique*, 143 (1953*b*), 334–341.

———. "Les Pouvoirs de la parole dans le Ṛgveda." In *Études Védiques et Pāṇinéennes*. Paris: E. De Boccard, 1955, I: 1-27.

———. *Hymnes spéculatifs du Véda*. Paris: Gallimard, 1956.

———. "Études sur Quelques Hymnes Spéculatifs." In *Études Védiques et Pāṇinéennes*, Paris: E. De Boccard, 1956, II: 55-59.

———. "The Enigma In The Ancient Literature of India," *Diogenes*, #29 (1960), pp. 32–41.

———. *Études Védiques et Pāninéennes*. Paris: E. De Boccard, 1964. Vol. XIII.

———. *Études Védiques et Pāninéennes*. Paris: E. De Boccard, 1965. Vol. XIV.

Robinson, Richard H. and Willard Johnson. *The Buddhist Religion*. Belmont: Dickenson Publishing Co., 1977 (2d ed.).

Viennot, Odette. *Le Culte De L'Arbre Dans L'Inde Ancienne*. Paris: Presses Universitaires, 1954.

Wheelwright, Philip. *Heraclitus*. New York: Atheneum, 1964.

———. *The Burning Fountain*. Bloomington: Indiana University Press, 1968*a*.

———. *Metaphor & Reality*. Bloomington: Indiana University Press, 1968*b*.

Wingfield Digby, George. *Symbol and Image in William Blake*. Oxford: The Clarendon Press, 1957.

Zimmer, Heinrich. *Myths and Symbols in Indian Art and Civilization*. New York: Pantheon Books, 1946.

———. "Death and Rebirth in the Light of India." In *Man and Transformation*, papers from the Eranos Yearbooks #5. New York: Pantheon Books, 1964, Pp. 326–352.

Index

NOTE: This index analytically lists items and concepts of interest to students of Indology, History of Religions, Comparative Literature and Philosophy, Comparative Civilizations, Literary Criticism, History of Consciousness, Art History, Psychology, and History of World View Thought in early civilizational development. In addition to being able to find specific items and topics herein, the reader can discover, by reviewing each topic's modifications, this book's major subjects, interests and its significant contents. Only major themes appear from chapter 6 and the footnotes.

Vedic accent is not noted in this index, though Sanskrit diacritics are. In the rest of this book, Vedic accent is generally recorded only in technical discussions or on technical terms (not usually for names and such). In quoted materials, Sanskrit diacritics (or lack thereof) and whether or not French accent is marked on capitalized letters remain as they are or are not in the original source regardless of correctness and without benefit of a *sic* notation.

Agni (fire god), 106–109, 111–112; and death, 115; as enigma subject, 35–37, 38–39; as ritual mediator, 75, 83, 108; as source of poet's inspiration, 12, 36–37, 42, 44–45, 54, 106–109. *See also* Insight; Inspiration
—Vaiśvānara (of all men): as ancestor to ātman conception, 145 n. 12, 168, n. 13; as patron of symposium, 7–8, 12, 17–22
Agnicayana (ritual), 8, 145 n. 12
Ajaṇṭa, 116, 118
Alaṃkāra (poetic ornament), in Ṛg Vedic scriptural style, 29–30
Ambiguity, 35, 36, 105, 130
Anderson, Charles, xvi
Archetype, xxii, xxviii, 27, 59, 60, 64, 71–72, 74, 76, 79, 103; of sun, 90, 96; of tree, 69–79; of wheel, 103–115, 119, 120
Arjuna, 63, 120
Asya vāmasya (hymn), 5, 53
Ātman (inner, essential self), xxii, 121, 122, 145 n. 12, 177 n. 35; ancestry of conception, 146 n. 16, 150 n. 35, 168 n. 13; as brahman, 124; and salvation, 169 n. 16
Autobiography, as rare Vedic genre reporting symposium experience,

12, 17, 23, 36–37, 42, 53, 54, 106–107, 108, 175 n. 13

Bachelard, Gaston, xii, 42
Basham, A. L., 72
Bashō (Japanese poet), xvi, 102
Bergaigne, Abel, 4
Bhagavad Gītā (Hindu text), 63, 72, 78, 98, 100, 120, 121
Bhāgavata Purāṇa (later Hindu text), 60, 61
Bhakti (devotionalism), 12, 73, 100; in Ṛg Veda, 147 n. 23, 148 n. 26
Bodhicaryāvatāra (Buddhist text), 101
Bolle, Kees, xii, 106
Bosch, F. D. K., 75, 78
Brahmā (Hindu creator god), 97, 123
Brahman (speculative symposium enigma): and Camus's "une énigme heureuse," 138–139; also power, 6, 56; reveals and conceals like bride's clothes, 16; Ṛg Vedic definitions of, 6, 144 n. 5; as speculative object, 5 ff., 26 ff.; of sun, 84–89; translation equivalent of, 130–141; of two birds, 100; of wheel, 107–113. *See also* Enigma
—as Upaniṣadic ultimate, 62, 78, 122–124
Brāhmaṇa (period and literature), 3; Aitareya, 98–101; and brahmodya, 10; Ṛg Vedic influence on, 7–8; on transmigration, 90, 94, 96–97; and wandering, 99
Brāhmaṇa (priest), in sacrifice and symposium, 9, 14
Brahma-sūtra, 97
Brahmodya (speculative or ritual question form): in Brāhmaṇas and Upaniṣads, 10, 62, 158 n. 13; Ṛg Vedic brahman in this form, 9–11, 21, 38–41, 156 n. 7
Brotherhood (of symposium companions), 9, 11, 12–17, 53, 55, 172 n. 25. *See also* Companion
Brown, N., 43–47
Buddha (also called Siddhārtha and Gautama), xx, 98, 99–100, 121, 125; enlightenment of, 63, 75–78, 96; on patronymic, 172 n. 26; on wheel of life, 116–118
Buddhacarita (Acts of the Buddha), 63
Buddhism, xxiv, 61, 72, 100, 102; contemporary Burmese, 121; cult of tree, 75; enlightenment myth of, 74, 75–78; of Han-shan, xiv–xv, Pali, xxiii–xxvi, 101; and Saraha, xx–xxi; and śramaṇa tradition, 99; Tibetan, 62; and transmigration, 90; its wheel of life ectype, 116–120; Zen kōan and symposium enigma, 56–57
Buitenen, J. A. B. van, 63, 90, 94

Camus, Albert, 114, 127, 129, 135, 138–140
Cart (bullock), 70–71, 103
Cārudatta (hero of *Little Clay Cart*), 103
Chadwick, N. Kershaw, xii, 63–64
Christianity: of Gregory of Nyssa, xxi–xxiii; Jesus as enigma, 136–137; medieval, on wandering, 102
Chuang Tzu (early Taoist philosopher), xxvi–xxvii
Circularity, in Sanskrit world conception, 73, 114, 120, 122
Cirlot, J. E., xxvi
Civilization: uniqueness of recurrent death idea in Indic, 90; and world view, 69, 72
Clarity, as element of style, 131, 136, 137–138. *See also* Language
Coleridge, Samuel Taylor, on enigma, 132–133
Companion (of symposium brotherhood, also called comrade), 9, 12–17, 45, 53, 55, 56. *See also* Brotherhood
Consciousness, ordinary and visionary, xxiii, xxvi, 6–7, 10–13, 15–17, 18–21, 24, 27, 57, 58, 64, 108, 155 n. 6, 156 n. 8
Contemplation: of image, xxiv, 23–24, 30, 34–37, 40–41, 81, 87, 89, 95, 133; of paradox and enigma, 32, 33, 39. *See also* Meditation

Contest (oratorical, speculative): Amerindian example, 162 n. 39; of Buddha, 78; as described in Ṛg Veda, 7–25, 45, 52–58, 83–89, 107–109, 148 n. 28, 149 n. 33; figurative and technical terms for, 7, 17, 24, 53–54; poetic, of classical times, 61, 144 n. 4; and Upaniṣads, 62–63, 152 n. 39. *See also* Symposium
Coomaraswamy, Ananda K., xxiii–xxv, 28, 29, 79, 98–102, 117
Creation: in Buddhist myth of, 116; in Christianity, 136–137; enigmas of, 62–63, 86–88, 95, 97, 107–116, 119; Judeo-Christian-Islamic, 72; and sacrifice, 16, 58; Sanskrit conception of, 73–74, 78, 83, 89, 104, 105, 106, 120–121, 124, 167 n. 11; scientific metaphors of, 74

Daniélou, Jean, xxi–xxiii
Dante, 81
Dave, K. N., 48–51
Day Lewis, C., xv–xvi
Death: in Buddhism, xxiv–xxv, 102; in Christianity, xxi–xxii; and dead birds image, 105; recurrent, 73, 90 ff., 94, 100, 105, 115, 116, 120, 124; refuge or escape from, 63, 65, 75, 76, 96, 115, 122, 137; in Ṛg Veda, 90, 95, 106, 115, 163 n. 1, 165 n. 8, 167 n. 13; and sun symbolism, 89, 91–97; in Upaniṣads, 93–95, 149 n. 30, 168 n. 15, 16, 177 n. 35; in wheel of life, 117, 118. *See also* Immortality; Rebirth
Delphi (oracle of), 34
Demiéville, Paul, 109
Dew, xxv–xxvi
Dhāman (dispensation of order), 24, 82–89
Dharman (manifestation of order), 83
Dialogue-dialectic: as feature of symposium, 57; influence on later traditions, 61–63
Dīrghatamas (Ṛg Vedic poet-speculator), 21–22, 31, 42–43, 52–54, 56, 63–65, 69, 74, 75, 78, 103, 105 ff., 119, 125
Divyāvadāna (Buddhist text), 116
Dṛṣṭānta (traditional simile), ectypes of two birds enigma, 59–61
Dugum Dani (New Guinea highlanders), 105
Duḥkha (dis-ease, unsatisfactoriness), in classical Sanskrit world view, 96, 119
Dunbar, H. Flanders, 81

Ecstasy: experience of, reported in Ṛg Veda, 151 nn. 35, 36; meditative, 78, 122; mystical, 124; of shaman, 64; and speculation, xxvi–xxviii, 100, 123
Ectype: Buddha myth as, 101; sun image as, 94, 96, 98–102; tree image as, 47, 74, 75–79; two birds image as, 59–61; wheel image as, 103, 116–125
Edgerton, Franklin, 5
Eliade, Mircea, 64
Endlessness, 73, 106, 111–116, 118–124
Enigma: auspicious, 138–141; defined, xvii, 32, 178 n. 5; English connotations of, 129–136; as extended image, xiii–xiv; in Greek symposium, 62; lucid, 134, 135, 138–140, 179 n. 9; and speculation, 67, 81. *See also* Brahman

Figures of speech, xiv, 3, 29–30. *See also* Language; Metaphor

Gandhi, M. K., 78–79
Gāyatrī (Hindu mantra), 81–82
Geldner, K. F., 3, 24, 43–47
Gonda, Jan, 9, 29, 30
Grassmann, H., 3
Guenther, Herbert, xx
Guru, 21, 57

Han-shan (Ch'an Buddhist poet), xiv–xv

Harappā (Indus Valley civilization), 69, 71, 72, 74, 75, 76, 82, 86, 103, 104, 167 n. 9
Hariśchandra (myth of), 98–101
Hartshorne, Charles, 1
Heestermann, J. C., 95
Heraclitus, xxv, 30, 33
Hermeneutics, xi, 49, 93–94, 163 n. 3
Hinduism, 72, 81–82, 120–121
Horner, I. B., 101
Horsch, Paul, 104
Huizinga, Johan, 61

Iconography, 85, 86
Image: archetypal, 75, 79, 90; as textual fossil, 59–61, 92, 95, 96; and hermeneutics, xii ff.; and insight, xxiii; of plumed serpent, 79–80; polyvalence of, 58–59, 105, 133; as root metaphor, 72; in scriptural style, 3, 136; in Shakespeare, xvi; and speculation, 27, 70, 74, 109, 122, 149 n. 32, 152 n. 40. *See also* Moon; Sun; Tree; Wheel
Imagination, as means of exploring reality, xv, xvii, 17, 23, 26, 87, 95, 132–133
Immortality: in Christianity, xxi–xxiii; in classical Sanskrit world view, 73–74; in Ṛg Veda, 18, 20, 44, 65, 75, 95, 169 nn. 16, 17; in soma experience, 12; in sun symbol, 89; in Upaniṣads, 123; in wheel symbol, 124. *See also* Death
Impermanence, in Buddhist wheel of life, 117, 118
Indo-Aryan (peoples), 82, 83, 103, 125
Indo-Iranian (peoples), 83
Indra, 85, 99
Initiation: and Buddha's enlightenment, 63, 78; as contest structure, 56–58, 63–65, 87; and shamanism, 64
Insight (into mystery): from Agni, 22–23; through enigma, 134, 138; and images, xx, xxiii–xxvi, xxviii; lack of, 14, 17, 107, 108; and salvation, 74. *See also* Inspiration; Agni
Inspiration: and enigma, xix, 132–133, 137, 138, 140; and immortality, 123; of poet in contest (usually associated with Agni), 7–9, 11–12, 17, 19–23, 42, 44, 53, 54–58, 108–109, 145 n. 11, 146 n. 14, 150 n. 35, 151 n. 36; in shamanism, 64. *See also* Insight
Interdependent arising (Buddhist conception of causation), psychology of, 120. *See also* Pratītya-samutpāda
Interpretation: and necessity of complex vehicle analysis, 50, 52, 84; model brahman example of, 43 ff.; and secondary tenors, 58, 82; using text and time specific information, 5, 7, 38, 60

Jainism, 72, 90, 99, 101, 121
Jātaka (Pali Buddhist collection), xxv–xxvi, 75–78
Jayanta Bhaṭṭa (Indic philosopher), 60
Jesus Christ, 63, 130, 136–137
Judaism, 130

Kabīr (old Hindī poet), 60
Kaivalya (uniqueness as salvation), 61, 63, 74, 118–119
Karman (consequentiality): and bondage to rebirth, 61, 73, 95–96, 118, 119; as orthodox action, 120–121
Kāvya (classical Sanskrit poetry), 5, 29
Knowledge, 57, 62, 63, 64, 75, 76, 83, 100
Kṛṣṇa, 96, 98, 104
Kṣatriya (warrior class), 76, 98, 99, 100
Kuiper, F. B. J., 9, 24, 45
Kumārasambhava (Sanskrit poem), 63
Kunhan Raja, C., 5, 21–22, 31–32, 43–47

Ladner, Gerhart, 102
Landscape, 69–71, 79
Language: and allusion, xii, 32, 130–136 passim, 164 n. 4; of brahmans, 27 ff.; literal/ordinary versus figurative, enigmatic: xiv, 27, 28–30, 34,

37–38, 131, 133, 134, 136, 137, 145 n. 10, 146 nn. 13, 14, 154 n. 5; relation to wonder and mystery, 21, 108, 136, 140–141; in Ṛg Vedic poetics, 2, 24, 28–30, 144 n. 7, 147 n. 22, 154 nn. 3, 4
Lucas, F. L., 137
Lunar, as symbolic structure, 119, 125

Madurai (city in Tamilnadu south India), 70–71
Maṇḍala (sacred pattern), 78
Mantra (verse), 6–7, 81, 84
Manu (Sanskrit law text), 72
Māra (death, Impermanence), 63, 76, 78, 117, 118
Māyā: in classical Sanskrit world view, 73, 106, 116; defined, 96–98, 170 n. 18; as power of contestant, 15; reveals and conceals, 171 n. 23; in Ṛg Veda, 86, 92, 148 n. 28
Meditation: in Chuang Tzu, xxvi–xxvii; at death, 93, 94; and experience of ecstasy, 124; on Gāyatrī mantra, 81–82; in Han-shan, xiv–xv; on image, xx, xxi–xxii, xxvi, 21, 27, 35, 100 (*see also* Contemplation on image); as insight means, 74, 122, 123, 151 n. 35
Metaphor, xii, xv, xxii; extended, xiii–xv, xix, xxvii–xxviii, 48, 52, 78, 89, 124, 177 n. 32; root, and world view, 72, 104–105, 106, 119; in Ṛg Veda, 3, 54; in speculation, xvii, 74, 125
Metaphysics, 27, 40, 59, 60–61, 101, 103, 109, 114, 115, 123–124
Mexico, 79–80
Mitrā-Varunā, 81, 82–87, 97, 98
Mokṣa (release), 63, 74, 96, 118–119
Monier-Williams (Sanskrit dictionary), 35, 123
Moon: full, 78, 96; as recurrent transformation, 48, 91 ff.; and sun, 81, 82
Mortality, xxii, xxiv, 34, 73–74, 76, 105, 106, 116 ff.
Mystery: of creation, 89, 97; evocation of, xiii, xix, 8, 23, 29, 30–38, 39, 113, 122, 123, 131, 132, 134, 137; in Sanskrit speculation, xvii, 39; in symposium, 12–15, 19, 20, 21, 27, 36, 55, 56–58, 83, 107–109, 153 n. 41, 175 n. 13
Mysticism, 119, 120; in Chuang Tzu, xxvii; defined, 146 n. 16; and ecstasy, 124, 151 n. 35; Sanskrit, 17–22, 23, 140, 145 n. 12, 165 n. 8; and soma experience, 12
Myth, 64, 75, 76, 78, 82, 86, 87, 96, 102, 105, 109, 112, 116

Naether, Carol (ornithologist), 50–51
Nicholson, Irene, 69, 79–80
Nikāya (collection of Pali Buddhist texts), xxiv
Nirukta (early Sanskrit text), 3
Nirvāṇa (release), 63, 74, 97, 117, 118–119, 152 n. 36

Obscurity, xvii, 4–5, 26, 30–32, 36, 37, 131
Old Testament, 70
Order (world), 21, 37, 69, 73, 81, 82–83, 92–93, 102, 104, 105, 106, 110 ff., 119–121. *See also* Ṛta
Ornithology, 44, 48–52, 56
Oxford English Dictionary, xvii, 129–136 passim

Paradox, 28, 32–34, 80
Pasternak, Boris, xvii
Pepper, S., 105
Philosophy, xi, 15, 28, 53, 61–62, 63, 72, 109, 119, 131, 134–135, 180 n. 16
Plath, Sylvia, xiii, xiv
Plato, 62, 109, 130
Play, 61, 97–98, 103, 105, 106, 125, 171 n. 24
Pound, Ezra, xii
Power: and knowledge, 63, 64; as non-aesthetic function of figures of speech, 29, 30, 57

Prajñā (ecstatic knowledge), 78
Pratītya-samutpāda (causation in Buddhism), 116–118. *See also* Interdependent arising
Psychology, 120
Puruṣa ("person" as spirit), 62, 63, 121–122

Rādhā-Kṛṣṇa (epos), 78
Rajagaha (site of Buddhist monastery), 117
Reality: in classical Sanskrit world view, 73–74, 105 ff., 116, 118; and ritual, 58, 82; and science, 105; solar and lunar images of, 81, 82; and speculation, xvii, xxiv, xxviii, 15, 18, 21, 23, 24, 27, 30–32, 34, 36, 58, 61, 70, 113–114, 148 n. 28; wheel image of, 78, 105 ff.; and wonder, xiii, 136; and world view, 72
Rebirth: continuance or end of, 73–74, 122; of moon, 92; realm, 73, 93, 94, 95, 101, 106, 116, 118, 121; as "redeath," 90; and wheel of life, 117–119
Release (salvation from recurrent death), 73–74, 94, 96, 99–100, 118, 119, 121
Renou, Louis, 6, 10, 24, 26, 28, 34–37, 38, 39, 43–47, 58, 67, 81, 82, 83
Richards, I. A., 27
Riddle, xvii, 28, 31, 33–34, 40, 61, 62, 63, 133, 155 n. 7, 178 nn. 3, 4
Robinson and Johnson, 72
Rohita, 98–100, 101
Ṛta (truth, order), 21, 24, 36, 82–89, 109, 110. *See also* Order

Sacrifice (Vedic), 3, 9–22 passim, 108; in Bhagavad Gītā, 120–121; and cosmos, 22, 27, 57–58, 82–83, 89, 110, 146 n. 16; as chariot, 53, 106–108, 149 n. 30, 176 n. 15; as means of continuance, 93, 95; preparation for, 27, 57; speculation on, 21–22, 40–41, 106–109
Sadhamāda (symposium), 8–9, 11, 44, 62
Salvation: Christian and Indic view of, xiii, 102; devotional, 100; and endlessness, 115–116, 124; and self, 122; sun ectypes of, 101; in Ṛg Veda, 60, 98, 115; in wheel of life image, 118–119, 124
Samādhi (meditative equipoise), 119
Sāṃkhya (Indic philosophy system), 59, 61, 119
Saṃsāra (phenomenal world), xxi, 63, 73–74, 78, 101; as endlessness, 115; and nirvāṇa, 149 n. 32; and wheel image, 105, 118. *See also* Rebirth realm
Saṃvega (aesthetic shock), xx, xxiii–xxvi
Sanchi (Buddhist monument), 71
Śaṅkara (Vedānta philosopher), 60, 61, 62
Śānti Deva (Buddhist author), 101–102
Saraha (Buddhist tantric poet), xx–xxi
Savitṛ (sun), 81, 82
Sāyaṇa (commentator on Ṛg Veda), 3
Science (modern), xii, 72, 74, 86–87, 105
Scripture, style of, xix–xxiii, 4, 28, 29–31, 138
Self: in Agnicayana rite, 146 n. 16; in classical Sanskrit world view, 74; essential, 121–124; existential versus essential, xxii, 59–61, 161 nn. 28, 29
Serpent, plumed, 79–80
Shakespeare, xviii–xix
Shamanism: and symposium, 63–65
Sharma, J. P., 45
Sharma, R. S., 45
Simile, xiv, xx, 4, 29
Śiva, 86, 98
Smith, Logan Pearsall, 137
Solar-lunar imagery: and death, 94–96, 101
Soma (inspiring extract), 11, 15, 16, 40, 44, 48, 57–58, 93, 123, 147 n. 19, 151

n. 35, 152 n. 36
Soteriology: in Burmese Buddhism, 121; in classical Sanskrit world view, 11, 73–74, 106, 116, 119, 121; mystical, 124, 165 n. 8; and recurrent death, 94–96
Speculation: beginnings of, in a civilization, 69–70; defined, 27, 69, 113–114, 153 n. 1; and images, xix, xxvi–xxviii, 74
—Sanskrit: early, 84, 89, 91–93, 95, 109, 130; and ecstatic vision, 123, 124; and enigmatizing images, xxiii–xxiv, 26, 28, 30, 34 ff.; first recorded context of, 25, 61–62, 108; and language, 4–5, 140–141; later, 96; and solar imagery, 98–102
Spirit (essential or inner self), as transcendent, 59, 60–61, 121–124
Spurgeon, Caroline, xvi–xvii
Śramaṇa (wandering mendicant): and release, xxv, 121, 123; and sun ectype, 99–101
Staal, Frits, 125
Śūdraka (Sanskrit dramatist), 102, 125
Sun: as enigma of life in Camus, 179 n. 13; and symbolism, 69, 81, 102, 167 n. 10; and transcendence, 91–98, 101; and wandering, 98–102
Sūrya (sun), 82
Sūrya's Bridal (Ṛg Vedic hymn), 91, 94, 96
Sutta Nipāta (Pali Buddhist text), xxiv
Svastika (solar well-being symbol), 82, 85
Symbolism: defined, xiv; of footprints, 175 n. 11; of four, 85; of full moon, 96; in Indic art, 158 n. 12; and meaning, xvi, 165 n. 7; ornithological, xxii–xxiii, 35–36, 64, 105; and reality, 82; of scripture, xxi–xxiii, 3; shamanic, 65; source of, 69–71; of sun and swing, 164 n. 6; of sun, wheel and tree together, 76–78; of tree in Buddha myth, 75–78; and the unknown, 133; of weaving, 14–15, 18, 19, 107, 153 n. 37
Symposium (Ṛg Vedic): compared with Greek equivalent, 11, 62, 161 n. 35; as described in Ṛg Veda, 42 ff., 52–59, 106–113, 175 n. 12; influence on later tradition, 42, 61–63, 79, 100; and saṃvega, xxiv; and self-transformation, xxviii. *See also* Contest

Tantra (yogic ritualism), 100, 104
Taoism, xxvii–xxviii
Tao Te Ching, 31
Tenor: of figurative language, 38; and interpretation, 50, 56, 58–59, 84–89, 94; and saṃvega, xx, xxiii–xxvi; in scriptural style, xx–xxii; and vehicle, xii–xv, xxiv, 6, 27, 54–56, 88–89, 110–113. *See also* Vehicle
Thieme, P., 43–48, 58
Thoreau, Henry David, xvi
Tibet, 116, 117–118
Time, xxvi, 165 n. 8; as endlessness in wheel enigmas, 110–116, 120; conceptions of, in Sanskrit world view, 73, 89, 120, 122
Tradition, 39, 71–72, 74, 79, 90, 94, 97, 125
Transcendence: of attachments, 73, 78, 121; in classical Sanskrit world view, 59, 60–61, 63, 73–74, 78, 114–115, 121–122, 124; images of, 59–61, 96; and insight, 17, 20–21; and lucid enigma, 137; and play, 98; sacrifice as vehicle of, 40–41, 149 n. 30
Transcience, xxiv–xxvi, 96, 118
Transmigration, 90–96, 166 n. 9
Tree, 64–65, 69, 74–79, 162 n. 4
Trident, 86

Unity, 10, 34, 39–40, 89, 110, 113, 114
Upaniṣads (early classical texts), 10, 47, 59–62, 72, 78, 93–94, 95–96, 99, 101, 121–125, 177 n. 31

Vāc (Holy Word), 12–16
Vajra (thunderbolt), 85
Vālakhilya (Ṛg Vedic text), 39
Vedānta, 35, 46, 47, 59

Vehicle: of Heraclitus aphorism, analyzed, 33. *See also* Tenor
Vidatha (enigma contest), 45, 49, 53–54, 57
Vision: in Buddha myth, 116; in contest, 16–19, 21, 54–58; language forms suited to, 32, 34–37; and power, 14; in shamanism, 64; and speculation, xxvi, 27, 35, 114; transcendent, 147 n. 17, 148 n. 29
Viṣṇu, 104

Waddell, L. A., 117–118
Wandering: as spiritual alternative, 98–102, 173 n. 33; as Ṛg Vedic metaphor, 17–19, 107
Warren, Henry Clark, 75–78
Watson, Burton, xxvi–xxviii
Well-being, 58, 82, 84, 85
Wheel: of creation (Upaniṣadic), 122–124; in landscape, 69, 71; of life (Buddhist), frontispiece illustration, 95, 103–104, 105, 116–120; as lucid enigma, 137; water, 103–104, 106, 173 n. 1
Wheelwright, Philip, xi, 30–31, 133
Whitehead, A. N., 69
Whitney, W. D., 10
World View: defined, 72; and images, 105; source in tradition and landscape, 69–70
—Sanskrit: and brahman images, 27, 87; classical, 73–74, 82–83, 89, 101, 106, 118–120, 173 n. 31; shift from Ṛg Vedic to classical, 59–61, 72–73, 90 ff., 115

Xenophon, 62

Yajurveda (early Sanskrit text), 38
Yama (god of death), 95, 115
Yoga, xxvi, 61, 74, 119, 122, 123, 145 n. 9

Zimmer, H., 91

Compositor: Trend Western
Printer: Braun-Brumfield, Inc.
Binder: Braun-Brumfield, Inc.
Text: Palatino, Linocomp
Cloth: Holliston Roxite B 53515
Paper: 50 lb. P&S Offset Vellum